MANAGING
HEALTH SERVICE
CONTRACTS

The Management of Health Care

Series Editors
John J. Glynn and David A. Perkins

Published:

Managing Health Care

Edited by John J. Glynn and David A. Perkins

The Clinician's Management Handbook

Edited by David M. Hansell and Brian Salter

Other titles in the series:

Achieving Value for Money

Edited by John J. Glynn, David A. Perkins and Simon Stewart

The GP's Management Handbook

Edited by Peter Orton and Clare Hill

MANAGING HEALTH SERVICE CONTRACTS

Edited by

Kim Hodgson

Director of Business Development
The Medway NHS Trust, Kent

with

R. W. Hoile

Consultant Surgeon
The Medway NHS Trust, Kent

WB Saunders Company Ltd
London   Philadelphia   Toronto   Sydney   Tokyo

W. B. Saunders Company Ltd   24–28 Oval Road
London NW1 7DX

The Curtis Center
Independence Square West
Philadelphia, PA 19106-3399, USA

Harcourt Brace & Company
55 Horner Avenue
Toronto, Ontario M8Z 4X6, Canada

Harcourt Brace & Company, Australia
30–52 Smidmore Street
Marrickville, NSW 2204, Australia

Harcourt Brace & Company, Japan
Ichibancho Central Building, 22-1 Ichibancho
Chiyoda-ku, Tokyo 102, Japan

A catalogue record of this book is available from the British Library

ISBN 0-7020-1998-4

Typeset by Paston Press Ltd, Loddon, Norfolk
Printed in Great Britain by WBC, Bridgend, Mid Glamorgan

CONTENTS

CONTRIBUTORS

Glenn Douglas BA(Econ), MBA, IPFA, MIHSM, Director of Finance and Information, The Medway NHS Trust, Kent, UK.

Michael Faulkner MSc, MI Mgt, Organisation Development Adviser, The Barbican, London, UK.

Elaine Hedgecock BSc, Managing Director, PDP Limited, Peterborough, UK.

Kim Hodgson MSc, DipN, RGN, Director of Business Development, The Medway NHS Trust, Kent, UK.

Lin Horley HISS Project Manager/Information Systems Manager, Chelsea and Westminster Hospital, London, UK.

Rose Lapping Residence 8, The Medway NHS Trust, Kent, UK.

Richard Long TD, MA, Solicitor, Secretary to the Trust, Trust Headquarters, North Kent Healthcare NHS Trust, Sittingbourne, Kent, UK.

Stephen Parsons AHSM, Locality Commissioner, West Kent Health Authority, Aylesford, Kent, UK.

David Poland BA, MBA, MHSM, DipHSM, Contracts and Marketing Manager, The Medway NHS Trust, Kent, UK.

Stephanie C. Stanwick M Phil, DipN (Lond), RGN, Director of Commissioning, West Kent Health Authority, Aylesford, Kent, UK.

Peter Webb BA, IHSM, Fundholding Manager, South Thames Regional Health Authority, Bexhill-on-Sea, East Sussex, UK.

Toni Wilkinson MA, DMS, Unit General Manager, Croydon Mental Health Service, Warlingham Park Hospital, Warlingham, Surrey, UK.

FOREWORD

R. W. Hoile

In 1995 the NHS Executive published a handbook on clinical involvement in contracting (*Clinical Involvement in Contracting. A Handbook of Good Practice*, NHS Executive, April 1995). Accompanying this handbook was a letter signed by the Chief Executive of the NHS Executive and the Chairman of the Joint Consultants Committee. In their letter they reinforced the need to involve clinicians in contracting, and they expressed the hope that the publication would encourage clinicians and managers to view the contracting process as a mechanism for improving the quality and effectiveness of services within the NHS.

Why should a clinician become involved in the contracting process? As Clinical Director it is not uncommon to hear one's colleagues, many of whom are also medical managers, state that contracting is one of those managerial chores which is best left to professional managers. It is my belief that this is no longer a tenable situation and that it behoves every clinical manager to understand and take part in the process of setting contracts – whether those be internal service level agreements between departments or other Trusts, or whether the contracts involved are large clinical contracts made with purchasing authorities, general practitioners etc.

The manner in which we can take our departments forward in a way that profits both our organization and the patients whom we serve is to work in partnership with our managerial colleagues, our information technology departments, in strategic linkage. This involves taking part in the planning, taking part in the actual contract negotiations, bringing in the innovations in medical care that only we as clinicians can see and understand, and helping our professional managerial colleagues by focusing on our strengths, linking these to a business strategy and thus developing robust and profitable contracts.

Contracts can be improved by aiming for specialty-based contracts with specific quality standards and this is where the clinical audit process can be used to produce informed negotiations with purchasers. These purchasers too need access to informed medical advice in order to develop purchasing and health strategies and thus the negotiation really should be a two-way exchange of information. The providers need to actively involve clinicians in agreeing the broad terms of contracts in order to promote ownership of that contract. The providers must also be required to make available the appropriate resources and business planning support to enable clinicians to be involved in the contracting and planning process. Much can be achieved by shifting away from a focus on finance and activity towards contracts based around good practice (supported by information from clinical audit), effectiveness and quality of service delivery. Contracts should take into account the role of continuing education and audit and should allow for non-clinical work to be done, such as work for colleagues, national professional work and accreditation visits. All of these matters can be covered during the negotiation phase.

If the contracting process is not robust and clinicians do not involve themselves in this process, the final result will be unsuccessful and to the detriment of the involved departments, directorates and Trusts.

If unsuccessful management processes are encouraged and contracts continue to focus on finance and activity alone, then things will go wrong. Imagine the situation where you do not involve yourself as a clinician in the contracting process. The information available to managers will be of limited use, and strategies which are developed will have to be defensive if the non-clinical managers are unable to interpret the market and predict changes and trends. This will produce a stagnant situation where contracts would be devised which provide a basic hospital provision, but in which there will be no innovation. The performance of the hospital or Trust will begin to go wrong. There will be losses, inefficiencies etc.; in fact the hospital or Trust will begin to decline and decay. If on the other hand successful management paths are built up, and clinicians involve themselves in the contracting process in a manner described above, there will be rich communication between clinicians and managers, with the development of good strategic planning, teamwork, strong strategic linkage between information sources and the planning process, and actions will be built up which encourage innovation. This will drive contracts which reward performance, increase efficiency and change the focus of the Trust, making it a living, growing organism. I know which type of organization I would rather work in.

I believe that this book contains a rich source of very valuable information which will help clinical managers become involved in the contracting process to the benefit of the organization they serve. It is only by taking part in the process of planning and contracting for your organization that you can shape its future structure and guide the direction in which it develops.

The best way to predict the future is to create it.
(Peter Drucker)

INTRODUCTION

This text is concerned with contracting within the NHS. This development originated in the attempts in the 1980s to create a competitive environment for a number of public services. During this time it was gradually recognized that it was possible to secure good quality public services by allowing the development of purchasing agencies which focused on the desired activity and outcomes rather than on the managerial processes by which those objects were achieved. By 1990 the Conservative administration had decided that the public would be better served if it adopted the market philosophy and applied it across the whole spectrum of health care, permitting the interaction of public and private hospitals and the cooperation of GPs and health authority purchasers. This move led to a number of important consequences. It was necessary to develop a new language and this drew ideas from the private sector—marketing, contracting, business planning—as well as more esoteric concepts such as reconfiguration and business process reengineering. Such a language drew the criticism that the values of the factory were being introduced to the health service and that this was inappropriate if not dangerous. The axiom that the money should follow the patient was adopted as a mechanism. The aim was to reverse the previous practice in which those services which were efficient in using their resources to treat large numbers of patients were effectively penalized. Since the variable costs of that activity were only recouped a long time after the event, there was a pressure on controlling the volume of work, rather than an incentive to pursue high levels of efficiency.

Fundamental to the introduction of the market was the need to distinguish between the roles of purchaser and provider and to restructure the existing authorities and hospitals so that they played a single role, i.e. purchaser or provider but not both. Individuals had to choose or be appointed to a purchaser authority or a provider institution; it was not acceptable to sit on the fence or to wear two hats. The new skills of purchasing had to be identified, developed and implemented. Successive reorganization of District Health Authorities was necessary to create purchasing authorities of adequate size and capabilities. Purchasers had a steep learning curve, and for some years it has been the case that the provider hospitals and their staff have a clearer perspective on the needs and activity of services than those purchasers who are supposed to pay the piper and call the tune.

No clinician can afford to ignore this development. Medical services are funded only if they are part of a contract or if an identified individual or agency has explicitly agreed to pay for them. The agreement of contracts determines what work is to be done. If clinicians ignore this development they may find that they are forced to work to inappropriate and inadequate contracts negotiated by administrators.

This book is not intended as a commentary on the rights and wrongs of the NHS reforms. It accepts that some form of internal market is here to stay regardless of the political complexion of the government in power. The authors believe that it is of critical importance to the future of the NHS (and to all of us) that clinicians should play a very active role in how the system works. Our intent is to provide clinicians and managers with practical guidance which will enable them to play their full part in shaping the future of health care in the UK.

SECTION I

CONTRACTING FOR HEALTH CARE

" I'M YOUR MOTHER! ~ STOP CALLING ME
A 'SEGMENT OF A HIGH COST AREA'."

INTRODUCTION TO CONTRACTING

Michael Faulkner

OBJECTIVES

◆ To introduce the reader to the NHS internal market.

◆ To explain the central importance of contracts in the NHS internal market.

◆ To provide a guide to the book as a whole.

INTRODUCTION

This book is designed for clinicians and managers working in the National Health Service (NHS). The NHS of today is very different from the NHS of even five years ago. It is likely that the NHS in five years time will be equally different from that of today.

Anyone who has worked in the NHS for more than five years, will have been affected directly or indirectly by a series of government initiatives which, taken together, have created an internal market within the NHS. A point which will be stressed throughout this book is that the internal market is in its infancy and is still very much evolving.

For hospital doctors in the NHS, the internal market will have affected how many patients are treated and in which order they are treated. It will probably have started to influence the way in which patients are treated. Hospital nurses will be very aware of the pressure to get patients in and out of hospital as quickly as possible. Most clinicians are probably very much more involved in the management of health care than they were in the past.

The freedom of general practitioners (GPs) to refer patients to particular hospitals and particular consultants will be constrained by the contracts which their local health authority has negotiated. Some GPs have decided to become fundholding practices, in which case they are negotiating contracts with hospitals and other providers to deliver care for their patients.

Some people will be doing jobs that did not exist before the internal market – business managers, contract managers, commissioners, marketing managers. Staff working in information and information technology will have seen their jobs moving centre stage and becoming critical to the work of the NHS.

Many of the people working in the health service as cleaners or cooks or porters have also been affected. Their services may have been contracted out to private sector suppliers and they may have lost their jobs completely or now find themselves doing much the same jobs but no longer as NHS employees.

Managers and clinicians have had to make difficult and unfamiliar decisions about which services are 'core' and should be managed within the enterprise and which can be bought in through a process of tendering. Similarly, managers and clinicians may have had to tender to go on providing existing services or to secure contracts to provide new services.

In summary, the creation of the internal market has touched everyone in the NHS and has had a dramatic effect on the way in which the service works and is managed. At the time of writing, the internal market is only four years old. It is likely that at least as much radical change lies ahead as has already been encountered in the past few years.

The book is designed to explain how one of the key mechanisms of the NHS system – contracting – works and to give some practical guidance and help to people who are, or ought to be, engaged in the contracting process.

If contracting is to work in the interests of patients rather than against their interests, clinicians must play a central role in the contracting process. This is far from common practice. In most Trusts and most health authorities, contracting is very firmly under the control of non-clinical managers. No doubt there are honourable exceptions but we are some way away from clinical led contracting being the norm in the NHS.

Does it matter? Contracting determines or very strongly influences decisions which have, until very recently, been regarded as fundamentally clinical decisions:

♦ What range of services should a particular hospital or community unit provide?
♦ How many patients should receive treatment or care?
♦ Which patients should be given priority?
♦ To which hospital and which consultant should a GP refer a patient?
♦ What models of clinical practice should be used?
♦ What proportion of patients should be cared for on a day surgery basis?
♦ What standards of care should we be providing?

At the extreme, contracting can determine whether or not your hospital or community Trust continues to survive.

If the world does not yet feel quite like that, it is because contracting and the internal market within the NHS have only existed for about four years. The first of those years was known as a 'steady state' year in which no major changes to existing patterns of service provision were permitted. It is quite apparent that contracting is becoming more sophisticated (or more invasive, depending on your viewpoint). Contracts are starting to specify in some detail the services to be provided, the admission and discharge criteria, the priorities and the standards of care. Contracts are also starting to be moved from provider to provider. Hospitals are losing whole services and, indeed, being closed down.

If the internal market is to be anything more than a political catch-phrase, it is important that contracting does exercise this kind of influence. Otherwise it is a completely empty bureaucratic exercise. However, unless clinicians are centrally involved in the process, it is very likely that contracts will be signed which, quite unintentionally, have extremely adverse effects on patient care. Our enemy is not the bureaucrats or the politicians, it is ignorance.

Looking to the future, the government has announced its intention to move in the direction of 'primary care led' purchasing (Department of Health, 1994). In this model, the bulk of contracts would no longer be between health authorities and providers (hospitals, community Trusts and so on) but between GPs or groups of GPs and providers. An immediate consequence is that we will have *more* contracts to negotiate and deliver. Primary care led purchasing will place a clinician on one side of the negotiating table. We believe that clinicians should be on both sides of the table.

Contracting has the potential to improve health care in the NHS. Handled well, it can take some of the 'luck out of the system' and help to ensure that services are developed to meet the needs of local populations. It can also help to drive up standards of care and the efficiency with which scarce resources are used. At its very best, it can avoid wasteful duplication of facilities and resources and may eliminate clinical practice that is of doubtful value. These are all issues which require clinical insight and involvement if the outcome is to be a positive one for users of the service.

It is already possible to detect a number of potential problems which will occur if the contracting process is not handled well:

1. Too much emphasis may be placed on numbers of patients rather than on the quality and benefits of care. Much of the language of contracting is about throughput, activity and contacts and very little about resolving or ameliorating health problems.
2. Dogma may replace clinical judgement and sound research. There is a prevalent view, for example, that hospital care is less desirable than community care, that day surgery is better than

inpatient surgery and that minimally invasive techniques are better than conventional techniques. Pressure is applied to both purchasers and providers who are 'failing' to meet national norms in these areas. Little regard is given to the mix of patients, the nature of the community or to the fact that not enough good research exists to justify such policies.

3. The goals and values of the organization may be displaced. The pursuit of contracts and contract income can easily become an end in itself. As a result, provider units find themselves taking on contracts which they are ill-equipped to deliver or which do not fit well with the main purpose and structure of the organization.

4. Competition gets in the way of patient care. Health care depends to a great extent on collaboration between agencies and between professionals within agencies. There is a tension between collaboration and competition and sometimes competition has got in the way of doing what would be best for patients.

For example, orthopaedic services might be improved by having a 'hospital at home' outreach element. The local community Trust insists that anything which happens in the community is 'theirs'. The acute Trust wishes to manage the service as an integrated service and to retain the funding which goes with it. The local purchaser declines to make a clear determination. The result is that the service stays as it is and probable gains in both the quality and efficiency of care are lost.

The beneficial effects of contracting all involve clinicians doing things differently. Clinicians must be in there in the thick of things managing that change process.

Where clinicians are not involved in the contracting process, they become disempowered and a sense of helplessness and poor morale quickly comes to pervade the organization. They are being told to do things they may not agree with. If they argue, they are told that that is what the contract says and that is what they have to deliver. Some protest that the contract is unfair, or unreasonable or even unethical. By that time, it is usually too late to put matters right.

If clinicians are to become involved in the contracting process, they need the skills and knowledge to enable them to do so effectively. There is no point in exchanging clinical ignorance for managerial ignorance. This book is intended to start building the skills and knowledge required to play a full part in the contracting process. It is a starting point. It cannot turn you into an expert negotiator overnight or even provide the depth of financial knowledge required to handle contract negotiations effectively. Fortunately, contract negotiation, as later chapters explain, is a team game. At the moment, accountants and managers are on the team, and all too often the clinician is missing. It is his or her clinical expertise and the practical knowledge of patient care that is needed, not another financial expert or manager.

In preparing this book, the contributors have tried to take a reasonably balanced view of how the contracting process is working currently and how they believe it is likely to develop over the next five years or so. It is very easy to criticize a system which is still very much in its infancy with everyone engaged in the process trying to climb a very steep learning curve.

It is my belief that some form of contracting process within the NHS has the potential to bring about real improvements in the care which the NHS provides.

This potential will only be realized if the contracting process moves away from being a ritual dance between two sets of bureaucrats and towards being clear and explicit understandings between clinicians who are working together to improve the quality and efficiency of a national healthcare system.

In this model of the contracting process, clinicians working in primary care will be agreeing with their colleagues in secondary and tertiary care the type, size and quality of provision which is required to deliver the best available health care from a finite resource allocation.

The conversations will not, of course, be easy. There are genuinely difficult issues concerned with matching finite resources to (arguably) infinite demand. There are balances to be struck between expenditure on prevention and promotion and expenditure on curative medicine. Clinicians working in hospitals will be torn between the wish to preserve the institutions to which they belong and the sense that the balance between institutionally based care and care in the community is shifting.

If the contracting process is to be beneficial it will require a change in work practices and that change will, inevitably, be uncomfortable.

The alternative to something like the contracting system is to carry on fudging difficult issues and muddling through. Although this has served quite well in the past, for the NHS is an outstanding achievement and one of the best and most efficient healthcare systems in the world, the pace of change in health care suggests that a more rigorous approach is required for the future.

The message in this book, is that clinicians, supported by their management colleagues, must lead the contracting process if it is to deliver real benefits to patients and to the population as a whole. To do this, they must understand the workings of the internal market and of the contracting process and they must demand a leading role in that process.

This chapter aims to set the scene. The first part is a very basic introduction to how markets work and how market principles are applied within the NHS internal market. This is followed by a 'who's who' for the internal market. It introduces the main players and explains their roles. The section headed 'the contracting process' outlines what happens during a contracting 'round' and introduces the notion of contracting currency. The chapter concludes with an excursion through likely developments in the near future and introduces the chapters which make up the main text of this book.

The book is not intended to be read from cover to cover. Depending on your role in the NHS, you may wish to go to those chapters which are of most immediate relevance and interest. However, as the chapter on negotiating indicates, successful negotiation depends on understanding the other side's agenda. So, even if you are a purchaser, you may wish to read the provider perspective and vice versa.

WHAT IS A MARKET?

Markets are the mechanism through which people with something to sell are able to do business with people who have a need and the resources to meet that need (Box 1.1).

Box 1.1
The market: key features

> ◆ A market is a way of bringing together buyers and suppliers – people who wish to have goods or services and people who can provide those goods or services.
>
> ◆ A market is a way of determining the *price* of particular goods or services – what is a fair exchange.
>
> ◆ A market encourages suppliers to make available the goods and services which people want.
>
> ◆ A market can be about what will happen in the future – instead of making our exchange immediately, we can agree or *contract* to make a certain exchange at a particular time in the future.

Anyone who has bought a house, or been to the supermarket or looked for a job has participated in a market. Markets are such a pervasive part of our lives that we hardly notice them. As soon as we need to exchange resources with someone else, we are probably participating in a market.

Often, when we make an exchange in a market, we enter into some form of *contract*. When we take a job, we undertake to carry out certain duties and to turn up at certain times in exchange for some money and other benefits.

Contracts are central to the operation of any market where the exchange is not *immediate*. If I give you £10 000 for your car and then drive it away, the deal is done and no contract exists. I still have certain rights as a buyer but there is no contract between us. If, however, I enter into a car rental agreement with you, a contract exists. You are undertaking to go on providing me with a car for a specified period into the future in exchange for a payment or payments from me. Contracting, therefore, entails making some judgements about the future. As making judgements about the future is an inherently uncertain business, a central issue in contracting is about how *risk* should be shared between purchaser and provider.

The car hire example may seem a long way from the NHS but it illustrates some of the fundamental points about markets which apply equally well to the NHS internal market.

HOW MARKETS
WORK

Markets are supposed to work in certain predictable ways. An underlying principle of any market is that it will seek to balance supply and demand – that is, the quantity of goods or services available and the quantity of goods and services which people want (and are able) to buy (Boxes 1.2 and 1.3).

Market forces should also stimulate *innovation*. In a market, it is very much in the interests of suppliers to develop and introduce cheaper and better products. If they are successful, they will attract

Box 1.2
Too much demand?

Suppose that people want more of a particular product than is currently available. A number of things might happen to resolve the imbalance between supply and demand:

♦ Existing suppliers will try to produce more. They know that, if they can produce more, there are buyers out there who would be prepared to buy extra products.

♦ New suppliers may enter the market. An existing company may decide to make different things or someone might start a completely new enterprise. A firm overseas might decide to start exporting its goods to meet demand in another country.

♦ Suppliers may increase the price of their products. This will tend to reduce demand as people decide that they are not prepared to pay the new higher price for the product which was attractive at the original price. The higher price will be sustained until demand has come into balance with supply.

♦ As prices increase, it becomes more attractive for existing suppliers to increase capacity and for new suppliers to enter the market.

Box 1.3
Too much supply?

> What happens if there is too much supply and not enough demand? To some extent the mechanisms outlined above go into reverse:
>
> ◆ Suppliers will reduce their prices to make their products more attractive so that demand will go up.
>
> ◆ Existing suppliers may cut back on their capacity and some may leave the market – voluntarily or by going out of business.
>
> ◆ New entrants will be discouraged from entering the market.
>
> ◆ Exporters will be discouraged from providing products for the market.
>
> Again, these processes should continue working until demand and supply are back in balance.

customers away from their competitors. If they fail, they will lose customers to their more successful competitors (Box 1.4).

Box 1.4
Innovaton: effects on the market

> What happens if a supplier finds a way of making a better product or a cheaper product which is just as good?
>   Existing suppliers will be under pressure to reduce the cost of their products or to make them attractive in other ways. If they are unable to do so, customers will stop buying their product and move to the better or cheaper alternative. In the long term, suppliers who are unable to keep up with their competitors will go out of business.

It is the skill of the supplier in reading the market and the demand either for the better product or for the cheaper version that will keep the supplier in business.

All of the mechanisms outlined above sound sensible and socially useful. They encourage innovation, they enable customers to get the best products at the keenest prices and they ensure that someone will try to supply what customers want.

This is the mechanism of *competition* which is supposed to work in the interests of the consumer and usually does. One of the most persuasive recent examples is that of British Telecom in the UK. The introduction of even modest competition coupled with major technological advances brought about both very worthwhile price reductions and significantly improved service. They apply in what economists call a *free market*. In a free market, the assumptions listed in Box 1.5 apply.

♦ Customers can choose perfectly freely between competing suppliers on the basis of the best product at the best price.

♦ Customers know about all the products which are on offer – they understand them and can make informed choices

♦ Suppliers can enter and leave the market freely to match supply and demand

As we will see in the next section of this chapter, the NHS is not a free market – it is a *managed market* and, as such, behaves rather differently to the free market with which we are all familiar.

Before moving on to look at the managed market of the NHS, let us look quickly at some of the disadvantages of free markets. We have talked blithely about suppliers going out of business if supply exceeds demand or if a better or cheaper product is introduced. What really happens is that hundreds or thousands of people lose their jobs. A more personal example has been the effect of falling demand in the housing market in the UK which has left a great many people owning houses which are worth significantly less than they paid for them and which may be worth less than the money they still owe on their mortgages.

Market forces can also produce strange effects. For example, there is an over supply of bus operators in some cities resulting from deregulation of public transport. In the longer term, the market should settle but the transitional period is very disruptive. In contrast, rural communities are often without satisfactory public transport because there is not enough demand *at the right price* to attract a potential supplier. This has enormous social impact on rural societies.

Market forces work quite well in the longer term and for the majority of people. Their side effects can be devastating in the short and medium term and for particular individuals or communities.

The concept of the managed market seeks to counteract some of these damaging side-effects and also to address some of the factors which differentiate publicly funded health care from the theoretical free market.

*THE MANAGED
MARKET*

Two key factors differentiate publicly funded health care from other sorts of markets:

1. The customer is not free to make informed choices between different suppliers. Rightly or wrongly, we make the assumption

that customers should only access most publicly funded health care through a professional adviser or intermediary – most frequently, the general practitioner. In the case of emergencies, the Accident & Emergency team act as gatekeepers for other healthcare resources.

2. The total amount of money to be spent on publicly funded health care is determined by the government as part of the annual public spending round. We are not free to do the equivalent of spending more on our holidays and less on our car, although the government can exercise similar allocation choices on our behalf.

Health care is also a highly political issue. People become deeply upset if their local hospitals close or if there are not enough neonatal intensive care facilities or if waiting times are too long. In the UK, the NHS is held in great affection and any serious movement away from NHS provision to private sector provision is controversial.

The professional staff groups, particularly doctors, within the NHS are unusually powerful and influential. In creating the internal market, the government has had to move at a pace which powerful staff groups would tolerate. It is not inconceivable that consultant medical staff could have withdrawn from their NHS contracts. It is certainly the case that active and coordinated opposition by the medical and nursing professions would have made the reforms virtually unworkable.

To reflect the particular characteristics of the publicly funded healthcare market, the government has created a managed market rather than a free market. In particular it has introduced controls on the operation of the market (Box 1.6).

In addition to these market regulatory functions, the government also issues a stream of detailed policy directives in terms of healthcare priorities, equal opportunities policies, information technology, education and training, research and development and so on.

As a result, health service managers and clinicians operate in a very complex world which has some of the characteristics of a marketplace and some of a government bureaucracy. Some of the issues concerning the balance of central direction and market forces are discussed more fully in the final chapter of this book.

WHO'S WHO IN THE INTERNAL MARKET   All citizens of the UK and visitors passing through are or are likely to be *consumers* of the services provided by the NHS. Most citizens are registered with a GP, they may receive hospital care either as an inpatient or an out-patient, they may consume medicines provided by the local chemist but paid for, in part, through the NHS. Many will use community services such as community nursing or health visiting and their children will be seen by school nurses and may

Box 1.6
Controls on the NHS
internal market

♦ Purchases are not made by individual consumers but by agents who act on their behalf. The agents, predominantly fundholding GPs and health authorities, act within cash-limited budgets.

♦ The government reserves the right to approve new entrants into the market and can also act to prevent suppliers 'going out of business'. It is interesting to note that, at the time of writing, no NHS supplier has been allowed to fail. The government also regulates mergers between suppliers and acquisitions.

♦ Pricing is dictated through a cost *plus* formula which is meant to prevent cross subsidization between products or services and which also constrain suppliers in their ability to raise prices to take advantage of excess demand.

♦ The financial performance of suppliers is very closely monitored to ensure that they do not run up liabilities which they cannot cover.

♦ Capital investment is very tightly controlled as part of the total control of government expenditure.

receive specialist help from speech and language therapists working in schools.

These services come from *providers*. Providers include GPs and dentists, hospitals, community units, ambulance services and so on. Most hospital and community services are provided by *NHS Trusts*. An NHS Trust is a unit within the NHS which is governed by a Board of Directors and which earns its income by contracting to provide particular health services. Most ambulance services in the UK are also provided by NHS Trusts. General practitioners, general dental practitioners, opticians and chemists, by contrast, are independent businesses which have contracts with the NHS to supply particular services.

Services are bought on behalf of consumers by two basic types of *purchaser*. Health authorities contract with providers to provide specified healthcare services for their local populations. District health authorities (DHAs) purchase hospital and community services and family health service authorities (FHSAs) contract with GPs, dentists and chemists to provide primary healthcare services. There is a certain amount of private sector purchasing of health care through organizations such as BUPA.

In many parts of the country, DHAs have joined together sometimes with FHSAs to form *commissioning agencies* which carry out purchasing on their behalf.

The second type of purchaser is the *fundholding* GP. Under the NHS reforms, GP practices of a certain size (originally 9000 and subsequently reduced to 7000) were allowed to apply to hold funds with which they could purchase specific elements of health care for the patients covered by their practices. Where GPs elected to become fundholders, the money for their patients was taken away from the district health authority and given to the GPs to manage directly.

The whole internal market is managed by the *National Health Service Executive* (NHSE) on behalf of the Department of Health and its equivalents in Wales, Scotland and Northern Ireland. The NHSE operates through a set of eight *regional offices*. At the time of writing, the regional offices also carry out the residual functions of the *regional health authorities* which are due to be wound up in 1996.

THE CONTRACTING PROCESS

Each year, commissioning agencies and fundholding GPs negotiate contracts with provider units. The contracts specify the quantity, type and quality of care which is to be provided and the money which the provider unit will receive in return for those services.

Purchasers are under an obligation to assess the health needs of their populations and to place contracts to meet those needs within available resources. In doing so, they are working under the constraints of national policy as expressed in directives such as *The Health of the Nation* (Department of Health, 1990) and *The Patients Charter* (Department of Health, 1991). Contracts may also be placed for education, training and research.

In the first year or two of the internal market, contracts were nearly all in the form of *block contracts* – a single payment to provide a comprehensive range of health services. As the market has developed and both purchasers and providers have become more skilled and more confident, more sophisticated forms of contracting have emerged. Contracts are often on a *cost and volume* basis. Cost and volume contracts specify the *number* of particular types of care to be treated and attach a price to each. Contracts often have *triggers* built into them which allow funding to be adjusted if the numbers of cases vary above or below certain specified levels.

A key issue in the contracting process is the question of *currency*. Oddly enough, currency does not refer to money but to the quantities in which different kinds of health services can be described and measured. What exactly is the 'product' of a health service provider which a commissioner is buying? In many community services and in professions such as physiotherapy, the currency has been the *contact* – how many times a healthcare worker and a patient come into contact.

There is an expressed wish on the part of both central government and purchasers to move towards contracting for *outcomes* or for *health gain* – that is, to stop paying for what providers *do* and to start paying for what they *achieve* – the benefit to the patient. Progress in this direction is inhibited partly by a paucity of research and reliable data on the outcomes of healthcare interventions and partly by the limitations of existing information systems. Clinicians will be very familiar with the methodological difficulties of measuring health status and health gain and the particular problems of associating particular changes in health status with particular health interventions. Many important variables such as economic status, housing, air quality and nutrition lie outside the control of clinicians within the NHS.

As with many aspects of the internal market, there is a tension between centralization and decentralization. The government is keen to ensure that purchasers obtain the best possible value for money and would like them to be able to compare the prices which their providers are charging with prices elsewhere in the country. Being able to compare prices nationally implies that there should be some standardization of the 'products' of the NHS. Currently work is under way to define *Health Resource Groups* (HRGs) which will group together types of patient who are likely to consume the same levels of resource. The development of HRGs builds on early experiments with DRGs (Diagnosis Related Groups) which were used extensively in the health system in the USA. If successful, HRGs would effectively become the standardized products of the NHS. The downside of this approach is that it makes it more difficult for local purchasers and providers to agree programmes of care which meet local needs or which cover both hospital and community elements. The wish to have uniform and comparable 'products' may tend to stifle innovation. HRGs and other forms of 'currency' are discussed more fully in Chapter 8.

Similarly, whilst contract negotiation is a local process, it takes place according to a national timetable driven by the government's overall annual budget process. The key steps in a typical timetable, for example, 1994/95 are shown in Box 1.7.

CONTRACTS IN THE NHS Although this book is primarily concerned with contracts between NHS purchasers and NHS providers, there are several other sorts of contracts which apply to the NHS (Box 1.8). The differences in law between various sorts of contracts are dealt with in Chapter 9.

Developments on the horizon The internal market is still in its infancy and the current rate of change and development is likely to continue for some time. The government has, however, announced three policy initiatives which it is worth exploring in some detail.

Box 1.7
The contracting
timetable

STAGE	TIME
Price procedures	May
Value for money market comparison	June/July
Preliminary purchasing plan	October
Service specification from purchaser	October
Consultation meetings	December/January
Contract negotiations	December/January/February
Firm purchasing plan	November/December
Formal proposals received	January
Negotiations concluded	March
Contracts signed	31 March

Box 1.8
Contracts in the NHS

Type of contract	Key characteristics
NHS purchaser:provider contract	Internal to the NHS and not enforceable at law
Contracts with GPs, GDPs, opticians and retail pharmacists	Legal contracts with independent businesses negotiated nationally between the government and representative bodies
Contracts of employment	Contracts between employers and employees. Governed predominantly by employment law and enforced largely through Industrial Tribunals
Contracts with non-NHS suppliers	Conventional commercial contracts

1. GP-led purchasing

The government regards GP fundholding as a major success story and intends to extend the scheme to the point where most purchasing is carried out through GPs (Department of Health, 1994). To enable this, the government has announced a series of proposals to make it easier for GPs to become fundholders. The government proposes to introduce three levels of fundholding which will both enable smaller practices to participate and enable GPs to gain experience with quite limited schemes before moving on to more ambitious levels of fundholding. The three schemes are:

♦ Community fundholding in which GPs will hold budgets for medication and for some community services but not for hospital care.

♦ Standard fundholding which is essentially the current scheme with some anomalies addressed. This will give GPs purchasing power for most elements of elective hospital work and community care.

♦ Total fundholding in which GPs will be responsible for purchasing accident and emergency care in addition to elective work.

At the time of writing a number of pilot studies are under way to assess the practical issues associated with each type of fundholding. Some of the issues associated with GP-led purchasing are explored in the final chapter of this book.

The government is also introducing changes to the funding arrangements for the management costs associated with fundholding and making it easier for small practices to form fundholding consortia.

2. New health authorities

As we indicated earlier, many health authorities have formed consortia called commissioning agencies. Currently these are informal in nature as changes to district health authorities and family health service authorities require primary legislation in the form of an Act of Parliament.

The government has announced its intention to introduce measures in Parliament designed to lead to the creation of new health authorities which will combine current district health authorities and family health service authorities. The role of the new health authorities will be very much to support GP-led purchasing rather than to undertake purchasing themselves.

Essentially, therefore, the purchasing role moves away from health authorities towards GPs and the role of the health authorities will be to support, regulate and monitor the GPs.

3. The NHSE

Regional health Authorities still formally exist although, for all practical purposes, they have been reduced to eight. The government intends to introduce legislation to abolish regional health authorities and to replace them with eight regional offices of the NHSE. It is important to recognize that these are branches of the Civil Service rather than locally accountable bodies. Their role is to *implement* national policy *not* to make local policy.

The NHSE through its regional offices will be responsible for:

♦ Making national policy for the NHS.
♦ Overseeing the work of the new health authorities.
♦ Monitoring the performance of NHS Trusts.
♦ Managing the internal market.

Taken together, these three policy initiatives will bring about a further step change in the operation of the internal market with all GPs playing a pivotal role in the contracting process. The government argues that these changes will introduce a measure of very direct local accountability into a system which has been criticized for its lack of local accountability. Patients (the consumers) have a direct and personal relationship with their GPs and will, therefore, be able to exercise a clear influence on the shape of health service which they receive. What is unclear, at the time of writing, is how the pressure from GPs responding to the wishes of their patients will be reconciled with more strategic health goals and with the needs of relatively small groups with special healthcare needs.

In addition to these major policy initiatives, a number of other trends can be predicted with some degree of confidence.

1. Mergers

There is some scope for merging smaller Trusts to acquire economies of scale and more comprehensive service provision. Again there is a tension between the wish to create fewer but larger units and the wish to maintain real competition in local market places.

2. Competition and collaboration

Under certain circumstances, competition interferes with collaboration between Trusts. A wish to provide a 'seamless service' between hospital-based care and community care can conflict with competition between (say) a hospital Trust and a community Trust each keen to maintain its independence and viability. One of the priorities for the NHSE in developing processes for 'managing the market' will be to address this sort of issue more sensitively than is currently the case.

3. Private sector participation

Relatively little progress has been made on collaboration between the NHS and the private sector. The government views private sector participation as an important source of capital for the NHS and we might expect to see increasing pressure on Trusts to develop such partnerships and on purchasers to facilitate a mixed provider economy. At the time of writing, most collaborative projects have tended to be in non-clinical areas such as car parking and energy. There are, however, a number of collaborations with voluntary sector providers in the area of long-term residential care for people with learning disabilities.

4. Cost pressure

Pressure on costs and a drive to secure better value for money will remain an imperative. Central government appears to believe that it is at or close to the threshold of tolerable taxation levels and demands from other elements of public expenditure such as social security suggest that there will be little if any increase in the real monies available to the NHS. Purchasers faced with a finite budget and growing demand respond by placing pressure on provider prices. The current rather rough and ready cost improvement programmes (CIPs) in which providers are simply asked to show a percentage reduction in their costs are likely to be replaced by careful and informed negotiation on the part of purchasers. In particular, more attention will be paid to the demonstrable benefits of particular forms of healthcare intervention.

5. Contracting for outcomes

As indicated earlier, there is scope for changing the basis for contracting away from activity – what we do towards outcomes, what we achieve. This will require a significant improvement in our understanding of the efficacy of particular clinical interventions and in the information systems which are available within the NHS. Outcomes research is high on the NHS research agenda and a national centre for disseminating outcomes research has been established. The implementation of HISS (hospital information systems) and their equivalents in the community and in primary care should facilitate this kind of development by enabling patient-related data to be captured more precisely and to be analysed more easily.

6. Longer contracts

At the moment, most contracts are set for a year at a time. It is probable that there will be a move towards longer contracts as purchasers and providers gain confidence. Longer contracts may support a less episodic view of health and be much more appropriate for clinical conditions in which the goal is relatively long-term care rather than treatment. Clearly, equitable sharing of risk between purchaser and provider becomes more important the longer the period covered by a contract.

SUMMARY

Contracting is the key process through which the internal market works. To date contracts have been relatively simple, focused on activity rather than outcome and drawn up between a relatively small number of providers and a smaller number of large purchasers.

With the advent of GP-led purchasing and the move towards contracting for outcomes rather than activity, there will be a step change in the level of complexity involved.

Instead of a small contracts department negotiating a big contract with a major purchaser, we are probably moving towards a situation in which individual services will have to negotiate contracts with a large number of GPs. The contractual conversation will increasingly be clinician to clinician rather than manager to manager.

It is imperative that clinicians have the skills and knowledge to do this effectively and efficiently and that they have access to the managerial support and information which will allow them to handle the process without prejudicing their clinical workloads. Alternatively, clinicians should recognize the time required to participate in the contracting process and allocate protected sessions within their work programmes for the negotiating and managing role.

This book is designed to provide a starting point for clinicians and managers who are to become engaged in the contracting process. The next three chapters examine the contracting process from the perspective of a commissioning agency, a GP fundholder and an NHS Trust respectively.

Chapters 5,6 and 7 examine the practicalities of the contracting process from preparation of the contract specification, through negotiation to the management of a contract once it has been signed.

Chapter 8 explores developments in information and information technology in relation to the contracting process.

Chapter 9 outlines the legal and policy framework of contracting in the NHS.

Chapter 10 looks at the other side of contracting – contracting out services such as cleaning, catering and security and less familiar examples such as pathology and other clinical services.

Chapter 11 looks at contracts *within* organizations – internal service agreements. These provide a mechanism for ensuring that the services within a hospital or community service are properly aligned with the contracts with external purchasers.

The last chapter takes an overview of contracting and the internal market and summarizes some of the successes of the process and some of the problems which are still unresolved.

Throughout the book we have tried to provide case studies and checklists which we hope will give practical guidance.

FURTHER QUESTIONS

The following questions identify some issues from this chapter which you may wish to consider or discuss further with your colleagues.

♦ How are clinicians involved in contracting in your organization?

♦ Does the involvement of clinicians need to be improved? If so, how?

♦ What are the barriers to the involvement of clinicians in contracting?

♦ What training and development might be needed by clinicians to enable them to lead the contracting process?

REFERENCES Department of Health (1990), *The Health of the Nation: A Strategy for Health in England*. London.

Deaprtment of Health (1991), *The Patient's Charter*. London.

Department of Health (1994), *Developing NHS Purchasing and GP Fundholding — Towards a Primary Care-led NHS*. EL(94)7a.

CHAPTER 2

THE COMMISSIONING PERSPECTIVE: THE ROLE OF DISTRICT HEALTH AUTHORITIES AS PURCHASERS

Rose Lapping

OBJECTIVES

- ◆ To trace the development of district health authorities (DHAs), from their original role of purchasing *and* providing, through to the new purchasing only approach and ahead to the continuing development of commissioning agencies and consortia.

- ◆ To outline funding arrangements and the likely impact of proposed changes in formulae.

- ◆ To describe purchasing strategies and arrangements for public consultation, and how commissioners go about the task of identifying health care, taking in the concept of priority setting and rationing.

- ◆ To discuss the role of GPs in influencing purchasing.

- ◆ To outline the issues associated with outcomes measurement, alongside contracting for health gain.

- ◆ To discuss the role of purchasers in relation to quality of care, the impact of the Patient's Charter, and the role of local authorities in purchasing health care.

- ◆ To outline the management of waiting lists.

- ◆ To cover how purchasers prepare for and conduct contract negotiations with providers, including the resolution of contractual problems and performance monitoring.

- ◆ To outline arrangements for extracontractual referrals, and competitive tendering for healthcare services.

INTRODUCTION   Purchasing is about change.

As people's needs change so must their health services. As new technology is developed, the new NHS must use that technology to best effect. People now live longer and their expectations of a quality lifestyle have increased; the health service must adapt to the particular challenges of this ageing population. Purchasers need to reach out to the future and not simply replicate the past.

Health services need to be flexible in order to respond to these developments. Purchasers must think ahead to the changing needs of patients rather than existing patterns of provision. The importance of purchasing lies in the ability to anticipate and adapt to change.

There is recognition that the purchasing function is not yet fully developed. Given the continuing environmental turbulence around the mergers of health authorities, both with each other and with family health service authorities (FHSAs), the planned abolition of regional health authorities and the substantial increases in the coverage of GP fundholding, this is hardly surprising.

The fundamental shift to a purchaser-driven system has required a radical change of attitudes and behaviour by all those involved in the health services. Purchasers have a responsibility to continue this pace of change.

THE CHANGING ROLE OF DISTRICT HEALTH AUTHORITIES   During the 1980s the future of the NHS came under critical scrutiny by the government. Administrative reconfigurations sought to tackle weaknesses in the organization and management of health services.

Following the 1982 reorganization, the NHS became a centrally directed and managed body with a very strong hierarchy existing between management levels.

Running alongside these changes was the ever increasing gap between government funding for the NHS and the rising demand to meet the needs of an ageing population and advances in medical technology. Fixed budgets for hospitals meant that increased productivity, and therefore expenditure, was not recognized, with the resulting highly publicized reductions in workload once the money ran out.

FUNDING ARRANGEMENTS   Before the NHS reforms were introduced, DHAs received a budget from the regional health authority (RHA) to manage their hospital units and community health services within their boundaries. Health authorities would only be funded for the amount of work carried out within these units. These fixed budgets were seen to penalize hospitals for any increased productivity as their expenditure increased in line with the number of patients treated, but their income remained static.

This often led to cost-cutting workload reductions at the end of the financial year, causing highly publicized bed closures and the cancellation of operations.

Under this system any 'cross boundary' flows of patients were funded by the RHA in the budget-setting process to ensure that the 'treating' hospitals were not penalized.

In the reformed NHS, funding is given to DHAs based upon the number of residents within their boundaries, adjusted for age and the incidence of disease. This formula for allocating budgets is known as weighted capitation. Merged health authorities would take on the revenue funds formerly allocated to the previously separate DHAs. Over the last four to five years, adjustments have been taking place in the budget-setting process to bring different DHAs to a weighted capitation target position based on their population.

These changes had very serious consequences for some health authorities. For example, some Inner London DHAs which contained large, teaching hospitals would, under the old system, have been allocated a substantial budget to pay for the 'out of area' patients they had treated for other DHAs. Under weighted capitation this money passed to those 'home' DHAs to purchase health care for their residents themselves.

The arrangements for securing resources at national level through the Public Expenditure Survey (PES) will be unchanged by the most recent structural changes. The abolition of RHAs will mean that the resource allocation for DHAs, FHSAs and GP fundholders will be handled by central management processes. New guidance is currently being finalized on a revised national capital allocation formula. Until this process is completed, the combined impact of these charges cannot be fully assessed.

NHS REFORMS   In response to these financial and other difficulties around the provision of health care, the government, in 1988, announced a cash injection for the NHS plus a far reaching ministerial review of the future of the NHS.

In January 1989 the White Paper *Working for Patients* (Department of Health, 1989a) was published. Its proposals, together with those of a second White Paper *Caring for People* (Department of Health, 1989b), were subsequently enacted in the NHS and Community Care Act 1990 and came into force on 1 April 1991. The health service reforms introduced the purchaser/provider split and required DHAs to perform a new role as commissioners of health care for their resident population. This moved authorities away from their old role as direct providers of hospital and community health services; this task passed on to the new NHS Trusts. The opportunity for larger GP practices to become purchasers of some hospital services for their patients as GP fundholders (GPFHs) was also introduced.

The philosophy driving the purchaser/provider split, rightly or wrongly, is one of improving public service through competition. Fundamental to all these changes was that money would follow the patients.

This process of commissioning health services highlighted the need for DHAs to develop a range of new skills and expertise as well as a different kind of organizational structure. Working relationships needed to be strengthened or formed with the general public and other agencies such as:

◆ GPs.
◆ Colleges of nursing/health and medical schools.
◆ Statutory and voluntary organizations.
◆ Community Health Councils (CHCs) and FHSAs.

Whilst looking to work closely and positively with local providers, the new style DHA had no operational responsibilities. They were funded to purchase health services for their resident population and needed to use their purchasing power and expertise to ensure that services were provided and developed in ways that were appropriate, effective and efficient.

To discharge their new responsibilities, DHAs needed:

◆ Sufficient purchasing power based on a large population.
◆ The scope to provide opportunities for GPs to select services within their geographical boundaries.
◆ To have as close a geographical and organizational link with local authorities and the FHSA as possible; to provide a local focus.
◆ To employ staff with the appropriate range of skills to properly assess local needs and views.
◆ to liaise and cooperate with local people and organizations who had a legitimate interest in health commissioning.
◆ To ensure that financial resources were used economically, efficiently and effectively.
◆ To secure measurable improvements in the health of the resident population.
◆ To monitor health and health care of their local population; to ensure quality of services.

MERGER OF DHAs   It was apparent quite early on in the process of implementing these challenging issues that many DHAs throughout the country would need to develop a different management configuration. The most common approach was the merger of several DHAs to form one central agency to commission on behalf of each locality within the newly extended boundaries.

While there were no plans at this time to allow the formal merger of FHSAs and DHAs, close working with the new agencies was encouraged. As mergers proceeded, many DHAs put in place the concept of localities purchasing to avoid the possible dangers of remoteness. Benefits of one larger commissioning agency were seen to be:

♦ Better utilization of scarce skills.
♦ Lower management costs.
♦ Reduced administrative complexity.
♦ Smoother contracting processes, with local providers only having to relate to a single commissioning authority.
♦ Strengthened commissioning through increased purchasing power.
♦ Centralization of public health functions.
♦ Improved ability to take a wider look at the need for health services across the various localities within the expanded boundaries.
♦ A single focus for the assessment of issues affecting a particular care group across the new authority.
♦ Greater financial leverage.
♦ Simplified policy-making.
♦ Greater degree of co-ordination across the boundaries of primary and secondary care.
♦ Integrated information systems and management.

The purchasing function comes of age only in 1996 with the new merged health authority. For the first time in NHS history a single public health authority will have responsibility for *all* health services.

THE ROLE OF GPs IN INFLUENCING PURCHASING

These new health authorities will continue to be responsible for implementing national health policies. They will still have overall responsibility for assessing the healthcare needs of the local population and for developing integrated strategies for meeting those needs across primary and secondary care boundaries. Health services can now be planned from their logical starting place – primary care. A key new role is envisaged in developing this role and forging constructive partnerships with GPs. Purchasers cannot plan their secondary care services without first asking what primary care can do.

As fundholding develops, GPs will become increasingly important as purchasers in their own right. The GP fundholding perspective is covered in more detail in Chapter 3.

To highlight this point a major expansion of the fundholding scheme was announced in October 1994, to come on line in 1996. Minimum list size requirement will drop from 7000 to 5000 and three types of fundholding are envisaged:

♦ Community fundholding:
  - a new option for small practices of 3000+ patients.
♦ Expanded version of the current scheme:
  - includes specialist nursing services;
  - almost all elective surgery;
  - outpatients (except very high cost, low volume cases).
♦ Total purchasing:
  - GPs in a locality purchase *all* hospital (including Accident and Emergency) and community services for their patients.

This latter option will be run as pilot projects for the time being as will the following:

♦ Maternity services.
♦ Osteopathy, chiropody and patient transport.
♦ Medical inpatients.
♦ Mental illness and other long-stay treatments.

The new style health authorities should support these moves towards primary care led purchasing and ensure that they work for the benefit of individual patients and the local population as a whole.

MANAGING THE NEW NHS

Responsibility for overseeing the implementation of the reforms, and actively managing the new NHS, was given to the newly formed NHS Management Executive (NHSME) within the Department of Health.

As the reforms have taken hold, it has become clear that the central management of the NHS must adapt to better serve the new style organization. A light touch approach, respecting the freedoms of both purchasers and providers at a local level is favoured, although a degree of strategic management is required to ensure accountability.

In 1993, following yet another review, the Secretary of State decided that the responsibility for the effectiveness of the NHS should be devolved as far as possible to the local level. This meant streamlining central management and consolidating joint working between DHAs and FHSAs. The main changes identified in the review were:

♦ To abolish the 14 RHAs as of 1 April 1996.
♦ To reorganize the newly named NHS Executive to include 8 regional offices, with approximately 135 staff in each.
♦ To enable the formal merger of DHAs and FHSAs (from 1 April 1996) to create stronger local purchasing authorities with the emphasis on primary care led purchasing.

KEY ROLE OF HEALTH AUTHORITIES

A key role of the new style health authorities is to assess their resident population's health needs and then to purchase healthcare at a sufficient level of quantity and quality to meet those perceived needs.

A distinction between these various activities – commissioning, purchasing, contracting – can be made by applying the following definitions:

◆ *Commissioning.* The strategic activity of assessing needs, resources and current services and developing a strategy to utilize resources.
◆ *Purchasing.* The operational activity of applying resources to buy services to meet needs.
◆ *Contracting.* The process by which commissioning and purchasing objectives are achieved.

An outline of how health authorities conduct these activities is set out in the following pages of this chapter.

HEALTH STRATEGIES

Health authorities are strategic bodies and in order for them to discharge their new responsibilities, they will need to adopt a systematic way of going about what is to be achieved. Health strategies, linking needs with action plans and effective use of resources have been found to be useful tools to succeed in this area.

The aim of an effective health strategy can be expressed as adding years to life and quality life to years.

The point of a health strategy is that it should create clarity about direction, long-term aims and how money will be allocated to provide healthcare services. It must be a strategy for *health* and not just health services. Health strategies are open to public consultation; this helps raise the level of public debate around decision-making and the critical choices that must be made. The views of those involved in influencing referral patterns and the choice of providers can also be gathered, focusing attention on key issues which need joint action with other local agencies.

Communication is a key purchaser responsibility and *must* be built in at every stage. Health strategies, as purchasing plans, can also give providers an early indication of any likely changes which could affect them in the medium- to long-term, thereby helping with their own forward-looking plans.

IDENTIFYING HEALTHCARE NEEDS

To enable DHAs to produce effective health strategies, they must be able to:

◆ Evaluate the current pattern of health care.
◆ Identify the need and options for change.
◆ Monitor the effect of their actions on the health of the local people.

In addressing needs assessment one can reasonably ask, whose needs should we look at – the individual or the population, the sick or the well, the users or the non-users, acute or chronic illness and so on.

Authorities will need to build on the work of their Public Health Directorates and look at:

♦ The population profile:
  - Working closely with the FHSA, the DHA will need to collect data to build up a picture of the size, distribution and nature of the population they serve.
♦ Health status:
  - How healthy are the local residents?
  - Are there any pockets of ill health?
  - How does the health of local people compare with national standards?
♦ Utilization of services:
  - Where does the resident population currently receive health care?
  - How are they treated?
  - Numbers of cases, both planned and unplanned.
  - Data on case mix.
♦ Identification of any unmet need:
  - Waiting lists and times.
  - As specifically expressed by patients.
  - Local professional assessment.
  - National, epidemiological approach through research programmes etc.

These ongoing studies will determine the nature, quality and quantity of services needed. Purchasers will need to assess the strengths and weakness of existing service providers whilst questioning current methods of delivery services and identifying any gaps. To do this they *must* seek and analyse the views of patients and the public generally, GPs, local authorities, CHCs and voluntary groups.

Case Study 1 at the end of the chapter outlines the work done by Hillingdon Health Agency in identifying healthcare needs. Other examples can be found in the NHSE (1994) publication, *Involving Local People*.

PRIORITY SETTING AND RATIONING

As in most things, it is never possible to achieve everything for everyone. Compromises have to be made. Judgements must be exercised locally by commissioners about exactly how, and what compromises have to be made, to get the best results in terms of health improvements, given the financial, human, equipment and other resources available.

Despite an ever increasing allocation of funds, the NHS has never been able to meet the needs of all patients on demand. Medical and technological advances, coupled with an increase in the public's expectations, have led to an ongoing imbalance between finite resources and infinite demand. The inevitable consequence is that limits have to be set on what services are provided within the NHS. Readers will be aware of the very public and emotive debates around funding for particular services, in-vitro fertilization (IVF) and the inserting of grommets being just two examples.

Prior to the NHS reforms, priority setting was a political process with national policies established by health ministers and passed down via central management to local health authorities. Strongly influenced by professional views, these national priorities and policies would then be interpreted for local use. Priorities could be hidden or 'shaded' by consultants' personal decisions and the manipulation of their waiting lists. The new commissioning role has bought the task of setting priorities and policies closer to the patient.

A systematic approach to making these difficult choices could be as follows:

1. Establish local health needs.
2. Identify those benefits for health which could *realistically* be achieved by particular interventions or approaches.
3. Compare results of 1 and 2 and then decide which are the most important to concentrate on.
4. Identify targets or milestones to enable a judgement to be made on progress towards the achievement/improvement being sought.

Case Study 2, at the end of the chapter suggests how this systematic approach to priority setting can be practically applied.

Using these steps and working through their local health strategy should provide commissioners with the answers to the following questions, enabling them to be confident that they are contracting for health gain:

◆ What are the priorities for improving health?
  - What interventions and approaches should be used to achieve these priorities?
  - How long before results become apparent?
  - How can success be measured?
◆ What resources will be used to meet the goals?
  - Does the health authority have sufficient finances to directly contract with providers?
  - How much work will need to be done to encourage GPs, voluntary agencies, local authorities etc. to use their own resources to provide services?

Priority setting and rationing of resources are difficult partly because information can be patchy or non-existent, but mostly because the task is inherently complex. Many authorities have little room for manoeuvre and must find new and innovative ways of considering healthcare priority setting and rationing of finances. The concept will continue, however, and health authorities must be able to explain the decisions they take to patients, service users and clinicians. More than that, patients and the public must be empowered and encouraged to have a say in decision-making.

OUTCOMES MEASUREMENT

The introduction of outcomes into the contracting process is essential to ensure the new NHS works in the interests of the public. For health professionals, the outcome is the result of an intervention designed to improve the health of the individual and the population. For the patient, an outcome is the continuing condition in which they find themselves after a series of contacts, investigations and treatments at the hands of specialists within the fields of primary, community and hospital care. Outcomes exist in a variety of forms:

◆ Short, intermediate or long term.
◆ Illness or treatment specific.
◆ Process, surrogate or generic.
◆ Clinical or social.

They may or may not be beneficial, depending on individual values, but should be measurable.

Where reliable information is available on the effectiveness of procedures and treatments in any one service, commissioners can then move directly into contracts with providers which flag up markers to identify quality care and quality outcomes. This process requires a structured approach and requires input from both management and public health experts. Together, they need to work towards appropriate opportunities for changing service provision rather than perpetuating what may be unhelpful interventions of unproven benefit.

Service objectives need to be clarified alongside an understanding of the process of care for the services in question. It requires sound management information and a literature search, combined with constructive dialogues with providers. Discussions with colleagues who may well have moved further down the road of determining better outcome measures are also useful. We are accustomed to thinking about healthcare provision in terms of input and output. The challenge is to think beyond output targets to the ultimate health outcome. This is the real measure of health service performance and the one by which the quality of the NHS will be assessed.

QUALITY To provide a good quality service is the shared objective of all those concerned with the delivery of health care. This applies to both the professionals responsible for individual clinical care and managers responsible for the organizational framework within which that care is made available.

Whilst there is agreement about this goal, the definition of what constitutes a quality service and how this is achieved prove to be more difficult.

Achieving high quality, cost-effective clinical practice – that is, improving patient care and preventing ill-health – is the NHS's main business. It provides a basis of teamwork and lies at the heart of the corporate agenda of all authorities, whether they are FHSAs, Trusts or DHAs.

As outlined in previous paragraphs, to provide quality health care, effective health strategies by commissioners should demonstrate the qualities listed in Box 2.1

Box 2.1
Effective health strategies

♦ Appropriateness

♦ Equity

♦ Accessibility

♦ Acceptability

♦ Efficiency

Source: Maxwell (1984).

Whilst these considerations provide a framework, they only go so far in defining good quality services and how to maintain and monitor them at an operational level.

One of the concerns expressed at the inception of the NHS reforms was that quality would be sacrificed by commissioners in the pursuit of increased activity and lower prices. As contracting has developed it has become evident that commissioners have incorporated a wide range of quality standards, including waiting times, medical/clinical audit and patient satisfaction.

QUALITY The need to develop new style high quality services is not an issue
SPECIFICATIONS for providers alone. Purchasers should take the lead in identifying the way forward and acting as catalysts for change through the contracting process. In recent years Trusts have been working alongside the commissioners in developing health strategies to span the next three to five years, working through the implications together.

In taking this forward, commissioners are working to bring together their approaches to specifying and assuring quality in primary, community and acute health care into a strategy outlining specifications for quality development. These specifications will need to include current standards and monitoring methods, with future priorities and objectives for improvements in quality. Central to these specifications will be the development of ways of involving service users in planning and monitoring contracts for health services. Building on these generic quality specifications, many commissioners have now included specific quality standards where they expect providers to make significant progress in the coming contractual year. As a basis for agreeing future contracts, local providers will be expected to have demonstrated, through rigorous reviews, that they have taken positive steps forward. From this baseline the commissioners will then expect to negotiate more challenging targets to ensure continuous quality improvement.

THE PATIENT'S CHARTER

Publication of the Patient's Charter in October 1991 put the government's Citizen's Charter initiative into practice in the NHS. This ensured that the emphasis continued to be placed on issues of access and patient convenience. The publication of league tables of the performance of providers based on Patient's Charter Standards is likely to ensure that quality is given even higher prominence.

In April 1992, the government introduced National Charter Standards and also asked each health authority to introduce local Charter Standards, with information on performance being published annually.

The Secretary of State launched the revised and expanded Patient's Charter in January 1995. The new document draws together the original rights and standards with improvements made since. The new Patient's Charter also introduces a new waiting time guarantee, a new right around mixed sex wards and a number of new national standards.

Purchasers will need to satisfy themselves that these new standards are implemented and performance is satisfactory. They will want to ensure monitoring arrangements are in place to prove this. For public information, purchasers' annual Patient's Charter reports should include information on providers' performance. Where performance does not continue to improve, purchasers will need to take action through the contracting mechanisms.

USE OF ACCREDITATION PROGRAMMES TO STRENGTHEN QUALITY ASSURANCE

Accreditation is a method used to evaluate the quality of health service provision. It is the professional and national recognition reserved for facilities that provide high quality health care. Participation in the process is voluntary. There are many examples of accreditation schemes from abroad. In the USA, health insurance companies insist on hospitals being accredited if they are going to do business with them. There are also well developed accreditation systems in Australia and Canada.

Accreditation comprises three main stages:

- The development of organizational standards concerned with the system and process of delivery of health care. Standards are developed in consultation with the relevant professional organizations and are revised annually to ensure they reflect current health trends.
- Implementation of standards. The various accreditation agencies provide support material and guidance on interpretation of standards.
- Evaluation of compliance with standards, by means of a survey conducted by a team comprising a senior consultant, manager and nurse.

Although still quite a new concept in this country, there are a number of different schemes by which providers can seek and achieve accreditation. Some of these, such as Clinical Pathology Accreditation, look at particular areas of health care while others have developed a broader approach – the King's Fund Organisational Audit, for example. Accreditation can be used to assure purchasers, both DHAs and GPFHs, that services are being provided to a good standard.

Purchasers have to tackle a wide spectrum of purchasing decisions with a range of different providers. These decisions will involve service costs and volume, access to services as well as quality. Whilst commissioning authorities have moved forward in developing quality initiatives among their local providers, expert knowledge around cost and volumes, access to services etc., is usually held within the provider unit. The purchasers have few details about exactly how specific services are provided in a given place. There is often no expertise about what constitutes best practice, especially when dealing with more remote providers or with specialist services not provided locally. In these cases, purchasers must rely on the quality mechanisms set up by the DHAs local to the provider concerned. GP fundholding can further complicate this picture. They have few facilities for monitoring quality and are therefore almost entirely dependent on local commissioning authorities.

A good accreditation system, laying out validated information about which standards a provider does or does not meet, can be very useful to commissioners wanting to develop services.

The provider unit management team will have early warning about where standards are not being met and commissioners will be able to target resources accurately. Where sound accreditation is in place, local people can be assured that safe, good quality services are available to them.

Medical and clinical audits are crucial and ongoing mechanisms to ensure continuing provision of high quality services to patients. Audit, designed to monitor and assess performance with the aim of improving where applicable, is undertaken either by single professions or on a multi-professional basis. Audit activities are already well established within provider units. Accreditation schemes aim to draw on the results of audit to provide generic standards and processes which will benefit patients.

In this way one process will add to and complement the effectiveness of the other.

CONTRACTING

Risk sharing with providers

Following the NHS reforms, contracts formed the link between purchasers and providers. It was envisaged that there would be three types of contract:

♦ Block.
♦ Cost and volume.
♦ Cost per case.

As purchasers and providers gained experience in contracting, the system became more sophisticated. Arrangements now included:

♦ Contracts for longer than one year.
♦ Specified floors and ceilings for workload levels.
♦ Introduction of a wide range of incentives and penalties.

Developing purchasing depends on the death of the block contract. Purchasing is about *change* and the block contract is incapable of delivering it. It is designed solely to protect providers' existing flows of resources.

Effective purchasing means shifting contracting from left to right along the spectrum shown in Box 2.2. Ideally from the point of view of effective purchasing all contracts would be cost per case – not achievable obviously.

Box 2.2
The contracting spectrum

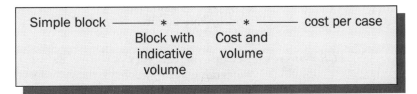

Implementation has in some ways been hampered by poor information and costing systems, but also by the reluctance of some purchasers to become involved in these more sophisticated agreements. Their view is that block contracts may be considered crude, but at least they can keep control of the expenditure and, to a certain extent, the performance of providers. The improved management of their workload by providers and the increased involvement of clinicians in contract negotiations have gone some way in allaying these fears.

One of the most controversial features of contracting and its associated risks has been the use of extracontractual referrals (ECRs). The term ECR signifies a referral by a GP or consultant to a provider unit for which there is no existing contract with the patient's 'home' health authority. The DHA manages the budget for these referrals.

There are three different types of ECR:

♦ Elective.
♦ Emergency.
♦ Tertiary.

Elective ECRs

As well as encompassing referrals to a provider unit where the DHA does not have a contract, elective ECRs are also those referrals to a provider unit which has specifically excluded from the contract the service requested. As part of the authorization process, providers and GPs are expected to contact health authorities to discuss 'out of contract' cases before making the referral.

Emergency ECRs

Emergency ECRs are those cases which have to be admitted into a hospital or treated within 24 hours. Prior approval is not required although, if possible, notification and discussion of the case would be considered good practice.

Tertiary ECRs

A referral not within existing contracts between consultants in different NHS facilities is known as a tertiary ECR. Providers do not have to obtain prior authorization from the DHA before accepting these cases for treatment. However, consultants initiating a tertiary referral need to complete a form to inform the DHA of all appropriate details.

ECR policies Because of the very sensitive nature of ECRs and the need to determine how much of their budget should be set aside, it is imperative that DHAs should develop sound procedures in discussion with local GPs and clinicians. To this end, DHAs have set up 'safe haven' offices, with named ECR managers as contact points and dedicated fax and phone lines on a very strict confidentiality basis. The following general principles are very useful:

- ECR procedures should be simple, quick and non-bureaucratic.
- Regular liaison between local GPs and clinicians is essential to ensure up-to-date knowledge of local referral practices and patterns.
- Any ECR process should complement good clinical practice.
- Information on individual patients should be treated in the strictest confidence.
- As far as possible the patient should not be aware of the administrative process of managing ECRs.

In the early days of contracting, the risks involved with ECRs fell squarely on the 'home' DHA, who had to find the cost of these 'unexpected' episodes of care from within their budgets.

Since then, steps have been taken and processes set in motion to enable these risks to be at least identified and shared, if not lessened. Dialogues between purchasers and providers have been encouraged with the aim of 'no surprise' policies being put in place. Joint discussions around priority setting and rationing have also served to maximize risk sharing.

THE ROLE OF LOCAL AUTHORITIES IN PURCHASING HEALTH CARE

As outlined in previous paragraphs, effective purchasing for new style DHAs require them to develop close alliances, to pool expertise and to develop the right balance of primary, secondary and community health services. Local authorities must be included in these discussions.

Alongside the NHS reforms, major changes to the financing and delivery of community care were introduced in the form of the White Paper *Caring For People*.

Local authorities were given lead responsibility for community care as purchasers of some kinds of care. Progress up to that time in developing services for vulnerable groups, such as the elderly and mentally ill, had been, at best, piecemeal. Local authorities were now being asked to prepare community care plans in conjunction with health authorities and other agencies. A huge amount of money had been transferred to local authorities to enable them to discharge their new responsibilities. One of the biggest fears, however, was (and still remains) the disputes around whether the care being provided was health or social and therefore which pot of money should be utilized.

Some DHAs have moved on from these early difficulties to establish and develop joint commissioning arrangements. This joint approach has promoted a move towards better understanding of local health issues, including special education needs, health promotion, child protection arrangements, and local needs assessment, as well as simplifying community care assessment policies. In some areas this approach has progressed through joint planning and needs assessment to the pooling of resources for particular services of care groups through locality working. Joint planning, objective setting and working should enable the following to be provided and evaluated on both health and social grounds.

- Personal care services.
- Primary health care.
- Adapted housing.
- Short-term care.
- Residential or nursing home placement.
- Prompt access to specialist acute care as and when needed.

DHAs must continue to forge these alliances. Strong partnerships should demonstrate the ability to answer the following:

- Are you sharing?
  - Money, skills, information.
- Are you working together?
  - Joint commissioning, joint public consultation.
- Are you achieving anything?
  - Improving services, identifying service gaps.

The ultimate objective should be to create a climate locally within which services can be provided to the local population in a coordinated way across social and health boundaries. This objective, in the most part, remains unfulfilled.

MANAGEMENT OF WAITING LISTS

The management of waiting lists continues to be a thorny problem. This has been exacerbated by examination of quality assurance alongside measurement and monitoring systems such as the Patient's Charter and the setting of specific quality standards in contracts. When added to a significant rise in public expectations, and the publication of performance figures, the difficulties can only increase.

Although GP fundholding and the establishment of NHS Trusts can be regarded as innovations, the acid test of the NHS reforms is what difference they have made for patients. Two factors constantly highlighted to demonstrate this positively are that more patients are being treated and that they do not have to wait so long for that treatment. Other examples cited to illustrate the overall improvement in quality within the NHS are improved access and initiatives to enhance patient convenience.

Some of the increase in activity is almost certainly the result of better information systems with Trusts improving their counting mechanisms and recording of the work done. However, the longest waiting times have indeed fallen (quite dramatically in some areas) and nationally there has been a reduction in the number of patients waiting between one and two years. To some extent these improvements have been achieved at the expense of those waiting less than a year. There is a school of thought which states that the management of waiting lists and achievements in cutting waiting times have been achieved more through specifically allocated funding and direct political intervention than by the success of the NHS market. One definite spur to deliver and demonstrate improved performance has been the identification of the responsibility for managing waiting lists as sitting squarely with senior management at the highest level within both Trusts and purchasers.

HOW PURCHASERS PREPARE FOR AND CONDUCT CONTRACT NEGOTIATIONS

The need to manage activity effectively has been a long-standing challenge for the NHS. Following the reforms, this needs to be exercised by DHAs and GPFHs through the machinery of contracting.

In adhering to a national contract negotiating cycle, affecting DHAs, FHSAs, GPFHs, NHS Trusts and RHAs, all contracts must be signed by 31 March. This signing off process is monitored by the NHS Executive via the RHA.

It is important that contract negotiations begin as early as possible with contract teams in both purchasers and providers able to reach agreements at an early stage. Chief executives are expected to take personal responsibility for ensuring this.

To ensure effective contracting processes are in place purchasers should encourage better working with providers. The purchaser/ provider relationship should not be restricted to formal negotiations; it must be constant and ongoing. Dialogues need to be developed in which purchasers and providers jointly work to achieve their objectives. One of the major failures of contracting to date has been the lack of recognition that cooperation achieves better results than conflict and coercion. A non-confrontational dialogue should involve:

♦ Openness about the service and financial context in which contracts operate.
♦ A joint approach to risk sharing.
♦ A shared understanding of who does what in each organization, with named contacts.
♦ An agreed approach to sharing information.
♦ The flexibility to adapt to changing circumstances.

Case Study 3 at the end of the chapter outlines an example of how these joint, nonconfrontational dialogues can be applied successfully.

Purchasers and providers need to involve clinicians and nurses fully in the contracting process; not simply in negotiating the contract, but also in managing it throughout the year. Realism in contracts can be achieved if clinicians' views on clinical need and practice, workload planning and medical developments are taken on board.

GPs, both fundholders and non-fundholders, also need to be closely involved in preparing for and conducting contract negotiations. Often described as the gatekeepers to health services, GPs are ideally placed to help DHAs monitor the quality of contracts.

In working up service contracts, purchasers need to be informed of robust provider prices at the earliest possible time (usually in November) with limited alterations before final prices are issued in January. In turn, purchasers have to be realistic about volumes of service to be purchased and the practicality and impact of changes in their purchasing intentions.

Unrealistic expectations can undermine both the providers' pricing policy and the adequacy of the purchasers' own reserves for ECRs. Change needs to be planned.

In moving services, and in preparation for contract negotiations, the purchasers should be satisfied that:

◆ The change is founded on local need, following consultation with GPs.
◆ The change will contribute towards the DHAs' ultimate goals.
◆ Any providers involved have the opportunity to discuss the implications, with both the purchasers and their own clinicians.
◆ Effective management information systems are in place to monitor the effects of the change.

Where a contract is to be withdrawn from one provider totally, there will need to be an agreement reached as to the timetable for the reduction of costs. Purchasers should be aware that fixed costs may not be able to be withdrawn immediately. Should a reduction in volume of activity be negotiated, the purchaser should suggest how demand is to be reduced and the provider must control activity to the agreed levels. Both parties must be responsible for managing the transition.

MONITORING OF CONTRACTS

Ultimately the responsibility for monitoring lies with the purchaser. In turn, they have their contract performance monitored by the RHA, both by formal reporting mechanisms and by joint meetings to discuss progress with contract negotiations.

The present systems of corporate contract monitoring and review will continue to operate until new arrangements come into effect following the decision to abolish RHAs.

Good practice requires that sound performance monitoring arrangements should be in place, with appropriate plans of action to manage activity discussed and updated throughout the year.

Chief executives, both purchasers and providers, need to keep in close touch with the processes of negotiation and monitoring as outlined above. They should ensure that negotiations do not falter and that the momentum is maintained.

Should negotiations fall down, there are established arbitration and conciliation arrangements with RHAs. However, purchasers should have their own milestones for agreement of contracts in place to ensure the speedy and timely settlement of contracting disputes within the year.

COMPETITIVE TENDERING An increasing number of DHAs are looking to market-test health-care services, within both the NHS and the independent sector. Purchasers are being encouraged to continue to look for better quality, more choice and improved value for money, and to market-test alternative providers.

Case Study 4 at the end of the chapter sets out an example of contract shifting and market testing.

In undertaking market testing, purchasers will need to ensure that:

◆ The concept of competitive tendering is taken forward as part of their wider purchasing strategy.
◆ They are clear about the objectives of the exercise.
◆ The process is open and fair, with wide consultation taking place.
◆ The exercise takes place within a realistic timetable.
◆ The results and the exercise are properly evaluated.

Although competitive tendering is a new contracting tool to the NHS, good practice guidelines are emerging to assist purchasers:

◆ Tendering processes will have a longer timescale than the annual contracting cycle.
◆ Ideally the outcome of a tendering exercise should be included in purchasing plans and contracting intentions, with clear time-tables and explanations of processes.
◆ Where a change in service results, these changes should be implemented, at a minimum, six months after the outcome of the tendering exercise.

Any resulting changes in service should also be discussed with all parties as outlined in previous paragraphs covering effective con-tract negotiations.

National guidance on market testing in the NHS is set out under cover of EL(93)55 with an update and outline of future plans set out in EL(95)29. The NHS Executive has established a Market Testing Team whose brief is to respond to market testing developments in the NHS and make a range of information available to the NHS and commercial sector in due course.

SUMMARY The fundamental shift to a purchaser driven system has required a radical change of attitudes and behaviour by all those involved in the health service. Purchasers have a responsibility to continue this pace of change. Their goal continues to be that of changing inappropriate ways of delivering clinical care and preventing illness. To achieve this they need to work for local people and be well informed about the health and consequent health needs of the local population. They also need to continue to develop contracting to achieve and maintain improvements in:

♦ Value for money.
♦ Effectiveness.
♦ Quality.

The changes in the NHS as outlined in this chapter were designed to create an internal market. The main features of this market are now in place:

♦ Purchaser and provider functions have been split.
♦ Providers have, in the most part, moved into Trust status.
♦ Financial allocations are now channelled through purchasers.
♦ New pricing and costing systems continue to be developed.

Further developments include DHA mergers, an expansion of the GPFH scheme, joint commissioning with local authorities etc. All these factors will be coming together to help build a complex network to manage the new NHS.

Key issues for purchasers around continuing this building process include:

♦ A strategic view
  – DHAs need to move beyond the annual contracting cycle to take at least a five year look forward at local and national priorities.
  – Purchasers need to give providers a picture of long-term plans.
  – Health strategies should contain clear health targets alongside clear identification of success criteria and measurement processes.
♦ Robust and effective contracts
  – Contracts must be appropriate to the services being purchased and the providers' ability to provide them.
  – Contract negotiations must involve the DHA, FHSA, local authorities as well as GPs and clinicians.
  – Purchasers must be confident that they are buying services that improve the quality of health care and make it responsive to the needs and wishes of their local population.
♦ Knowledge-based decisions
  – Purchasers must ensure they have sound mechanisms in place to collect robust, accurate information and intelligence.

- There must be an openness and explicitness about health services and the financial context in which contracts operate.
- Doctors must be included in negotiating and managing contracts.

♦ Listening and responding to local people
- Purchasers should improve the public's awareness of local health and health service issues.
- Patients and the public must be empowered and encouraged to have a say in decision-making.
- Purchasers must ensure that relevant patient rights and standards are driven firmly through contracts, with the publication of performance and progress.

♦ Mature relationships with providers
- There needs to be a creative tension, and robust negotiations, between purchasers and providers.
- The purchaser/provider relationship should provide ongoing discussions throughout the year and not be restricted to formal negotiations around the contract signing period.
- There should be joint understanding of who does what in each organization with identified contacts.

♦ Local alliances
- Strong partnerships should be encouraged and developed between health authorities and the local statutory and voluntary agencies.
- Purchasers can then build on these strengths to move towards joint commissioning with local authorities.
- One in three patients nationally are with fundholding practices; health alliances are essential with this strong purchasing force.

♦ Organizational fitness
- This relatively new science of purchasing needs a new approach to developing scarce managerial and organizational skills.
- Purchasers must establish and maintain a good image to attract high quality staff.
- Purchasers must be able to provide, through national circuits if applicable, the education, training and development to enable their staff, and thereby their organizations, to succeed.

CASE STUDIES

Case Study 1. Identifying health care needs

A purchasing agency set up a systematic programme of reviews on a locality basis to ensure that local need, which differed across the catchment area, was identified and that current patterns of health care were evaluated.

Specialties were individually addressed, looking at perceived needs, current provision and options for change to inform the agency's strategic and operational plans.

Multi-agency teams, consisting of:

♦ public health officer from the purchasing agency,
♦ service development manager,
♦ local GPs, both fundholders and non-fundholders,
♦ local CHC member,

took between two and four months to complete each review.

The CHC's contribution was highly valued and they were extremely proactive in feeding in patients' views, identifying those specialties presenting particular problems, and arranging and leading patient discussion groups. The agency found that having GPFHs on board also increased leverage with providers.

Once the reviews were completed, the teams moved on to monitor services and negotiate any changes with providers.

The agency were able to create a picture of what an 'ideal' service would look like from a patient need point of view and then move on to discuss with providers who would be best placed to meet those specifications.

Contracts have been shifted between providers and specific patient quality issues have been included in contracts.

The impetus is now on achieving radical changes (where appropriate) rather than simply 'tweaking' current provision.

Case Study 2.
Priority setting and
rationing

Many health authorities are faced with a need/supply mismatch with regard to the provision of health services. This is especially difficult when dealing with services such as those associated with assisted conception.

Health Authority A had established that a number of women and couples within their catchment area were in receipt of or had requested these services. Government studies, supported by experts in the field, had already ascertained that IVF, for example, was a relatively effective intervention compared with tubal surgery. Due to the high costs, access had historically been limited by the waiting lists.

This approach became unsustainable with the advent of the Patient's Charter and central government's determination to have no-one waiting more than 18 months.

This raised both service provision and ethical issues, the health authority having to balance national rules with purchasing services to meet local demand.

In consultation with providers and public health colleagues, Health Authority A produced a policy for assisted conception services, setting out specific criteria that patients would have to meet in order to be eligible for treatment. These were centred around:

♦ Lower age limit.
♦ Upper age limit.

♦ Number of treatment cycles to be funded.
♦ Proviso that all other avenues of clinically indicated treatment had been pursued.
♦ Number of children from previous/current relationship.

Case Study 3.
Purchaser/
provider dialogues

Purchaser A was asked by Hospital A, a local provider within the purchaser's boundaries, to support a capital development to extend the obstetric unit. This support would be in the form of buying more episodes of care.

Due to capacity problems, the purchaser had traditionally bought obstetric care at Hospital A and Hospital B, which was located in a neighbouring health district.

There was a degree of concern on the purchaser's part due to the lack of robust data around the number of women who would wish to continue to use obstetric services at Hospital B.

Following joint discussions between the purchaser and both providers, a proposal was worked up to ensure the risk was shared. Clear protocols were established and the capital development as a whole was well supported by local women, GPs and MPs.

The purchaser agreed to buy more finished consultant episodes (FCEs), in effect all their obstetric activity, from Hospital A but would remain responsible for paying for any continuing activity at Hospital B.

Should a woman's GP refer her to Hospital B, they would then approach Hospital A (*not* the purchaser). Hospital A would then contact the GP and the patient to discuss agreement to divert the referral. If this was appropriate and acceptable, the obstetric services would be within contract; if not Hospital A would pay hospital B an agreed price to cover the cost of the episode of care.

Case Study 4.
Contract shifting
and market testing

A purchasing authority undertook to review arrangements for Ear, Nose and Throat (ENT) services in the light of future health needs and current service deficiencies.

Following an epidemiological study and costing exercise the principal reasons for reviewing the service were:

♦ The changing nature of clinical practice in ENT, with services increasingly provided on an outpatient or day treatment basis. This had the effect of leaving inpatient care reduced in volume but requiring a greater concentration of special skills.
♦ The need for new inpatient arrangements to enable these specialist skills to develop, and to meet junior doctors' hours targets and training accreditation requirements.
♦ A recognition that the poor fabric of Hospital A, which historically had provided all ENT services to patients within the purchasers' boundaries, could no longer sustain modern acute hospital services.

As well as keeping local GPs in the picture, the purchaser then moved on to hold informal discussions with providers within the health authority boundaries whose clinicians and managers generally acknowledged and supported the proposed service changes.

Following these discussions a broad range of options were identified and reviewed. A clear agreement emerged that the 'hub and spoke' model was appropriate in this specialty. It was envisaged that this would involve two inpatient centres (location had not been addressed fully at this stage) backed up by more and better local day care and outpatient facilities.

The discussions then moved on to a more formal basis with Trusts A, B, C and D putting forward their business cases to bid for the new style ENT services. Clear objectives and realistic timetables for this market testing exercise were set out by the purchasers before carrying out an extensive analysis of service quality, access and financial implications. CHCs, GPs, Trust clinicians and managers were actively involved.

Two options – NHS Trusts A and B versus Provider C and D – were chosen as viable ways forward and then submitted for further review.

On service and access grounds, the two options were finely balanced and had real strengths although the costs were significantly different, with the Trusts C and D option coming out at £1.5 million more per year than that submitted by Trusts A and B.

A decision was then made that from a specified date ENT services would be provided by Trusts A & B. Main inpatient units would be sited in provider units within both Trusts with day and outpatient treatments at a range of local hospitals.

Following several open public meetings to answer questions from the general public, GPs, CHC etc., and continuing discussions with clinicians and managers, this proposal has recently gone out for a formal and public three-month consultation period.

FURTHER QUESTIONS

The following questions identify some issues from this chapter which you may wish to consider or discuss further with your colleagues.

♦ How can purchasers ensure, through their health strategies, that as many people as possible receive high quality care using available resources?

♦ How can purchasers judge the performance of the NHS in terms of effectiveness and quality?

♦ How can purchasers build and maintain sound knowledge bases and information systems?

- How can purchasers feed back to their local population details about what contracts have been negotiated and the services being purchased as a result?

- How can purchasers develop an environment in which they work jointly with providers to achieve objectives?

- How can purchasers learn from working with GPFHs?

- How can purchasers develop new skills within their team and ensure they have the right people in the right job?

REFERENCES

Glennester, H. (*et al.*) (1992), *A Foothold in Fundholding*. King's Fund.

Department of Health (1989a), *Working for Patients*. London: HMSO.

Department of Health (1989b), *Caring for People*. London: HMSO.

Department of Health (1991), *The Patient's Charter.* London: HMSO.

Ham, C. (1994), *Management and Competition in the New NHS.* Radcliffe Medical Press.

Maxwell, R. (1984), *Dimensions of health care quality. British Medical Journal.* 12 May

NHSE (1994), *Involving Local People*. Health Publications Unit.

NHSME (1993), *Purchasing for Health – A Framework for Action*. Health Publications Unit.

South Thames Regional Health Authority (1994), *Priorities and Planning Guidance 1995/96.*

Spry, C. and Griffiths, S. (1992), *Developing a Health Strategy.* South West Thames Regional Health Authority.

CHAPTER 3

THE GP FUNDHOLDING PERSPECTIVE

David Poland, Peter Webb and Toni Wilkinson

OBJECTIVES

- ♦ To understand how the GP fundholding scheme operates.
- ♦ To explain how a GP fundholding practice prepares for contract negotiation.
- ♦ To outline future development of the GP fundholding scheme

INTRODUCTION When the fundholding scheme was first proposed back in 1989, it was heralded as the most radical development of the NHS Review. Four years after its introduction it remains, perhaps, the most significant and far-reaching of the NHS reforms. It has not proven to be the 'wild card' that was originally suggested by some sceptics, although it is still too early to judge if the full benefits propounded by its supporters have been achieved. What it has undoubtedly demonstrated is that committed GPs are able, not just to influence the type of care provided for their patients, but to direct through the contracting process, changes in the range and accessibility of services available.

The first part of this chapter outlines the history of the GP fundholding scheme and the government's rationale for introducing it.

The chapter explains the entry requirements and scope of the scheme, together with pilots which are currently under way to test possible extensions to the scheme in the future.

This is followed with an outline of how fundholding practices prepare for contract negotiation and indicates the sort of contracting objectives which are likely to be important to fundholding GPs. It also explains the parts likely to be played by the GP partners and by the practice, or fund, manager.

The chapter outlines the various approaches to GP fundholding such as multi-fund or consortia arrangements and indicates how these differ from single practices.

The advantages and disadvantages of fundholding for GPs and their patients are identified and discussed. The chapter stresses the importance of GP fundholding to many providers and offers guidance on how provider units should manage their relationship with fundholding GPs.

Finally, the chapter looks forward to likely developments in both fundholding and in GP-led commissioning. It also discusses, in outline, the likely changes in the role of existing health authorities as district health authorities (DHAs) and family health service authorities (FHSAs) merge to be replaced by single authorities in April 1996.

THE FUNDHOLDING SCHEME

GP fundholding was initially proposed in the White Paper *Working for Patients – Caring for the 1990's* (Department of Health, 1989), which was published in January 1989 after a major review of the National Health Service by the government.

Following the White Paper, the National Health Service and Community Care Act 1990 was introduced. This gave GPs who meet certain criteria the opportunity to purchase a defined range of health services for the benefit of their patients and to manage a budget to enable them to do so. The scheme was, and remains, voluntary and GPs are free to join or leave the scheme at any time.

On 1 April 1991, 294 funds throughout England became the 'first wave' of fundholders by taking responsibility for their own budgets. By 1 April 1994, this number had risen to 1673 funds. Out of a total of 9100 practices in England, over 2000 were in the scheme. It has been estimated that during 1994/95, fundholders' budgets totalled over £2800 million, or about 9% of total NHS resources (Source: National Audit Office, 1994).

The scheme now covers a substantial proportion of the population with percentages varying across the former English health regions from 46% in Oxford to 20% in NE Thames.

MANAGEMENT RESPONSIBILITY FOR FUNDHOLDING

Statutory responsibility for the management of the fundholding scheme lies with the regional health authorities, but many functions have been delegated to FHSAs. These include data validation for budget setting and the training of practice staff. Additionally, FHSAs have a statutory responsibility for monitoring fund expenditure and can initiate an audit and review of fundholding practices where they feel that this is necessary.

GPs are themselves responsible for the purchasing and coordinating of services on behalf of the patients on their list, within the limits laid down by the 1990 Act and subsequent regulations. For those aspects of fundholding where those interested or involved in the scheme require further guidance, the responsible FHSA should be approached.

MAIN OBJECTIVES OF THE FUNDHOLDING SCHEME

Working for Patients recognized that GPs are 'uniquely placed to improve patients' choice of good quality services' because of their relationships with patients, hospitals and other providers of health care.

The government's rationale was to give GPs the opportunity to take more direct control of the NHS resources provided for their patients, and by so doing, to improve the quality and efficiency of care provided.

The main objectives of the fundholding scheme are to allow GPs the opportunities listed in Box 3.1.

Box 3.1
GP fundholding:
objectives

♦ Improve the quality of healthcare services available to patients.

♦ Stimulate hospitals, and other healthcare providers, to be more responsive to the needs identified by GPs and their patients.

♦ Improve the balance of care between the primary, community and hospital settings and reduce duplication between the sectors.

♦ Improve value for money in the use of scarce NHS resources.

♦ Develop the existing practice environment for the benefit of the practice and its patients.

ENTRY REQUIREMENTS

Working for Patients initially suggested that only those practices with lists of at least 11 000 patients (twice the national average) would be eligible to join the fundholding scheme. Smaller practices could join together to achieve this number by forming 'consortia'.

When the scheme was introduced in 1991 the qualifying list size was reduced to those exceeding 9000 patients. This requirement was later reduced to 7000 patients and the ability to form consortia remained.

The rationale behind allowing practices to form consortia was that smaller practices, who would otherwise be barred from joining the fundholding scheme, would be allowed to take part. A large consortium embracing, say, four or five small practices, could have fairly considerable purchasing power. Specific services, such as outreach clinics, would become more viable for both GPs and providers as sufficient patients would be available to sustain regular clinic activity.

A consortium becomes an entity in its own right and, therefore, money allocated to the fund can be spent on the patients who are on the lists of the constituent practices. There is no requirement, from an audit point of view, to spend funds in proportion to the number of patients who are on the various practices' lists. A great deal of cooperation is therefore required within the consortium to ensure that purchasing is equitable across all practices who make up the consortium.

Until April, 1995, the requirements listed in Box 3.2 were necessary.

Box 3.2
Fundholding
requirements

◆ Minimum list size of 7000 patients.

◆ All partners in the practice to be 'signed up' to fundholding, the application having been made by all partners.

◆ Capability to manage a fundholding budget effectively and efficiently. This means that the practice will need to possess, or have access to, computer equipment and appropriate management expertise.

◆ In effect the practice would have to demonstrate to the regional health authority that it would be able to deal with the additional administrative burdens associated with the fundholding scheme. They would have to possess the necessary information technology to track patients and monitor the practice budget.

Department of Health Circular EL(94)79, *Developing NHS Purchasing and GP Fundholding*, announced three new types of fundholding for those entering the preparatory year from April 1995:

1. Community fundholding which may be taken up by small practices with 3000 plus patients.
2. Standard fundholding for which the list size is reduced from 7000 to 5000.
3. Total purchasing which is to be piloted in approximately 30 locations.

Further details of these changes are given later in this chapter.

LEGAL POSITION Fundholders are responsible for purchasing services included in
OF GP the *List of Goods and Services* covered by the scheme (see below).
FUNDHOLDERS Fundholders may collaborate with other purchasers in setting joint contracts, but they would still retain accountability for fund
Statutory expenditure.
responsibility

Liability in civil law   General practitioners as providers of care have always borne professional liability for their own acts or omissions and have been required to have professional indemnity cover, either through membership of a defence body or through an appropriate insurance policy.

As employers GPs have also been vicariously liable for the negligence of their employees.

The assumption of fundholding status introduces a new dimension to the GP's liability in civil law as a commissioner and purchaser of care. The commissioning function involves recognizing and evaluating needs, and contracting accordingly. The purchasing function involves ensuring that services purchased are adequate and appropriate.

It should also be noted that since commissioning and purchasing are management, not clinical activities, the professional medical indemnity held by GPs will not necessarily provide cover in the event of a claim which alleges negligence in these areas. GPs should clarify the position with their defence/insurance organizations.

As fundholders, GPs continue to be vicariously liable for the negligence of their employees, but this liability will become more extensive as fundholders directly employ increasing numbers and variety of staff.

SCOPE OF THE SCHEME   The services which fundholders may purchase as part of the scheme are set out in the *List of Goods and Services* which was issued under the terms of the NHS and Community Care Act 1990. The list is revised from time to time. The current list was issued under the auspices of Department of Health circular HSG(94)25. There may be regional variations to the list which will require clarification from the local FHSA.

Expenditure under the scheme can fall into one of four categories:

◆ Hospital services
◆ Prescribing.
◆ Practice services (including staffing).
◆ Community services.

Fundholders have the choice to allocate funds between each of the four headings as they consider appropriate. In this way resources can be planned and targeted in accordance with the needs of the practice patients.

Fundholding budgets are used to purchase the goods and services listed in Box 3.3.

The National Audit Office (1994) estimate that in 1993–4, fundholders were responsible for purchasing approximately 20%, by value, of the hospital and community health services used by their patients. District health authorities purchased all other

Box 3.3
Fundholding
expenditure

1. Specific hospital services comprising a defined list of:

◆ Certain elective procedures set out in the *List of Goods and Services*

◆ All outpatient procedures, except
 – First outpatient attendances following emergency or self-referral attendances
 – Chemotherapy or radiotherapy
 – Renal dialysis
 – Genitourinary medicine clinic attendances
 – Antenatal attendances

◆ Diagnostic services (e.g. radiology and pathology) provided on an outpatient basis, except:
 – Breast screening or cervical screening where these are carried out under national screening programmes

◆ Direct access services such as:
 – Physiotherapy
 – Speech therapy
 – Occupational therapy
 – Chiropody
 – Dietetics
 – Counselling services

2. Community and other services such as:

 – Domiciliary consultations
 – Health visiting
 – District nursing
 – Mental health counselling
 – Learning disabilities

3. Drugs and appliances prescribed by the practice

4. Non-medical staff employed by the practice

services for fundholders' patients not included in the scheme, including emergency treatment and services for patients whose treatment cost in excess of £5000 per year. The limit on cost was increased to £6000 per year for 1994/5.

THE PREPARATORY YEAR   The year before full fundholding status is achieved is known as the 'preparatory' year. All potential fundholders must successfully complete a preparatory year in order to achieve full fundholding status. The preparatory year is an opportunity for the practice to familiarize itself with the requirements and regulations of the scheme and for the responsible FHSA to support the practice in preparing for the first full year as a fundholder.

A practice must make a formal application to the regional health authority to join the scheme. Practices should liaise with their local FHSA as their support will be essential during the application process. Applications must be signed by all partners within the practice or a proposed consortium.

All potential fundholders must have the support of the regional health authority and have successfully completed their preparatory year before they can attain full fundholding status. Applications may be refused but there is an appeals procedure to the Secretary of State. In reality, applications can only be refused in exceptional circumstances and such cases are rare.

If successful in their application, a practice will receive formal notification together with details about how it can claim the preparatory year management allowance. The management allowance will then continue for each year that the practice remains in the fundholding scheme.

Preparatory year objectives   A structured approach should be adopted during the preparatory year encompassing the areas shown in Box 3.4.

Box 3.4
Preparatory year: key areas

◆ Hospital referrals

◆ Community services

◆ Prescribing

◆ Staffing

◆ Computer requirements

◆ Management allowance

◆ Training

This will enable the practice to have a clear understanding of the number and type of referrals that it is making, the providers used and an indication of how they wish to develop goods and services which they may purchase over the subsequent year.

Staffing   The staff budget is set in the same way as for all non-fundholding practices, but is cash-limited. Fundholding practices are, however, responsible for determining their own priorities on how the staffing element of the budget will be spent.

The management allowance may be used to develop the skills available to the practice by recruiting qualified/experienced staff or training existing employees.

Computer requirements   During the preparatory year practices will be looking at their computer requirements.

If the FHSA approves applications for reimbursements of the costs of computer purchases, the centrally determined rates are currently as follows.

Practice management systems

These are computer systems specifically designed to manage the wide range of general activities associated with general practice such as:

♦ Staffing records.
♦ Patient database.
♦ Prescribing.
♦ Call/recall systems for cytology or mammography.

The system is usually networked throughout the practice premises and is available to every GP in the practice.

The practice can claim for up to 50% of all costs (hardware, software and maintenance) of these systems.

Fundholding systems

These are systems designed to enable the practice to manage their fund. It is used to keep records of patient activity and costs of treatments incurred as part of the GP fundholding scheme.

Ideally, the fundholding system should be integrated with the practice management system, but in many funds they are not.

The practice can claim reimbursement for 100% of software and training costs and up to 75% of hardware costs, including maintenance for these systems.

Management allowance   The management allowance is a means of reimbursing practices for additional administrative costs incurred as a result of taking on the responsibility for managing a fund. Prior to April 1995 the preparatory year management allowance was set at 50% of the full year fundholding allowance. From April 1995, there will be a more complex formula to reflect the three new forms of fundholding. Under the new rules, GPs will be able to claim from the locum allowance for up to one day a week spent managing the fund, without actually having to employ a locum. The new scheme is summarized in Box 3.5.

Training   The purpose of undertaking training during this preparatory year is fourfold:

♦ Familiarization with the objectives and requirements of fundholding.
♦ Introduction to the techniques required for successfully commissioning, purchasing and contracting for services.

Box 3.5
Management
allowance

List size	Basic fee (£)
5 000	36 658
6 000	38 538
7 000	40 418
8 000	42 028
9 000	43 638
10 000	45 248
11 000	46 858
12 000	48 379
13 000	49 899
14 000	51 419
15 000	52 940
16 000	54 110
17 000	55 280
18 000	56 450
19 000	57 620
20 000	58 790
21 000	59 961

PLUS: £1400 for each practice in the fund in excess of one;
£650 per branch surgery; and up to one day's GP time from
the locum allowance without having to employ a locum.

Source: Bruce and Davies
(1995)

♦ Instruction in day-to-day management processes, such as financial monitoring and reporting, upon which the efficiency and
viability of the practice depends.
♦ Understanding the implications of the NHS Executive fundholding accountability framework which is (at the time of writing)
out for consultation. The key requirements of this framework
are summarized in Appendix 1.

***GP FUNDHOLDER
BUDGET
ALLOCATIONS***

The 1989 White Paper indicated that it was the government's
intention to set GP fundholder hospital budgets on a capitation
basis. This would mean that reference would be made to the
number of people on a GP's list, which could be adjusted to take
account of age, sex and epidemiological factors. By using this
methodology, fundholders' budgets would then be calculated in
the same way as DHAs'.

In practice, however, the NHS Executive have adopted a more
cautious, incremental approach to budget setting which is still
progressing towards a capitation method. The reason for this
approach was that there was a need to avoid a situation where

some practices would receive sharp gains in funding whilst others received reductions in services for their patients.

The compromise, therefore, was for hospital budgets to be set which would enable fundholders to buy services to a similar level that they had received in the previous year. The NHS Executive's intention was that budgets should be allocated based on data collected on the number of treatments and diagnostic tests carried out for the practice during the fundholder's preparatory year.

Capitation benchmarks At the time of writing, the NHS Executive are considering a move towards a capitation based system as an alternative to historical funding. A system known as capitation benchmarks is currently being developed. Further details can be found in Department of Health Circular EL(94)84.

These benchmarks are based on average treatment and prescribing levels and it is anticipated that they will help inform fundholder budget setting at a local level. Over the next few years budgets should be based on these benchmarks although they can be adjusted further for local factors such as indicators of health need and the proportion of patients on the practice list with private health insurance.

FINANCIAL ACCOUNTABILITY The NHS Executive expect fundholders to manage their financial affairs within the budgetary allocations set by the regional health authority unless there are unforeseen circumstances, and to adhere to the financial requirements set out in the GP fundholders' Manual of Accounts.

Underspends Where fundholders underspend their budget allocations, they have a statutory right to keep their underspend provided these savings are used for the benefit of the patients on their list. Savings can be held by the FHSA on behalf of fundholders for use in future years and may be carried forward for up to four years.

Underspends can be of three different types:

◆ Planned – which can be made from planned improvements in efficiency within the practice.
◆ Unplanned – from unplanned variations in the expected referral or prescribing activity during the year.
◆ Windfall – when a budget has been based on incorrect data or when hospitals have failed to raise invoices within the approved timescale.

In the past few years, the NHS Executive have requested that regional health authorities identify those practices with windfall underspends and negotiate their 'voluntary' return. There is then no statutory requirement for practices with windfall underspends to return their savings to the centre.

Savings have to be used for the benefit of the patients on a practice list, as detailed in Box 3.6.

Box 3.6
Budget savings:
approved purchases

> ◆ The purchase of additional services covered by the *List of Goods and Services*.
>
> ◆ The purchase of material or equipment which:
> - Can be used for the treatment of patients of the practice.
> - Enhances the comfort or convenience of patients.
> - Enables the practice to be managed more efficiently and effectively.
>
> ◆ The purchase of material or equipment relating to health education.
>
> ◆ The improvement of any premises from which the members of the practice carry out their practice whether by improving the structure of the premises or the purchase of furniture and furnishings.

Overspends

Overspends can arise for a number of reasons. For example, a chronically ill patient who requires expensive drugs may join the practice list in-year; the budget may have been set using inaccurate data; or there may be in-year problems of managing patient referrals to provider units.

Overspends at year-end may be met from contingency funds held by district health authorities, where provision has been made for these. Overspends cannot automatically be deducted from future fundholding budgets but can be taken into account in future assessments. Continued and unjustified overspending may lead to a fundholder being removed from the scheme by the regional health authority.

PREPARING FOR CONTRACT NEGOTIATION

Fundholding gives GPs new responsibilities as commissioners of health care. In addition to providing clinical services directly, in accordance with their general practitioner contracts with the FHSA, a specific fundholding budget is allocated for the purpose of purchasing health services. This budget is quite distinct from GMS (General Medical Services) money and has to be accounted for separately.

The commissioning process for fundholders, as for DHAs, comprises three distinct but linked elements – needs assessment, purchasing and contracting. Guidance on how GPs will perform these tasks is given below.

Individual needs assessment
At the individual level, GPs have always been involved in assessing patients and delivering, or organizing, services on the basis of perceived needs.

Following the extension of fundholding into community health services from April 1993, fundholders have had greater freedom to exercise care management functions. For example, they are able to directly employ community nurses and the GP is able to purchase community nursing services for individual patients. This should take place within the framework of local agreements between all the community care agencies involved. Fundholders should not bypass these systems nor, indeed, the systems set up in conjunction with local authority social services departments. It is the responsibility of the FHSA and local authority to make sure that all GPs are aware of the agreed procedures for accessing community care 'packages'.

Assessment of population needs
The assessment of a population's healthcare needs has been described as 'the science behind the art of commissioning'. It is the start point of the commissioning process. Once population needs have been established, priorities may be embodied within a purchasing strategy and contracts drawn up with providers. Contracts are monitored and performance evaluated, which then enables needs to be reassessed.

For the practice population as a whole, fundholders have to aggregate individual needs in order to arrive at a global assessment of the nature and scale of the health needs of its patients. This assessment can then be used as the basis for prioritizing need and developing a purchasing strategy.

Assessment of population needs is a specialized task and outside expertise (e.g. epidemiology, health economics) may be valuable.

In reality, in preparing for contracts a practice will consider its patients health needs based on assumptions around historical referral rates to local hospitals and services and will base its purchasing intentions on these activity figures. The practice should not assess its patients' needs in a vacuum. Many other agencies have an interest in the same individuals – other health commissioners and providers, social services (who have the lead responsibility to pull together community resources under the NHS and Community Care Act 1990), housing, education and voluntary groups.

The fundholding practice therefore needs to collaborate with others in working towards a unified framework for assessing needs. The importance of joint assessment will increase as the number of fundholders grows. Fundholders will be expected to have an effective dialogue with other commissioners in order to ensure that care services within the locality are comprehensive, complementary and coherent.

Purchasing The prioritization of the health needs of a population will lead to the formulation of a purchasing strategy, hopefully arrived at in collaboration with other commissioners. Fundholders have two obligations – firstly, to develop their own purchasing strategy, and secondly, to contribute towards a purchasing strategy produced by all commissioning agencies (which includes participating in community care planning).

Department of Health Circular EL(92)47 requires DHAs, with FHSAs and GP fundholders, to develop clear health strategies, providing at least a five year context for purchasing strategies.

The ultimate aim should be to develop a five year strategy for purchasing services with other commissioning partners, but the process of working with others is as important as the production of a plan.

Fundholders are not expected to be able to produce a five year purchasing strategy when they commence fundholding, but by the end of the first full year there should be significant progress towards a practice strategy, and clear evidence of joint working with other agencies to develop a locality strategy. The draft accountability framework for GP fundholding (December 1994), which is summarized in Appendix 1, further strengthens this responsibility by requesting practices to produce annual practice plans, and to signal major shifts in purchasing intentions.

When considering its purchasing intentions the practice will need to be aware of the number of patients on providers' waiting lists, the achievement of Patient's Charter standards, price and the accessibility of services. These matters will be as important to the practice as more strategic issues mentioned above.

Contracting There are a variety of types of contract which may be used. The most common are block, cost and volume, and cost per case. 'Non-attributable fixed price' contracts are specific to some fundholding services where information on usage and referrals is poor. The advantages and disadvantages of each type are examined in Chapter 4. Employment contracts may also be used for services within the surgery (e.g. physiotherapy, chiropody).

The different types of contract are:

♦ *Block*. High volume activity such as diagnostics (pathology and radiology). Can also be used for outpatient activity if there is certainty about referral patterns.
♦ *Cost and Volume*. High volume activity, but where GPs wish to retain a degree of flexibility over some of their referrals and part of their budget; i.e. outpatients, inpatients or day cases.
♦ *Cost per case*. Low volume activity where GPs wish to retain full flexibility over their referrals and budgets; i.e. outpatients, inpatients or day cases.

♦ *Non-attributable*.   High volume activity where costs of providing services will not change during the contract period; i.e. community activity.

The content of the contract should identify, in a measurable way, what providers are expected to deliver and should reflect both parties' expectations about quality, outcomes, prices and payment. The contract should address Patient's Charter issues and specify how complaints will be dealt with. A full description of what should be included in a contract is shown in Box 3.7.

Box 3.7
Contents of a contract

> The nature and *level of services* to be provided
>
> ♦ The *duration* of the contract
>
> ♦ General or specific *population characteristics*
>
> ♦ The *locality* of services
>
> ♦ *Criteria* for admission and discharge of inpatients/outpatients and day cases
>
> ♦ Locally agreed *community care referral* procedures
>
> ♦ *Quality standards*, measures and quality monitoring mechanisms
>
> ♦ *Information* requirements
>
> ♦ Contract *monitoring* methods, including access to premises and data
>
> ♦ *Billing*, authorization and settlement

Contract objectives GP fundholders' contracts are public documents and from time to time members of the public or other NHS organizations, such as the Community Health Council, may wish to see them. To relieve GPs of the administrative burden of having to make arrangements for the contract to be viewed, the NHS Executive has asked DHAs to be responsible for dealing with requests from those wishing to see fundholders' contracts. The practices are, therefore, required to send a copy of their contracts to their local FHSA, who will then pass them on to the local DHA.

Personal details should, of course, be removed from 'cost per case' type contracts to safeguard clinical confidentiality.

A fundholding practice's objectives should be clearly defined and achievable and these will be reflected in the negotiated contract. The contract should identify, in a measurable way, what the providers are expected to deliver. Box 3.7 shows what should be specified in the contract.

An example of a GP fundholder agreement with an NHS Trust is shown in Appendix 2.

The private and voluntary sector

GP fundholders may place contracts with non-NHS providers such as private bodies, independent contractors, charities or voluntary organizations. Such contracts are different to contracts with NHS providers as they are legally enforceable in the courts. It is therefore recommended that fundholders take legal advice before entering into such contracts. The local FHSA should be kept informed about non-NHS contracting proposals through the practice's annual business plan.

Role of practice staff

When considering fundholding, practices will need to identify two key individuals who will play an important role in the future management of the scheme and in the preparation and management of contracts.

The lead GP partner

As the practice moves towards full fundholding there will, of course, be detailed discussions with, and amongst, all GPs within the practice. However, during the preparatory year a single GP (the lead GP) will normally be identified from amongst their number. The role of the lead GP is to represent other members of the practice and take responsibility for reporting progress to partners.

The fund manager

Similarly, a lead member of staff (usually called the fund manager) will be identified to work closely with the lead GP. The fund manager who can also assume the role of practice manager will take on the day-to-day operational tasks associated with running the fund.

In some cases the fund manager can be 'bought in' as an outside consultant to help manage the fund only, with the operational work of the practice being left to a separate practice manager.

There is no clear guidance on where responsibility should lie and, to an extent, the involvement of the lead GP will depend upon their interest in the scheme and the amount of time they are prepared to devote to it.

Some lead GPs will be happy to leave the contracting, budget negotiations and monitoring entirely to the fund manager, whilst others will adopt a more 'hands-on' approach to every aspect of the fundholding scheme.

The practice manager

Some fundholder practices employ both a fund manager and a practice manager. The practice manager is responsible for the day-to-day management of the practice clerical staff and premises, but they have no responsibility for the management of the fund.

*DIFFERENT
APPROACHES TO
FUNDHOLDING*

According to the National Audit Office (1994) during 1993/94, 71% of practices in England had patient lists below the current minimum size for fundholding status to be accorded (7000 patients). The NHS Executive are encouraging smaller practices to join together to form larger groups to enable them to enter the scheme.

There has been no single model through which a practice may enter fundholding. Practices qualifying with 7000 patients have been able to enter in their own right. Where a practice has failed to meet the minimum list size requirement of 7000 patients, it has been able to choose to combine for fundholding purposes with one or more other practices. In this model, sometimes known as a 'consortium', the fund which results is a single entity and a high level of cooperation between the practices is required. Separate funds may also decide to work together in order to increase their purchasing power. These are usually called 'multifunds' or 'cooperatives' and may operate on either a formal or informal basis. In such arrangements it is common for individual funds to specialize in contracting for particular services.

The response of the NHS Executive to the evolution of these various forms of fundholding has been the announcement of an expanded range of fundholding options to commence from the preparatory year in April 1995. For the time being, new fundholders may choose the range of services they wish to purchase, and with the reduction in list size from 7000 to 5000 there should be less need for standard fundholders to group together in consortia. In addition, about 30 pilot projects will look at the feasibility of fundholders purchasing all hospital and community health service care for their practice.

Such developments will give GPs much greater influence contractually over the services which are provided to their patients. This will call for increased responsibility and recognition of the effects of moving contracts, adequate notice of contract changes and a high level of cooperation between the GPs and practices involved.

*ADVANTAGES OF
THE
FUNDHOLDING
SCHEME*

As fundholding purchasing power increases, views are likely to become even more polarized on what the advantages or disadvantages of the scheme are. If increasing uptake can be used as a reliable indicator of the scheme's merits, then many GPs are expressing the scheme's popularity. Fundholding can deliver the following benefits:

♦ Shifts the balance of decision making from the secondary care sector to primary health care and enhances opportunities for integration. GPs are able to make informed decisions about their patients' secondary care requirements and may be able to improve the link between the two sectors.

♦ Allows shifts in resources enabling money to follow patients and links resource investment to clinical decision-making in primary care.

♦ Enhances the communication between GPs and hospital services through a system of direct negotiation. GPs and hospital clinicians are encouraged, through the contracting process, to meet to discuss contract proposals on activity and quality.

♦ Ensures that practices prepare business plans which will set out primary healthcare team objectives, health needs assessment and investment criteria. The business plans will enable the practice to become more pro-active in the way that it carries out business on behalf of its patients.

♦ Innovation in care provision with GPs contributing creatively to health service development. It is felt that GP fundholders are more flexible in their approach to service delivery. It is therefore easier for them to be innovative and experiment with various projects. If successful, these projects may be copied by health authorities for the benefit of all patients and not merely those whose GP happens to be a fundholder.

♦ Empowers practices to organize themselves to meet the individual and collective needs of a practice population. For example, GP fundholders have the purchasing power to request providers to be more responsive to the needs of the practice's patients through the provision of outreach clinics.

♦ Places the resources and decision-making process at the closest point to the delivery and assessment of health care. GPs are therefore immediately aware of the cost implications of their clinical decisions.

♦ Enables the movement of resources between hospital, prescribing and practice staff elements within the fundholding budget. If a practice has an underspending under one budget heading, it may transfer resources to another to enable it to pay for unexpected pressures during the course of the year (virement).

♦ The management allowance enhances practice management and reinforces practice based administration. Improved, better quality practice administration will enable the practice to be more efficient.

♦ Enhances family practice based information systems. Many GP fundholding practices have been able to take advantage of FHSA financial assistance to introduce or improve information technology.

♦ Improving quality of care, e.g. lower waiting times for operations, consultants operating local 'outreach' clinics and better clinical information to GPs.

The scheme has created a means for shifting both activity and resources from secondary to primary care. It has released creative energy among GPs for the benefit of their patients in developing a range of accessible services which did not previously exist. It has acted as a spur to DHAs to improve their purchasing on behalf of their constituent GPs. Fundholding will increasingly represent core business for the FHSAs, and it will continue to stimulate provider units to improve the quality of their services and information systems.

DISADVANTAGES OF THE FUNDHOLDING SCHEME

Conversely, the policy has its critics and these can be grouped under the headings of equity, perverse incentives, overheads, fragmentation and specialist training.

Equity

The equity of a two tier service has been made more explicit by fundholding practices demanding more and more responsive care for their patients. This, it is claimed, widens the differentials between fundholding and non-fundholding practices' waiting times for inpatient and outpatient care.

Perverse incentives

Unfortunately, the scope for distortions occurring in the achievement of strategic aims due to cost shifting (i.e. fundholders negotiating discounts for service contracts) and micro purchasing (i.e. purchasing against historical referral patterns or outside the NHS) are facets of the reforms that now need market management. It would, however, be unfair to criticize GPs who are just learning how to make tactical purchasing work on their patients' behalf.

Overheads

The administrative overheads associated with fundholding are considerable, and increasing paperwork and bureaucracy are taking their toll. Large increases in efficiency would be required to justify these new burdens. The scheme has been criticized for incurring increased administration costs. Indeed, it has been calculated (Davies, 1995) that the annual cost to the NHS of managing fundholding can reach £80 000 per practice.

Fragmentation

Achieving collaborative purchasing between DHA/FHSA and social services departments will involve a good deal of liaison, goodwill and a genuine desire to work together. Unfortunately, different systems and different cultures all need nurturing and this takes time and resources if the stakeholders are to feel appropriately engaged. If this does not happen, purchasing will become fragmented and this would prevent effective and efficient resource utilization for health for the population as a whole.

A further problem of fragmentation may occur in introducing national healthcare policy. An example of this is the recent recommendations contained in *Changing Childbirth* (Department of Health, 1993) where nationally the government wishes to introduce changes to antenatal care which is being followed by DHAs. GPs, on the other hand, may have a different view of how the recommendations should be introduced and this may result in *Changing Childbirth* being introduced piecemeal in different parts of the country. An area of particular concern is the nomination of 'lead professionals' to expectant mothers as this has been hotly disputed between GPs and midwives.

SPECIALIST TRAINING   The contract emphasis on consultant input, outreach clinics and contracts with non-NHS providers has diluted the experience for trainee specialists. This may have serious repercussions for the NHS in the future in that it will create a shortage of specialists in certain areas. A case study illustrating the advantages and disadvantages of fundholding can be found at the end of this chapter.

THE PROVIDER/ GPFH INTERFACE   The separation of purchasing and providing functions has forged new relationships and styles of working at all levels in the NHS. The introduction of GP fundholding has focused attention on purchasing for relatively small practice populations, and has given fundholders a powerful lever with which to shape services provided by local Trusts. This interface between providers and fundholders presents opportunities for achieving some of the most significant benefits such as shifting the balance of care from secondary to primary care sectors, but this process has to be managed through contract negotiations and monitoring.

As the coverage of fundholding has spread there are now few providers who do not regard fundholders as central to their marketing strategies. Similarly, fundholders depend upon providers responding to their requirements in order to provide appropriate services for their patients. This interdependency has been recognized in the draft accountability framework for fundholders which states that 'fundholders' may use NHS resources to achieve the most appropriate care for their patients, but 'unjustified or persistent breaches of the framework may lead to expulsion from the fundholding element'.

A prime responsibility of fundholders will be to produce an annual practice plan, which may include an outline longer-term view, and also to announce major shifts in purchasing intentions in the same way as district health authorities. This is both to assist health authorities form an overview of the combined effect of purchasing plans (and feed this back to GPs), and to assist providers to plan more effectively for the coming year.

Although fundholding is not designed to make life secure for providers, there is clearly a need for advance information on the level and type of services required in order to allow the provider to make any necessary changes. The provider should ensure that they receive all relevant information they need during the contracting process to enable them to sensibly plan a comprehensive portfolio of services. Individual fundholders will not be able to convey the total picture and therefore FHSAs and commissioning agencies should also be brought into the providers' overall contracting process at an early stage.

The involvement of clinicians in the negotiations between fundholders and providers is important in order to validate service proposals, and also to ensure that the professional staff who are expected to deliver services have been involved in the decisions which have determined the contracts.

There should be trust on both sides and confidence that both parties to the contract are seeking to achieve the best possible service for patients. This understanding should evolve as the relationships between the Trust and its fundholders progress and mature.

If there is little mutual understanding and respect the system cannot be expected to withstand the strains which will inevitably be experienced. Regional arbitration, or referral of disputes to the Secretary of State, should be avoided by resolving disagreements between the parties involved as early as possible.

FUTURE DEVELOPMENTS IN FUNDHOLDING

As part of its strategy to develop purchasing, the NHS Executive issued further guidance on how the GP fundholders scheme may develop in the future. EL(94)79 *Developing NHS Purchasing and GP Fundholding* represented a significant step towards a primary care led NHS.

In summary, the Executive letter set out the following proposals:

1. A major expansion to the options available for GP fundholding (which will remain voluntary).
2. A continuing and important role for DHAs and FHSAs (and for the proposed new health authorities which will replace them).
3. A stronger partnership between health authorities and all GPs (both fundholders and non-fundholders).

Expanded GP fundholding

There will be three types of fundholding:

1. *Community fundholding* – which will be a new option for small practices with 3000+ patients or for those who are not ready to take on standard fundholding. This option will *include* staff, drugs, diagnostic tests, and most of the community health services in the standard scheme (excluding mental illness and learning disability services). It will *exclude* all acute hospital treatments (including outpatient attendances).

2. *Standard fundholding* – an expanded version of the existing scheme. In addition to existing services, this option will include specialist nursing services (e.g. diabetic and stoma care), and virtually all elective surgery and outpatients (with a few very high cost exceptions, e.g. heart transplants).

The *minimum list-size requirement* for standard fundholding will be reduced from 7000 to 5000 patients.

There will also be pilot projects in the following areas to help inform decisions about future options.
   - Maternity services will be piloted in six sites with standard fundholding as well as the 'total purchasing' option described below.
   - Osteopathy, chiropractic and patient transport services to the surgery will be piloted within standard fundholding and
   - Medical inpatients, mental illness and other long-stay treatments will be piloted for possible inclusion at a later stage

3. *Total purchasing* – where GPs in a locality purchase all hospital and community health service care for their patients.

The role of the new health authority

It is proposed that existing DHAs and FHSAs will be replaced by a single new health authority at local level accountable to the Secretary of State through the NHS Executive regional offices. These new health authorities will be responsible for implementing national health policy. They will have overall responsibility for assessing the healthcare needs of the local population and for developing integrated strategies for meeting those needs across primary and secondary care boundaries.

Currently, DHAs have a major role as direct purchasers of hospital and community health services. The new health authorities will continue to have a significant direct purchasing role, for example for those services requiring a broad population base and for services outside the fundholding scheme.

As fundholding develops, however, GPs will become increasingly important as purchasers in their own right. Health authorities should support this move towards primary care led purchasing and ensure that it works for the benefit of individual patients and the local population as a whole.

This will enable health authorities to undertake their strategic, monitoring and support roles more effectively as follows:

♦ *Strategy.* Health authorities will develop strategy in collaboration with GPs, local people and other agencies (particularly local authorities) to meet national and local priorities. They will remain responsible for discharging public health functions, for establishing a local population perspective of health and healthcare needs, and working with others to ensure this influences local health strategy. Health authorities will also be expected to involve the public in developing local strategy and to increase public understanding about health and the changing nature of health services.

♦ *Monitoring*. Within the national framework, health authorities will advise on budget allocations to GP fundholders and ensure that the way in which GPs fulfil their providing and purchasing role is in the interests of patients and local people. The health authorities will be responsible for ensuring that national policy and local strategy are implemented effectively.

♦ *Support*. Health authorities will provide support to GPs in both their primary care provision and fundholding capacities through the provision of advice, investment and training. They will purchase direct those services which require a broad population base. They will also provide information to practices to support GP purchasing decisions.

♦ As GP fundholding develops, health authorities will need to shift the balance of their activity towards these strategic, monitoring and support roles. New partnerships will be formed between general practice and health authorities. The health authorities' role outlined above requires *all* health authorities to understand and support primary care provision, to work closely with existing fundholders and enable other GPs to become fund-holders, and to ensure all GPs contribute to the development of local strategy.

Accountability   Although fundholders' formal line of accountability will be to the regional offices of the NHS executive, most of their day-to-day contact with NHS management will be through the new health authorities.

Fundholders are already required to publish major purchasing intentions six months before the start of the financial year and to produce annual practice plans. Health authorities and fundholders around the country have also developed a variety of ways of reviewing progress and reporting on achievements. The government is, at the time of writing, consulting on a draft accountability framework for GPs. This will set out the principles and core requirements for that accountability and for the relationships between fundholders and the new health authorities. The draft framework can be found in Appendix 1.

SUMMARY   If GP fundholding has brought decision making closer to the patient and the scheme provides incentives for them to operate

cost effectively, they may soon be viewed as the explicit rationer of care which may undermine their advocacy role. During 1994/5 there were over 2000 fundholding practices with over 8500 GPs bringing the coverage of fundholding to now over 35% of the UK's population. More practices joined the fifth wave in April 1995, so the number has increased further.

This has been coupled with increasing resources being given to fundholders that will reduce some of the arbitrary distinctions between procedures that are in the fund and those that are not, since the total resources given to fundholders could add up to 100% of the health authority's budget!

However, total fundholding is only likely to become a reality if the negative elements of fundholding are minimized, such as masses of paperwork, and complex administrative systems.

Furthermore, GPs must be seen to retain their role as the patients' advocate which must not be usurped by their fundholding duties to act as rationers of care services.

For the DHAs and FHSAs, the concept of locality purchasing may become an even more powerful engine for change. The NHS is one of many factors which influences the health status of the population. Health is profoundly influenced by the environment, life styles, social conditions and economics. The importance of these environmental factors, together with the fact that over 90% of health care is provided at practice level, places primary care at the heart of healthcare purchasing. This message is reinforced in our system of health care which ensures that most secondary care is accessed through general practice.

Certainly DHAs and FHSAs and non-fundholding GPs all have an interest in hearing and nurturing this message. What will be interesting is which train reaches the station first, fundholding or locality purchasing, and whether either will be derailed before their journey is complete because they failed to recognize that all purchasing will be primary care led and the mechanics is of secondary consideration.

CASE STUDY

Advantages and disadvantages of fundholding

A GP fundholding practice situated about 14 miles from a major acute Trust, Hospital A, wants to purchase General Surgical 'Outreach' clinics. It specifies that it would like to hold regular consultant clinics within the surgery. The benefits for the patient are that they will not have to travel to the hospital for their consultation, but can be seen at their local GP's practice. There will also be teaching benefits for the GPs as they will be permitted to sit in on the consultations with the hospital consultant. Therefore, there will be an opportunity for improved communication and liaison between clinicians and an enhanced working relationship between the practice and Hospital A.

Furthermore, the GP fundholder contract with the hospital specifies that the practice's outpatients referred to the hospital must normally be seen by a consultant at their first appointment. If they are not, then the patients must not be seen by a doctor of a lower status than a senior registar. If they are seen by a senior registrar on their first attendance, then the patient must be seen by a consultant at any subsequent attendance.

It can be seen, therefore, that the practice are improving the quality of services that they are purchasing for their patients.

If a number of GP fundholders follow this example, however, and insist on the same level of service for their patients, then there could be heavy implications for both Hospital A and on patients of non-fundholding GPs.

When consultants attend outreach clinics, their services will obviously not be available within the hospital. Their urgent specialist advice will not be on-hand and neither will they be available for clinics attended by non-fundholder patients. There is also the travel time and travel costs to practices to consider.

With regard to outpatient clinics, there will be an effect on training for junior medical staff. The learning opportunities in outpatients will be removed if senior house officers and registrars do not follow up their own patients because fundholders insist that consultants do it. This will affect the availability of specialist skills within the NHS in the future.

If senior doctors are committed to seeing GP fundholder out-patients only, then their availability to see non-fundholder patients will be curtailed. Non-fundholding patients will therefore be seen by more junior medical staff which may have implications for the hospital in terms of its services.

FURTHER
QUESTIONS

The following questions identify some issues from this chapter which you may wish to consider or discuss further with your colleagues.

♦ Are all the members of your team familiar with the GP fundholding scheme, particularly what is included in the *List of Goods and Services?*

♦ How do you keep abreast of developments and changes to the GP fundholding scheme?

♦ Do you know what proportion of your unit or directorate income comes from GP fundholders?

♦ How do you ensure that you identify GP fundholders' activity and that appropriate and timely invoices are raised?

♦ How do you ensure that you take part in GP fundholder contract negotiation meetings?

♦ Do you know what activity and quality measures are included in your GP fundholder contracts?

REFERENCES   Bunce, C. and Davies, J. (1995), What the changes will mean for you. *Fundholding* January: 18–19.

Davies, J. (1995), How much does the scheme cost? *Fundholding* January: 22–23.

Department of Health (1989), *Working for Patients*. London: HMSO.

Department of Health (1993), *Changing Childbirth*. London: HMSO.

Department of Health Circular EL(94)79. *Developing NHS Purchasing and GP Fundholding*.

Department of Health Circular HSG(94)25. *GP Fundholding: List of Goods and Services*.

Department of Health Circular EL(92)47. *Priorities and Planning Guidance 1993/94*.

Department of Health Circular EL (94)84. *General Practice Fundholding – Guidance on setting Budgets for 1995/6"*.

National Audit Office (1994), R*eport of the Comptroller and Auditor General – General Practitioner Fundholding in England*. London: HMSO.

South East Thames Regional Health Authority (1993), *GP Fundholding Handbook and Reference Manual*.

Williams, S. (1994), *The Way Forward – Fundholding 1994*. Publishing Initiative Books.

APPENDIX 1   DRAFT ACCOUNTABILITY FRAMEWORK FOR GP FUNDHOLDING (December 1994)

Summary of key requirements
Management accountability:

♦ preparation of an annual practice plan
♦ signalling major shifts in purchasing intentions
♦ preparation of an annual performance report
♦ review performance with the health authority within the national framework

Accountability to patients and the wider public:

♦ publishing information (e.g. annual practice plan and performance report)
♦ involving patients in service planning
♦ ensuring an effective complaints system

Financial accountability:

♦ preparation of annual accounts for independent audit
♦ providing monthly information for monitoring by the health authority
♦ securing health authority agreements to use of savings
♦ stating planned contribution to the local efficiency targets set by the NHS Executive

Clinical and professional accountability:

♦ participating in clinical audit of GMS activities
♦ ensuring appropriate clinical audit of purchased hospital and community health care

APPENDIX 2   *FORM OF AGREEMENT*

This Agreement is made between

(The GP Fundholder)
and the Trust
(The Provider)

for the provision of services specified in the attached document for a period of 12 months commencing on 1st April 19   and is renewable thereafter subject to negotiation and agreement on revised terms.

Signed on behalf of the Fundholding Practice
by: ....

Name:
Position:
Date:

Signed on behalf of the Trust
by: ....

Name:
Position:
Date:

GP fundholders agreement with NHS Trust

SECTION A

General Terms and Conditions

A.1   These are as agreed between the Trust and the host District Health Authority for the period 19

A.2   Section A of the latest host Health Authority Contract will form the basis of the quality/performance specifications of this Contract unless otherwise specified within Section B of this Contract.

SECTION B

General Agreement Specifications

B.1   Prices will be fixed for the year of the Agreement in accord with National guidelines. The Purchaser will only pay for work that has actually taken place.

B.1.2   The Agreement for in-patients will be
Invoices will be raised according to the prices detailed in the tariffs which are attached to this document at Schedule 2.

B.1.3   The Agreement for out-patient services will be

B.1.4   The Agreement for Diagnostic and other clinical support services will be

B.1.5   The Consultant sessions (out-reach clinics) held within the GP's surgeries will be priced to include all reasonable elements of cost. The diagnostic and other support services costs resulting from these sessions (out-reach clinics) will be covered by the Agreement for such services as specified in section B.1.4

B.1.6   The out-patient attendance costs within the Trust will include all diagnostic tests normally carried out within the Trust.

B.1.7   The first out-patient appointment in the Trust will normally be with a Consultant and no out-patient will be seen for their first appointment solely by doctors of lower than Registrar status. If the first out-patient appointment is with a Registrar then the second out-patient appointment, if required, will be with a Consultant.

B.1.8   If a Consultant is unable to attend a GP surgery session (out-reach clinic) he/she will notify the practice and agree alternative arrangements. The practice will be informed at least seven days prior to the designated session if the Consultant cannot attend, unless in mutually agreeable exceptional circumstances. Should the Trust be unable to notify the Purchaser within the specified seven day period there will be a reduction of 50% of the next GP surgery session (out-reach clinic) price for that Consultant. This will cover the administration costs of re-arranging the session.

B.1.9   In circumstances relating to Section B.1.8 it is the Consultant's responsibility to notify his/her business manager to ensure correct invoicing takes place.

B.1.10 The provider will make every effort to reduce the number of follow-on attendances, but not to the detriment of clinical need. The Provider agrees to provide accurate and timely information so that the Purchaser will be able to monitor the number and type of attendances.

B.1.11 A fully completed encounter form will be sent to the practice each month listing all encounters for the previous month period. This encounter form will be sent to the Purchaser within 15 days of the start of the current month and will relate to all encounters during the immediate preceding month.

B.1.12 The following minimum information set will be provided on the encounter form:

a) Out-patients   Date of appointment
                      Specialty
                      Grade/Name of clinician seen
b) In-patients   Date of admission
                      Proposed operation
                      Appropriate OPCS code

B.1.13 There will be no charge for non-attenders at out-patient clinics or in-patients (DNAs).

B.1.14 Invoices will be submited monthly in arrears to the Purchaser. The invoices will only be accepted with a minimum data set detailing the following:
a) Patient's Acute Unit Number
b) Patient's Surname and Initial
c) Practice and Hospital identifier codes
d) Full operation details
e) All relevant operation codes in OPCS latest format
f) Clinical data in the form of a comprehensive and detailed discharge summary or a fully completed discharge letter

B.1.15 Authorisation of payment will occur only once the Purchaser has adequate evidence that the contracted work has actually taken place and that the minimum data set information relating to the contract has been fully completed as specified in section B.1.14.

B.1.16 On receipt of the invoice the practice will authorise payment and will pass the invoice to the Family Health Services Authority within two weeks of receipt of the invoice, retaining a copy for the practice record. The FHSA will only pay invoices which have been authorised by the practice. In circumstances where the practice disputes one or more items on the invoice, these will not be paid for until additional information has been made available by the Provider. However, the remaining items on the invoice over which there is no dispute will be authorised by the practice and sent to the FHSA in the normal way for payment.

B.1.17 A fully completed preliminary discharge form will be handed to each patient on leaving hospital, for information purposes.

B.1.18 Letters to GPs will be received within two weeks of the time the patient is seen in the out-patient department.

B.1.19 Hospital admission discharge summaries will be received normally within two weeks of the date of the patient's discharge. However, this will, at most, never be more than one month after the patient's discharge date.

B.1.20 Within the specialties purchased, tertiary referrals from one consultant to another in the Trust are chargeable. Details of the tertiary referrals will be sent to the relevant GP

Fundholder via an encounter form as soon as possible, which at most will be within two weeks of the tertiary referral being made.

B.1.21 Tertiary referrals outside the Trust may be made without prior authorisation being sought from the GP Fundholder. Consultants initiating a tertiary extra contractual referral MUST ensure that the relevant GP Fundholder is informed when the referral is made (ref. EL(92)97).

B.1.22 The provision of drugs to a patient, whether it be following an out-patient attendance or discharge from hospital, shall strictly follow the National and Regional Health Authority guidelines (EL(91)127) & (EL(95)5).

B.1.23 Patients who are referred by their GP by letter to a Consultant shall hear from the Trust regarding their out-patient appointment within 2 weeks, after Consultant prioritisation.

B.1.24 The Trust will provide the Purchaser with the following accurate information on an on-going monthly basis during the duration of the contract:

a) Current waiting times, by specialty, from receipt of initial referral for outpatient appointments

b) Current waiting times, by specialty, for admission.

c) An updated waiting list of the individual patients on the practice list, waiting for admission.

B.1.25 Any variations/amendments to this Agreement must be on the attached variation form signed by both parties.

GPFH AGREEMENT VARIATION

GPFH PRACTICE: ....

CONTRACT REF: ....   VARIATION NO: ....

....

This is to confirm the agreed variation. Please sign below to confirm your agreement to the changes.

Reason for variation: ....

EFFECT ON CURRENT AGREEMENT VALUE	REVENUE	CAPITAL	TOTAL
Current Value			
Variation			
New Value			

EFFECT ON CURRENT AGREEMENT ACTIVITY	IP	DC	OP	OTHER
Current Activity				
Variation				
New Activity				

Signed on behalf of   Signed on behalf of
the Purchaser   the Provider

Signed ....   Signed ....

Name ....   Name ....

Position ....   Position ....

Date ....   Date ....

SECTION C

C. DURATION OF AGREEMENT

C.1   The Purchaser has the right to cancel all or part of this Agreement if the Provider *consistently fails* to meet agreed service levels specified within this Agreement. It is the Purchaser's responsibility to draw shortcomings to the attention of the Provider. These sanctions are aimed to particularly cover:

a) Late submission of monitoring data

b) Excess waiting list times above those agreed in specialty Service Level Agreements within this Agreement

c) Excess out-patient appointment waiting times above those agreed in specialty Service Level Agreements within this Agreement

d) Failure to provide discharge documentation within the agreed period.

e) Failure to meet quality/performance standards contained within Section A of the latest local Health Authority Contract.

C.2   This Agreement may be terminated by either party, giving three months' notice.

C.3   This is a one year Agreement renewable annually by mutual agreement and supersedes any previous Agreement held with the Provider.

SCHEDULE I

GPFH AGREEMENT – ACTIVITY MANAGEMENT PROTOCOL

1. PRINCIPLES

1.1   The Provider will agree with the Purchaser a protocol for the management of contract (or Agreement) activity during 1995/96. In agreeing the protocol, the guidance contained in EL(93)10, EL(93)103 and EL(94)88 has been considered.

1.2   The guidance sets out a series of key action points based on good practice, namely:

◆ Contracts/Agreements for acute elective work must contain agreed thresholds and the necessary trigger mechanisms to ensure that Contracts/Agreements are managed and controlled throughout the year.

◆ Monitoring arrangements need to be agreed by the Provider and Purchaser if thresholds are reached in order to re-negotiate or manage activity back to within agreed levels. These arrangements have to be explicit in the Contract/Agreement and agreed before signing off.

2. CONTRACT TRIGGER MECHANISM

A) Principles

A.1   Actual activity should reflect agreed target activity levels and fall within a band, defined by tolerance levels above and below this target. There is a need to ensure that any potential in-year variances can be adequately managed to the satisfaction of both parties. This section describes the mechanism for making adjustments to the contract value should activity consistently be outside the trigger threshold, despite Provider action to manage elective workload evenly throughout the year.

A.2   The Provider accepts that the main objective of managing the contract will be to ensure contract fulfilment. The Provider will not plan to use the trigger mechanism as a method of securing new income, nor will it seek to manipulate activity to the same purpose. The trigger mechanism exists in the first instance, to enable variations, or anticipated variations from the target activity to be managed with flexibility by both sides, and in the second instance to ensure that any significant activity variations are matched by an appropriate payment variation.

B) Timetable

B.1   On a quarterly basis the value of actual activity on each contract category will be calculated and compared with the value of target activity to give a variance. Where appropriate this will involve consolidation of the value of activity for each contract category. Purchaser and Provider will consider the variance and its financial consequence at each quarterly review and they will agree any necessary action. In advance of the first and second quarterly review there will be no adjustment to value should tolerance levels be exceeded. If by November (after the second quarter contract review), the Purchaser and Provider decide that it is still not possible to manage activity in accordance with the protocol set out, then financial adjustments become chargeable over the remainder of the financial year and the Provider will revise the contract value using the mechanism described below.

C) Description of Trigger Mechanism

C.1   The trigger mechanism will be activated if the value of activity deviated by more than plus or minus 2.5% of the target value of the Contract/Agreement.

C.2   For the purposes of this Contract/Agreement, the target value of activity will be as follows:

ACTIVITY	TYPE	TARGET INCOME (£)
DIAGNOSTICS – PATHOLOGY – RADIOLOGY	BLOCK BLOCK	
IN-PATIENT DAY CASES OUT-PATIENT	COST + VOLUME/BLOCK COST + VOLUME/BLOCK COST + VOLUME/BLOCK	

C.3 *BLOCK*

Should the trigger mechanism be activated for Block contracts, the adjustment to the contract value will be as follows:

i. calculate the monetary value of actual activity (at the 1995/96 tariff rate)

ii. calculate the monetary value of the excess beyond the threshold

iii. calculate the marginal value of the excess by applying a marginal cost price percentage (70%) to give value of additional payment

iv. adjust value of contract to reflect increase in activity

C.5 It should be noted that the above actions will also apply to under-activity where a repayment will be given to the Purchaser.

C.4 Should the trigger mechanism be activated for cost/volume contracts, the adjustment to the contract value will be calculated as follows:

i. calculate the monetary value of actual activity (at the 1995/96 GPFH tariff rate).

ii. calculate the monetary value of the excess beyond the threshold.

iii. calculate the marginal value of the excess by applying a marginal price percentage to give value of additional payment.

C.5 It should be noted that the above actions will also apply to under-activity where a repayment will be given to the Purchaser.

C.6 An example of how the trigger mechanism will work is illustrated in the Appendix to this section.

3. CONTRACT ACTIVITY MANAGEMENT PROTOCOL

3.1 The Provider will issue activity reports showing projected and actual activity and value in each of the contract categories. These will allow both Purchaser and Provider to monitor deviations from agreed target contract activity levels and will be used at quarterly contract review meetings to facilitate discussions between the Purchaser and the Provider about what action to take to manage contract activity.

3.2　Action to manage over-activity

If the year-end projected activity, based on data from the first two quarters, is shown to be greater than the upper threshold limit and in the absence of alternative agreed action between both parties, the Provider will, at the express request of the Purchaser, begin to defer work until after 31 March 1996. In the first instance, work will be deferred only if a patient is on the waiting list for non-urgent treatment, has not been given an admission date and would not otherwise be an 'over-eighteen-month waiter'. If these measures are not effective, then it is assumed that the contract trigger mechanism (described in Section 2C) will automatically be invoked.

3.3　Action to manage under-activity

If the year-end activity is below the low-trigger point, the Provider will agree action with the Purchaser. The Provider and the Purchaser will be expected to share any relevant information which would explain why there was a reduced workload.

The provider will be permitted to offset over-activity in one contract category against under-activity in the other.

Appendix: GPFH Agreement. Cost and volume agreements, 1995/96 schedule

PRACTICE:

TARGET INCOME:　£250 000 (100%)

87.5%　= £218 750 lower threshold level

90%　= £225 000

92.5%　= £231 250 higher threshold level

92.5%　= 100% (GP gets at 70% marginal cost)

100%+ = £250 000 + (GP gets at 30% marginal cost).

A PROVIDER PERSPECTIVE

CHAPTER 4

Kim Hodgson

OBJECTIVES

♦ To explain how the NHS internal market works.

♦ To describe the role of contracts in the internal market, the different types of contract, and the contracting currency.

♦ To discuss the role of clinicians in the contracting process.

♦ To give practical guidance on successful contracting.

INTRODUCTION Since April 1991 both purchasers and providers have been struggling with the implications of the new healthcare market in the area of contracting. Central to the change was the introduction of a managed market which has exposed those involved to a whole range of new approaches and activities aimed at securing and delivering quality health care, at a reasonable cost and with equity of access, to the population.

For a provider, typically an NHS Trust, contracts are the means by which the income is secured to pay for the buildings, the equipment and materials to be used and the staff who will be employed to deliver the contracts. In most NHS Trusts, many costs are relatively fixed and have to be covered regardless of the number of patients treated. The absolute priority, therefore, for a provider unit is securing enough contractual income to enable the unit to pay its bills.

There is no point, however, in signing up contracts which the unit is unable to deliver. For providers, contracting is about securing adequate income through contracts which can be delivered.

Those who are engaged in contract negotiation in provider units are also engaged in a series of internal negotiations. Clinicians always have good ideas about improving existing services or introducing new services. Perfectly understandably, their focus is upon their own specialty area and their own patients. Successful contract negotiation in a provider unit is, therefore, also about satisfying, as far as possible, the aspirations of clinical staff within the provider unit.

The first part of the chapter explains the theoretical background to contracting from a provider perspective. Towards the end of the chapter is some practical guidance on handling the contracting process.

The chapter starts by recapitulating how a market works and examines the key differences between the *managed market* of the NHS and the sort of market in which commercial enterprises work.

This is followed by a discussion of the main players in the internal market – providers, purchasers and consumers. The chapter examines the *contract* as a formal agreement between purchasers and providers and outlines the content of a contract.

The objectives of NHS Trusts in the contracting process, including the need to ensure financial viability, the maintenance of a range of services and meeting their obligations for training and education, will be discussed.

A number of important contracting issues are then covered: the appropriate units of measurement in health care, how to estimate activity levels in contracts and how to deal with quality and pricing.

The pitfalls associated with the process of contracting and pricing will be highlighted, together with an action list for providers to help them identify the key difficulties, with guidance on how to avoid them.

Finally, the chapter discusses the organizational arrangements for contracting and stresses the need for clinicians to 'own' the contracts which they are expected to deliver. This section also discusses the issue of encouraging clinical directors to 'run their own businesses' whilst maintaining a corporate perspective.

The summary highlights the key issues in contracting from a provider perspective.

THE INTERNAL MARKET

This section builds upon the concept of the internal market detailed in Chapter 1 and its place within the National Health Service.

A market is a place where people trade. Sellers offer the goods and services which they would like to sell and buyers purchase what they need. A market offers a mechanism through which the needs of both sellers and buyers can be met. A market works well when both parties are satisfied with the deal which has been struck.

At least in theory, a market should perform a number of functions:

◆ It should ensure that sellers or producers only make what people want to buy. The market ensures that producers are *responsive* to the needs of customers.

♦ It should ensure that goods and services are produced efficiently and offered at the lowest possible price. Clearly, if producer A is able to offer the same service at a lower price than B, customers will start to buy from A instead of B. B will then have to find ways of reducing the price, make the services more attractive than A's or will have to give up and go out of business. Only efficient producers should survive in a market.

♦ It should encourage innovation (Manning and Dunning 1994). Customers are always on the lookout for new or better products and services. If a particular supplier can introduce a new product or a superior version of an existing product, again customers will switch their purchasing behaviour to the new provider thus stimulating existing providers to innovate as well.

♦ It should match capacity to demand. If customers only want so many of a particular product, suppliers will have to reduce their capacity to that level or be left with unsaleable goods. Similarly, if demand exceeds supply, existing suppliers will increase their capacity or increase their prices and new suppliers will enter the market, attracted by the higher prices which are available.

To a large extent, these theoretical considerations work in practice. There are many examples from the marketing literature of market forces changing the behaviour of products to the benefit of customers. Companies which have introduced products which nobody wanted have had to withdraw them or go out of business (one example is the Sinclair C5); prices have been driven down by new competitors entering the market and innovation stimulated by market forces.

All of these benefits, however, come from a *free market* and a free market has particular characteristics:

♦ The consumer has purchasing power which he or she can use freely – the consumer can decide where to spend his or her money.

♦ There are competing providers chasing consumers. Without competition in the market, none of the benefits will be realized. The absence of competing providers is called a *monopoly*.

♦ New providers can enter the market and unsuccessful providers are forced to leave it.

♦ The consumer has the *information* required to make rational choices between competitive offerings.

In a sense a market has been created by the NHS reforms. The key elements of a contracting mechanism, which establishes quality and price, are in place. There is evidence of changes in resource allocation and therefore service provision with some contracts being moved from provider to provider based on a comparative view of each organization's performance.

The health service market is not, however, a 'free' market. Young, Samual and Chambers (1993), a leading consultancy firm, identify eight features which affect the NHS market mechanism (Box 4.1).

Box 4.1
Features of the NHS
market system

1. Monopolistic conditions - where a single provider for a particular service exists. This particularly applies in remote areas.

2. Relatively mobile consumers - people generally want local provision and access to services. This may mean further development of the outreach service concept.

3. Dispersed control of referral patterns - GP fundholding has created a degree of uncertainty around purchasing decisions and the ability of providers to guarantee the retention of resources which were normally allocated to them through the health authority system.

4. High switching costs - the move of services from one provider to another can have huge implications in terms of the human, financial and political costs.

5. Politics - a public service demands public accountability which can reduce the risk that some organizations are willing to take in advancing service changes.

6. Poor information - this is a major problem for some providers and purchasers and becomes more critical as contracts become more sensitive to volume.

7. Weak purchasing - lack of experience and of strategic direction may be holding back the operation of the market.

8. Limited incentives - survival is the main incentive. For service developments one-off rewards are given but it tends to be clustered around the same provider units where the managers and clinicians are most active. This potential allows for gaps in service provision and therefore inequality to emerge.

The global position is similar to that in the United Kingdom in that demand for health care outstrips the ability of any economy to meet that demand. Demand is driven by public expectations, by political considerations, by medical innovation and by the changing characteristics of the population.

At the time of writing, it is still unclear to what extent the creation of an internal market and its associated reforms will deliver substantial benefits. There is some evidence of progress on driving up efficiency and stimulating innovation but the concept of increased patient choice remains notional, a subject to which we will return later in the chapter.

The internal market of the NHS is *not* a free market – it is a *managed market*. In a managed market, market mechanisms are moderated by other processes such as political decision-making and the influence of strong professional groups.

Another important difference between the managed market of the NHS and a free market is the tension which exists between healthcare choices for *individuals* and healthcare choices for whole populations.

The players   There are three main players in the market:

Providers are any organizations which provide healthcare services. These include NHS Trusts and Directly Managed Units (DMUs) but also include providers in the private and voluntary sectors.

Purchasers include any individual or body which is responsible for purchasing healthcare services for a particular group of people. The main purchasers in the NHS are commissioning authorities and fundholding GPs. Commissioning authorities are consortia of district health authorities that have agreed to work together to commission or purchase services for their populations. In the longer term, commissioning authorities will probably be replaced through full mergers of district health authorities. Purchasers could also include local authorities, other NHS Trusts, private companies and voluntary agencies.

Consumers are the members of the public who actually use healthcare services. The word consumer is used in preference to *patient* because there are areas of healthcare provision such as health education, maternity services and services for people with learning difficulties which deal with individuals who are not ill.

The fundholding   The fundholding GP (GPFH) is, to many providers, a serious threat
GP   to financial viability. The number of fundholding GPs is growing and many are testing their power by changing their traditional referral patterns. The resources which many providers would have naturally assumed would come to them are now in the market and is available to anyone who can offer the best deal.

GPs have three very distinct roles: that of referrer, of purchaser and of competing or collaborating provider.

1. The GP as a referrer

In many cases and particularly in group practices, GPs are not aware of the overall pattern of referral. Nor are they aware of the long-term plans for public health improvement by the development of local services. In the main their focus is on short-term access and, if they are fundholding GPs, on cost per patient treated. If they are not fundholding the primary concern appears to be the apparent inequality of access between their patients and those belonging to fundholding practices.

2. The GP as a purchaser

Many GPs are active in determining exactly what they will buy. For example, many wish to diagnose and merely to pay the consultant for the actual procedure, often without an initial outpatient consultation. For those who have outreach clinics in their surgery the issue of who 'owns' the patient is paramount. For example, if the hospital consultant sees the patient in the surgery and the patient subsequently requires surgery, to which provider should the patient go and whose choice is it? Some patients could be treated in the private sector, in the GP surgery or at another provider unit. The ownership of the patient still needs to be clarified.

3. The GP as a competing or collaborative provider

There is some evidence of shifts between the acute and the primary care sectors; however, there is no overall strategic framework and little collaboration between practices.

CONTRACTING FOR CARE

In the NHS, health care is purchased not by the consumer but by a purchaser acting on behalf of a group of consumers. A health authority or commissioning authority purchases services for the residents of its area and a fundholding GP purchases services for patients registered with the practice. In most cases, services are purchased *in advance* of their being consumed – rather like making a block booking with a hotel. You do not know exactly who is going to stay but you know that you are likely to need 300 bedrooms.

The mechanism through which this purchase is made is a *contract* between the purchaser and the provider. Contracts within the NHS are like any other form of contract *except that they are not enforceable in law*. It is probable that the government was nervous about a series of court cases between its health authorities and its NHS Trusts – essentially one part of the state suing another.

Like any other contract, an NHS purchaser:provider/contract will spell out:

◆ What services are to be provided.
◆ How much is to be provided.
◆ To what quality standards services are to be provided.
◆ When services are to be provided.

◆ How much will be paid for the services which are to be provided.

In addition, a contract may address questions such as:

◆ How will performance be monitored?
◆ What information will have to be provided as part of the contract?
◆ What happens if something goes wrong?

The contracting timetable
The contracting process in the NHS takes place to a timetable set by national government and is driven by the public spending round. Until the government decides how much is available to spend on the NHS, the process of contract negotiation cannot really start.

The timetable broadly runs from April to April and is set out in Box 1.7 in Chapter 1.

CONTRACTING FOR WHAT
When a purchaser places a contract with a provider, what exactly is the purchaser purchasing? How are the goods and services which an NHS provider produces described?

The terms in which the goods and services of NHS providers are described are referred to as the *currency* of the system – the units of health care used in setting contracts and managing performance. At the moment, most units are measures of throughput or activity rather than outcome. Currently *finished consultant episodes (FCEs)* are the most common form of currency for acute care and *contacts* the most common form of currency for community care.

For the provider there is an incentive to develop detailed contract currencies as, the more accurately the work they do can be measured, the more likely payment in full can be secured.

When the internal market started, the nature of the currency was largely defined by what hospital information systems could measure or attempt to measure (Raftery and Gibson 1994). This tended to reflect the Korner system, a system of performance measurement established in the NHS on the recommendation of the Korner Commission in the late 1980s. The main units of currency were:

◆ Finished consultant episodes (FCEs) also known as completed consultant episodes (CCEs).
◆ Surgical procedures.
◆ Outpatient attendances.
◆ Patient contacts.

A finished consultant episode referred to the care which took place from the point at which a given patient was admitted under the care of a named consultant to the point at which that patient was discharged *from the care of that consultant*. Before contract discussions take place the definition would need to be clarified and agreed. In addition FCEs do not normally recognize that one patient could have several procedures at considerable cost during one FCE.

Surgical procedures were relatively simple to define and not too difficult to count, as were outpatient attendances.

Patient contacts applied primarily to community services and to the work of the professions allied to medicine such as physiotherapy.

At the start of the internal market, most contracts were based on *average specialty costs*. Under this system, a specialty such as General Medicine would take its total costs and divide this by the number of finished consultant episodes. The result was the price that would be charged for a finished consultant episode in General Medicine. Over time, average specialty costing, whilst having the virtue of simplicity, started to cause real problems. It only required a fairly small change in the mix of patients treated (*case mix*) for the price to become unrealistic. If, for example, we started to treat patients who needed to stay in hospital longer or who needed more expensive medication, the average specialty cost would no longer be a good way of setting price and the provider would find that not enough money was coming in to cover the costs of care. Box 4.2 shows how a change in case mix can lead to a shortfall in resources.

Box 4.2
Changes in case mix

		Scenario 1	Scenario 2
Procedure	Cost	Volume	Volume
Complex major	£5000	25	30
Major	£3000	25	30
Moderate	£1500	25	20
Minor	£500	25	20
		100	100
	Average cost	£2500	£2800
	Total cost	£250 000	£280 000
	Total income	£250 000	£250 000
	Effect	£-	(£30 000)

Increasingly, providers have sought to move away from average specialty costing and to quote prices for particular procedures or for particular types of patient usually defined by diagnosis. Much greater progress has been made in surgical specialties where it is easier to cost particular procedures than it is in non-surgical specialties.

Similarly, pricing in contracts is increasingly starting to differentiate between inpatient, day case and outpatient care and, for outpatients, between initial attendances and follow-up attendances.

Difficulties arise when using contacts as a basis for pricing in community services and in the professions allied to medicine (PAMs). The problem is similar to that of average specialty costing. A 'contact' could be anything from saying hello to a patient in his or her own home through to carrying out a major nursing procedure. Only the ethics of the professionals involved prevent them from responding to the pressure to drive up 'efficiency' by doing more 'pop ins' and less real care delivery.

The government is currently piloting a new form of currency – the HRG (Health Resource Group). By the end of 1994/5 provider units are expected to have developed HRGs in at least one specialty. An HRG seeks to group together types of patients and procedures which are thought to consume similar amounts of healthcare resource, particularly in terms of inpatient bed days. The aim of HRGs is to enable purchasers to compare like for like prices amongst providers throughout the UK. HRGs are a development from the earlier DRGs (Diagnosis Related Groups) which proved unreliable indicators of cost as there was little direct relationship between diagnosis and care delivered. HRGs take into account the procedure likely to be carried out as well as the diagnosis.

Although there is still considerable ambiguity about contracting currency, there are three cardinal rules, the minimum costing standards, which can be seen in Box 4.3.

Box 4.3
Minimum costing standards

1. Contract prices should be based on actual costs excluding any profit element.

2. Contract costs should be established on a full cost basis.

3. There should be no planned cross-subsidization between specialties, procedures, and contract.

However much these forms of measurement are refined, measuring is still about *what we do* rather than what we *achieve*. Over the next five years or so, it is likely that there will be a steady move towards *commissioning for health gain*. In this model, the currency will be the benefits delivered in terms of the health state of the patient or client. Instead of commissioning a thousand hip replacements, commissioners will commission *programmes of care* which result in the achievement of agreed levels of mobility and freedom from pain.

Commissioning for health gain will offer a number of significant advantages:

♦ It will encourage innovation in clinical practice in terms of both efficiency and effectiveness. For example, if a commissioner was to purchase a specific outcome which is not yet regularly being achieved, it would encourage providers to seek ways of ensuring that certain outcomes are met, if they wish to secure the contract for the work.

♦ It will tend to drive out interventions of doubtful efficacy – if you cannot show what it does commissioners are not going to buy it. One example is for arthroscopy, where concerns are being raised about its role in diagnosing and subsequently treating disorders of the knee.

♦ It will promote integrated models of health care which bring together hospital-based and community-based elements of care, for patient groups with chronic conditions such as multiple sclerosis or those with long-term effects of a cerebral vascular accident (stroke).

♦ It will enable health promotion and disease prevention to be contracted for in the same way as curative medicine. An early example of this is the way in which HIV services are contracted.

♦ It will be a better model for chronic conditions.

HOW MANY WOULD YOU LIKE? The business of contracting is still in its infancy. Many of the hoped for benefits have not yet been realized as the mechanisms for achieving those benefits have still not been fully established.

In the early stages of contracting, activity purchased often reflected actual activity undertaken in the previous year. As contract activity was not based on future need it rarely took account of developments in clinical practice or of the health needs of the local population. Over-activity tended to be due to emergency workload and, therefore year on year, the emergency element of the contract increased and the elective element remained stable or reduced.

This had the effect of increasing waiting lists if the purchaser was unable to meet the demand for both elements of the contract. This problem has in part been offset by the introduction of more challenging targets for day surgery.

Price was normally uplifted for inflation with basic cost-drivers such as the number of bed days used or the amount of time spent in the operating theatre being the main denominator of price. This lack of sophistication in pricing meant that provider units were not recovering the full cost of providing more expensive procedures and therefore resulted, at the end of the financial year, in a deficit against contract income.

Today, the type of contracts in place vary but the main *block* contract prevails. The main reason is that they require relatively little information and are cheap to administer.

Trusts with better information systems are pushing for more volume sensitive contracts which effectively guarantees funding for additional work undertaken, a feature more common than under-activity performance. For the purchaser this type of contract carries more risk and it is likely that funds will be held back to cover any over-performance. Providers must be careful not to rely upon funding for additional work to cover their fixed costs as purchasers may insist that such work is carried out on a marginal cost basis.

Most contracts specify a *volume* of services to be provided. A Trust might be contracted to carry out 500 hip replacement procedures or to carry out 500 FCEs in General Medicine. Box 4.4 summarizes the main advantages and disadvantages of different types of contract from purchaser and provider perspectives.

Increasingly, contracts are differentiating between *emergency* and *elective* cases. Thus the contract might specify 400 emergency and 100 elective episodes of a particular sort.

Some contracts place *tolerances* around the contracted volumes. Thus a typical contract might specify 500 episodes *plus or minus 5%*. The tolerances are designed to allow for the difficulty in predicting patient flows with complete accuracy.

In agreeing volumes, the provider needs to be sure that the contracted volume for emergency work reflects the likely pattern of emergency admissions. If insufficient capacity for emergency work has been contracted, emergency admissions will keep displacing elective admissions leading to patient dissatisfaction, under-performance on the elective side of the contract and lengthening waiting lists.

The provider also needs to consider the impact of contracted elective volumes on waiting lists. If contracted capacity is less than required, waiting lists will lengthen which will make the provider unpopular with local GPs and their patients.

The contract should specify very clearly what happens when it becomes apparent that there will be a significant variance from contracted volumes. If fewer patients are coming through than anticipated, discussions need to take place with the purchaser to understand the reasons and to address these if appropriate. If the reduction in activity cannot be corrected, then the provider will probably want to negotiate to allow the funding to be spent on something else.

Some contracts do not deal with patient volumes as such. Instead, they specify when a service has to be available and to what standards it has to operate. Accident and Emergency services are contracted for in this way as are self-referral services.

In practice there is tremendous variability in the nature of contracts from one organization to another. The main factors which influence the effectiveness of contracting can be summarized as:

Box 4.4
Advantages and
disadvantages of
different contracts

	Advantages	Disadvantages
Block contract		
Purchaser	Certainty of financial commitments	Funds are committed, even if the contract is not fully used
	Easy forecasting	Difficult to force providers to change
	Minimum effort to monitor	
Provider	Certainty of cashflow	Little incentive to over-achieve
	Easy forecasting	Need to manage both costs and activity
	Minimum effort to monitor	
Cost and volume contract		
Purchaser	Tighter specification ensures priorities are addressed	Contingency funds need to be identified
	Provides incentives to perform better	Greater effort to monitor
Provider	Greater incentive to achieve more	Greater effort to monitor
	Ability to take advantage of under provision in the market	Dependent upon referrals above minimum being made to recover costs
Cost per case contract		
Purchaser	For low-volume high-value business	Demand may outstrip contingency funding
	Where demand is low but unpredictable	Monitoring load heavy
Provider	Actual costs recovered in direct proportion to the work carried out	Monitoring load heavy
		Nominal guarantees of business

Adapted from Owens and
McGill (1993) with
permission.

1. *The information systems available*. If the information system cannot measure the activity undertaken, the type of contract and its performance cannot be adequately monitored. This may result in gross under- or over-activity with the resulting financial consequences, usually with the provider unit carrying most if not all of the risk.
2. *The contract type*. A block contract has benefits in that it enables shifts between specialties but it is not sophisticated enough to ensure that all work undertaken is paid for. For example, a surgical inpatient admission will be more expensive than a gynaecological day case. If more work is undertaken in surgery than gynaecology then the provider unit is again at risk financially.
3. *The approach used to costing and pricing*. In deriving the price for a particular episode of care one or more cost drivers are used. These may include the average length of a patient's stay, the cost of a prosthesis or theatre time. The right approach is critical if the price is to reflect the cost.
4. *The length of the contract*. Most contracts run for a one year period. This makes it very difficult to invest in service developments which will, in the longer term, have significant benefits in either patient outcome or in cost.
5. *The realism of expected outcomes*. The purchaser and the provider must agree on what exactly they are expecting to be achieved from the contract. If there are differing views these must be clarified before the contract is signed.
6. *The attention to process and quality issues*. It is critical that the quality standards of the contract are explicit and that there are adequate monitoring tools to ensure that problems are identified early. Again, it is essential that quality standards are only agreed when both sides understand what is being asked for and are confident that it can be delivered.
7. *The process of establishing agreement*. Clinicians must be involved in the contracting process from the early stages to the final agreement and subsequent delivery. Ideally all specialty doctors should have an opportunity to influence purchasing decisions and make commissioners aware of their services, both the good and the not so good aspects.

PERFORMANCE MONITORING

In most cases, the contract will specify what information the provider has to give the purchaser, known as the *minimum data set* (MDS). Typically, this will consist of a monthly or quarterly report of activity against the contract specification.

The question of quality standards in NHS contracts is one of the most contentious areas of contract negotiation. Some purchasers issue quality specifications of awesome complexity requiring large amounts of information. The effort put into very detailed reporting against quality specifications can divert resources away from patient care.

Some quality standards have been imposed by the government through the *Patient's Charter* (Department of Health 1991; NHSE 1995). Box 4.5 summarizes the main requirements of the Charter.

Box 4.5
The Patient's Charter

To receive health care on the basis of clinical need regardless of the ability to pay.

Respect for privacy, dignity, religious and cultural beliefs.

You have the right to be told before you go into hospital whether it is planned to care for you in a ward for men and women.

Clear explanation of any treatments proposed including risks and alternatives available.

Immediate assessment (within five minutes) in Accident and Emergency Departments.

Patients to be seen within 30 minutes of appointment time in outpatient departments.

Patients whose operations have been cancelled for non-medical reasons to be admitted to hospital within one month of cancellation.

Guaranteed admission for treatment by a specific date no later than 18 months from the day placed on the waiting list.

All patients to have a named nurse, midwife or health visitor responsible for planning their care.

Patients to be given rights of access to their own health records.

Discharge of patients should be planned prior to discharge taking into account continuing health or social care needs.

Nine out of ten people can expect to be seen within 13 weeks. Everyone can expect to be seen within 26 weeks.

Ensured access to services for all including people with special needs.

Patients to be offered the choice whether or not to take part in medical research or medical student training.

All complaints about any NHS services to be fully investigated and responded to in a written reply from the chief executive.

If admitted to Accident and Emergency you can expect to be given a bed within three to four hours.

The pursuit of high quality health care should be a shared goal between purchaser and provider and it is appropriate to develop a joint strategy on quality assurance. Such a strategy should aim to set achievable and worthwhile goals and to eliminate duplication of effort between purchaser and provider. A good quality assurance strategy should not involve either party in the preparation and analysis of large amounts of data.

In the longer term, there may be a move to an *accreditation system* in which providers are accredited, perhaps by an external body, as providing services of satisfactory quality. This would relieve purchasers of the onerous and expensive task of writing quality specifications and developing monitoring systems to ensure compliance. Chapter 5 discusses issues of quality in more detail.

A key objective of NHS Trusts in the contracting process is to ensure financial viability. In addressing this issue, a Trust will consider the distinction between its 'core' income and income which can be considered at risk.

'Core' income can be described as the income the Trust receives from its main activities provided to its main purchasers, the DHAs. A provider may have one main purchaser from which it receives the bulk of its contract income or, as in the case of London teaching hospitals, it may have several purchasers who each spend large amounts of income.

Other sources of funds, such as GPFH and ECR (extra-contractual referral) income, are considered to be more 'at risk' as GPFHs are able to change referral patterns more quickly and, by their very nature, ECRs remain uncertain. These sources of income can represent a fairly large proportion for Trusts and careful consideration will need to be given to how this risk will be managed.

RESOLVING PROBLEMS

Problems and disputes do arise over performance against contracts and it is important to be clear about how these will be resolved. Contracts in the NHS between public sector purchasers and providers are not legal in the sense that they are enforceable by law. The Secretary of State can, however, impose a solution which is binding to both parties. The intermediate tier for the resolution of disputes is currently the regional health authority which has the role of conciliator. This role will, in future, be undertaken by the regional offices of the National Health Service Executive.

The most common form of dispute tends to be about volume. The contract anticipates a certain pattern of referrals to the provider but neither purchaser nor provider can directly control that flow. GPs are still free to refer to wherever they think most appropriate for their patients and the ability to predict patient flows for relatively small populations is still poor. It takes only a relatively small shift in the number of emergency referrals to throw a contract off balance (Box 4.6).

Box 4.6
Resolving disputes

Commissioner 'A' has traditionally purchased most of its acute activity at local district general hospitals 'B' and 'C', both of whom have major Accident and Emergency (A & E) departments.

Rationalization plans, however, will close the A & E department at hospital 'C' which will have the effect of increasing emergency activity, not only at hospital 'B' but also over the health authority's border at hospital 'D'. Hospital 'D' would like the anticipated increase in emergency referrals to be reflected in their forthcoming contract. The commissioner, however, does not have detailed information to support the hospital's claim and does not want to/cannot afford to purchase at the levels requested by hospital 'D'. It would prefer instead to support an increase in emergency referrals at hospital 'B'.

Negotiations are held during January to March to determine the correct emergency levels but no agreement can be reached between the two parties.

This outstanding issue means that contracts cannot be signed within the timescale laid down by the RHA and so the chief executives from both the commissioning authority and the Trust hospital are summoned to the offices of the RHA who will act as an arbiter on the dispute.

In addressing this kind of problem, providers need to recognize that purchasers do not in general have a 'slush fund' from which they can simply pay out for additional work. Similarly, purchasers need to recognize the ethical dilemmas which clinicians face when there is a mismatch between the number of patients turning up on their doorsteps and the theoretical demand set out in the contract.

The key steps in resolving disputes for both parties are:

♦ Understanding exactly what has happened.
♦ Trying to understand why it has happened.
♦ Agreeing actions to minimize damage to patients.
♦ Learning for next time.

ROLES IN THE CONTRACTING PROCESS
Management at the highest level is still, in many places, internally focused. The process of contracting demands that attention is directed outwards to the customer and to the purchaser of the services.

Each department in a hospital has a key role in play in ensuring that its services are communicated and understood. The main players in the contracting process are described below.

The chief executive

Here rests the responsibility for strategic skills and direction. The strategy should be targeted at both the external market and the internal organization. In many cases the Trust chief executive is adept at informal influencing which can produce significant benefits during contract negotiations.

Finance

We have yet to see fully developed finance departments which support the needs of the business and yet allow for internal devolution of both authority and responsibility. Basically, the role of the finance team should be to act as advisers, rather than the more familiar gatekeepers, to those who manage and deliver the service.

Contracting department

The main function of the contracting department is to coordinate the process of securing income and delivering services which meet the requirements of the purchasers of services and of the provider unit itself. It can provide advice on types of contract and documentation best suited to the individual service being negotiated.

Business manager

The business manager, who is more usually attached to a particular directorate or group of directorates, undertakes to ensure the delivery of the activity agreed within the contract. They will monitor the contract both in terms of quantity and quality and take corrective action where appropriate.

Marketing

Although in some hospitals a separate marketing function has been established, it is often seen as working closely with external agencies such as commissioners rather than focusing equally on the development of an internal marketing culture.

Clinical director

The involvement of clinicians in the contracting process is perhaps the most important goal to achieve. It is still viewed by many managers as a problem and one which many would not like to see happen.

One method of ensuring clinical involvement at all levels is that of the clinical directorates, headed up by a consultant clinical director (Box 4.7).

The role of the clinical directorate will be discussed fully in the next section.

Box 4.7
Clinician involvement
in the contracting
process

Study 1
A chief executive has no support amongst his clinicians for the NHS reforms. The consultant staff believe that the reforms threaten their clinical freedom and will not be involved in contracting or agreeing anything which might give management a foothold into their territory.
    The staff within the Trust feel uncertain about the future of their jobs as the work is being taken away to providers with whom communication and cooperation is better.

Study 2
A clinical director negotiates on behalf of his clinical team for contracts. Although there is little growth money available to purchasers, by agreeing changes to the case mix he has been able to secure funding for the development of a new service whilst also meeting the strategic objectives of the Trust.

THE ROLE OF THE
CLINICAL
DIRECTOR

The role of clinical director varies enormously between provider organizations as does the method of their appointment. In some units a single person heads up a range of specialisms; others have a director who is responsible for a narrow range of specialties who is supported by a business manager and a nurse manager.

In some cases the director is appointed by his or her peers (sometimes in his or her absence!) and in others by the chief executive. It is probably most beneficial for the former to be the rule as the director is then seen as a representative of doctors rather than as a representative of management, even though he or she will be paid for the time spent.

The key function for a clinical director is to manage relationships upwards to a medical director and the chief executive and laterally with autonomous colleagues and general managers.

The contribution of the clinical director to the contracting process is critical. Clinical directors should lead the contracting process for their own directorates. This does not mean that the clinical director has to be present at each and every meeting in the contracting process. It does mean that anyone who represents the directorate is perfectly clear about:

◆ The fact that he or she is *representing* the directorate.
◆ What can and cannot be agreed to on the directorate's behalf.
◆ The directorate's objectives in contract negotiation.

It is desirable that the clinical director establishes face-to-face contact with the people who are contracting for services. The clinical director will have a unique perspective on the reality of the clinical situation. He or she will be dealing with real patients and real staff – not just sets of numbers. The clinical director should be able to interpret the numbers and translate them into practical healthcare terms.

Most importantly, the clinical director should not *agree any contract unless they are confident of their ability to deliver it.*

It should, however, be recognized that doctors in management is a relatively new phenomenon. Doctors need to gain experience in general management and to receive ongoing training to enable them to cope with the complexities of the market. In the meantime additional support from the executive members of the Trust will be required to ensure that the best deal is secured.

Chapter 6 'Negotiating a Contract' offers some practical guidance on how to achieve what you want.

PREPARING FOR CONTRACT NEGOTIATION

Negotiation is the process through which two parties starting from different positions come together to an agreed position with which they can both live.

If the starting positions are identical, no negotiation is needed. If agreement is not reached with which both parties can live, then the negotiation has failed and failed for *both* parties.

The key to successful negotiation is good preparation. Many professional negotiators use the *Like – Intend – Must* as a framework for preparation.

Like to have

These are things which you would *like* to achieve in the negotiation but which you would be prepared to concede if necessary. They are the bargaining counters of the negotiation process. Like pawns in chess, they can be sacrificed but should not simply be thrown away.

Intend to have

These are the things which you fully intend to get from your negotiation. If absolutely necessary, you may give in on some of these if the negotiation would otherwise fail.

Must have

These are the things without which the negotiation will fail anyway. Contracting for a level of activity which you can meet and securing the resources which you really need fall into this category.

What do you need to know before the negotiation

Before you start to negotiate with the purchaser you must be sure that aspirations for your service do not conflict with those of other specialties. The Trust's annual business plan, which details how services will be provided and developed throughout the year, will give information about how associated services will operate. The corporate overview will be contained in the Trust's objectives and will form part of the five year strategic plan. It is important to ensure that directorate plans reflect the needs of the organization as a whole.

Within the directorate you will also need to negotiate with your own management colleagues before you start negotiating with the purchaser. Make sure that they will give you the information you need and will do the arithmetic for you. None of it is difficult, but it is time-consuming.

You need to have some feel for the types of service which the purchaser may want to commission from you and the quantities involved. This will mean looking back over your activity figures to find out what kind of demand exists and being clear about current waiting list levels. You may also want to read the *purchasing strategy* which commissioning agencies usually produce.

You need to have proper costings for each of your services and to know how these will be affected by changes in volume. Ask your assigned finance officer to prepare a table of costs for each of your services for various volume assumptions.

You need to think about any service developments which you may wish to advocate and you need to be clear about the benefits which you are claiming for these. Service developments which will result in reduced costs per case or measurable improvements in clinical outcomes will be a powerful bargaining tool. The onus is on you to demonstrate the benefits of the developments you want to introduce.

You need to find out how competitive your prices are both locally and nationally. If your prices are out of line with other local providers, there is a good chance that you will lose the contract unless you can show that your higher price really is justified in concrete terms like re-admission rates or postoperative infection rates. If you cannot show that you are better, then, quite rightly, the purchaser will buy the cheaper service. If your prices are out of line with national figures, again you are likely to come under pressure to justify your higher costs.

Try to put yourself in the purchasers' shoes: What are their *must haves, intend to haves* and *like to haves*?

MANAGING THE NEGOTIATION   As well as a senior clinician, the negotiating team should include the business manager and assigned finance officer. In some cases you may also want to take a senior nurse or other specialist.

Agree with your team that they will only contribute if you ask them to. You are a negotiating *team* and you are the captain.

Set out your arguments as clearly, reasonably and persuasively as you know how. Try to agree the basics first. For how many cases of what sort should we be contracting?

Listen carefully and politely to any counter arguments. If the purchaser thinks less capacity is required than you do, ask them to explain why. Have they evidence that the incidence of a particular condition is on the decline or that GPs are recommending different treatment?

Put your prices on the table and explain them. Stress any reductions in prices which you have been able to achieve through changes in clinical practice or greater efficiency. If you have been forced to increase prices, explain why this has been unavoidable and stress the off-setting savings which have been made elsewhere.

Put forward your proposals for improving the quality of care. Stress the benefits to patients. Point out the consequences of *not* making these improvements.

Put forward your proposals for service developments and explain how these will benefit patients and benefit the purchaser.

Throughout the negotiation process:

♦ Argue persuasively.
♦ Listen attentively.
♦ Behave politely.

Be prepared to *bargain*. This might involve linking things together.

'If you can agree to … we might be able to …'

Unless the issue is very straightforward, do not agree to anything on the spot. Take it away and work it through carefully before responding. Very few contracting issues can be safely resolved on the spot with a pocket calculator.

The following case study illustrates the fundamental points which have been raised in this chapter.

CASE STUDY   A hospital Trust is due to meet with their main commissioner to discuss the contract for renal services. There has been a steady increase in activity over the past few years as new patients join the renal programme and existing patients have transplants requiring subsequent years maintenance.

The commissioners, who have been funding additional activity for a number of years, now require a clearer understanding of what they are actually purchasing on behalf of their residents. They have indicated that they are not prepared to fund additional activity without this understanding and furthermore, they are considering moving towards a single 'preferred' provider for all of their residents' renal services.

Contract preparation is, therefore, critical to the successful outcome of the forthcoming contract negotiation meeting.

In *preparing* for the meeting, the hospital's contracts manager must obtain detailed information on the number and type of renal patients that have been treated over the past two or three years. In this way, the hospital will be able to identify trends in activity and also the likely level of activity that will be required for the forthcoming year. The commissioners' Purchasing Plan will also be read to ascertain the level of renal services being purchased at other hospitals.

An assumption must be made of the capacity within the hospital to ensure that it can not only deal with the year-on-year increase in activity, but also additional activity should the hospital become the commissioners' 'preferred provider'. The contracts manager must, therefore, liaise with his clinical and nursing colleagues to ensure that they can deliver the anticipated activity levels. He will also discuss with the finance department the funding that will be required to undertake additional activity and to ascertain whether discounts can be offered as inducements to the commissioner if they purchase larger volumes of renal work.

Before the meeting, the contracts manager will prepare an agenda for discussion and agree this with his commissioning counterpart. This will ensure that the key issues are discussed at the meeting. The meeting will be held at the hospital within the Nephrology Department.

On the day of the meeting, the Trust will field a team comprising the contracts manager, consultant nephrologist, finance officer and quality assurance manager.

The contracts manager will agree to 'chair' the meeting, thus ensuring that the key points that he wishes to make are discussed in full. Hospital staff have also agreed to 'take the minutes' so that decisions or action points are properly recorded.

The contracts manager will introduce his 'Team' and invite the consultant nephrologist to give a brief overview of renal services within the hospital, how individual patients are cared for at each stage of their treatment and how he proposes to deal with any additional workload.

The *opening* phase will then continue with both the commissioner and the hospital giving a position statement. This may be some distance from what both sides are prepared to accept as they may feel that the more they ask for at this stage, the more they are likely to get.

The negotiations will then proceed to a *testing* phase where both the commissioner and the hospital will test assumptions around their expectations – 'We can undertake all of your renal workload and offer you a marginal cost of £XXX'.

The next phase will be the *movement* phase which is really what the whole negotiating phase is all about. The ideal result for the provider is to obtain the maximum degree of movement from the commissioner, whilst at the same time, minimizing movement from the Trust's position.

Finally, if there is movement towards each other's position, the negotiation will enter its *conclusion and agreement* phase.

However, it can sometimes be difficult to know that any kind of agreement has been made. It is, therefore, helpful to quickly summarize any conclusions or agreements as clearly as possible at the end of the meeting.

As the hospital has taken a responsibility for the 'minutes' it is advisable to put any conclusions or agreements in writing as soon as possible.

SUMMARY

Over the last four years hospital and community units have been involved in the process of maintaining the delivery of their healthcare services whilst embracing a large and complex agenda of health reforms. One particular aspect of that change is the business of contracting. Providers no longer have a guaranteed budget but have to participate in a competitive process of securing resources which will pay for the services they wish to deliver.

The chapter has highlighted a number of fundamental points.

♦ The internal market in the NHS is a *managed market*. It differs in a number of important ways from the *free market* in which commercial organizations operate.

♦ *Purchasers*, in the form of *health authorities, commissioning agencies* and *fundholding general practitioners* place contracts with *providers* to deliver particular healthcare services.

♦ A contract specifies the *price* which will be charged by the provider to the purchaser. The government has specified that within the NHS:

> *Price must always equal cost and the same price must be charged to all NHS purchasers.*

♦ One area of development in contracting is the *currency* of the contract. What are the most appropriate units for measuring health care?

♦ There is a *national timetable* for contracting linked to the government's own public expenditure decisions.

♦ Contracts determine the *resources* which will be available for patient care.

♦ Contracts determine *priorities* in health care and often specify the *number* of patients for whom you are expected to provide care.

♦ Contracts are *negotiated* between purchasers and providers.

♦ Good *preparation* is the key to successful negotiation.

♦ Contracts are of such fundamental importance to the success of your unit and your ability to provide good patient care that clinical directors have to *lead* the contract negotiation process.

CONCLUSIONS   Contracting for health will lie at the heart of the National Health Service for the foreseeable future. The contracting process will be the engine of change in the development of health care in the UK, particularly as GP fundholders come to control an increasingly large part of the purchasing function.

At the time of writing, contracting is still at a fairly primitive level. Patterns of health care have not changed radically, no major providers have 'gone out of business' and there is still very little public debate about rationing and priorities in health care.

Within the next five years, the following are likely to have happened:

♦ GPs will be the main purchasers within the NHS. As a result, the contracting dialogue will be between GPs and fellow clinicians rather than between managers.
♦ There will be less emphasis on what we do (throughput) and much more on what we achieve (outputs).
♦ There will be some level of public debate which will make healthcare rationing decisions more explicit.
♦ Providers which are not able to demonstrate that they are delivering worthwhile health benefits at a reasonable cost will 'go out of business'.

The practical lessons from what has been discussed in this chapter for clinical directors are as follows:

♦ Make sure that you and your colleagues in other clinical disciplines are in the driving seat of contract negotiation and contract management.
♦ Make sure that you have a management team which is geared up to *support* you, not *control* you.
♦ Take the lead in developing more cost-effective models of care and make sure that you are able to demonstrate the real benefits of what you and your colleagues do.

CONTRACTING   ♦ Does a clinician clearly lead the contract negotiations for your
CHECKLIST   directorate?
♦ Do you have accurate and well-presented information about the demands on your service and the levels of work which you have done?
♦ Do you have accurate financial information which enables you to see the true costs of each type of care which you provide?
♦ Do you have accurate financial information which lets you see the effects on costs of different volumes of activity?
♦ Do you have a support team to help you in preparing for and conducting contract negotiations?

♦ Do you have accurate and timely information which enables you to monitor the performance of your directorate against its contracts?

♦ Do your clinical colleagues accept the need to work within a contractual framework?

♦ Have you a process in place to assess the value of the work which you do so that it can be clearly demonstrated ?

♦ Do you have a rolling programme of 'product development' which enables you to develop and implement models of care which are demonstrably more cost-effective?

♦ Do you have a strategy for moving towards providing complete packages of care?

FURTHER QUESTIONS

The following questions idenify some issues from this chapter which you may wish to consider or discuss further with your colleagues.

♦ What training and education would be appropriate to enable clinicians to play a full part in the contracting process?

♦ What improvements, if any, need to be made to information systems to support the contracting process?

♦ What factors would influence GP fundholders in their contracting decisions?

♦ How should we help clinical directors to balance the interests of their own directorates against the interests of the Trust as a whole?

FURTHER READING

Quality

♦ Koch, H. (1991), *Total Quality Management in Healthcare*. Longman Press, London.

♦ Koch, H. (1992), *Implementing and Sustaining Total Quality Management in Healthcare*. Longman Press, London.

Although these two books are expensive, they provide valuable information on a wide range of quality topics and are useful tools for dipping into to find examples and guidance for developing quality initiatives.

♦ *The Patient's Charter – raising the standard*. Department of Health (1991)

This booklet provides full details of the rights and standards set out in the Patient's Charter.

> ### Contracting
>
> ♦ NAHAT (1994), *Developing Contracting*.
> Results of a survey of district health authorities, Boards and NHS Trusts.

REFERENCES Department of Health (1991), *The Patient's Charter - raising the standard.*

NHSE (1995), *Revised and Expanded Patient's Charter Implementation* HSG(95)13.

Manning, S. and Dunning, M. (1994), Every day in every way. *The Health Service Journal* 10 March: 27–29.

Owens, J. and McGill, J. (1993), *Putting Patients First.* National Association of Health Authorities and Trusts (NAHAT), Birmingham Research Park, Vincent Drive, Birmingham.

Raftery, J. and Gibson, G.(1994), Banking on knowledge. *The Health Service Journal* 10 February: 28–30.

Young, Samual and Chambers (1993), *Effective Purchaser-Provider Relationships.*

SECTION II

MANAGING CONTRACTS

" YOU'LL HAVE TO EXCUSE ME ~ THIS IS THE ONLY WAY
I FEEL COMFORTABLE DISCUSSING CONTRACTING. "

CHAPTER 5

CONTRACT SPECIFICATIONS IN THE CONTRACT PROCESS

Stephen Parsons and Stephanie Stanwick

In dreams begins responsibility

OBJECTIVES

◆ To explain the purpose of a contract specification.

◆ To describe the process in preparing a specification.

◆ To provide suggestions for the structure of a specification.

◆ To highlight pitfalls to avoid when preparing a specification.

◆ To identify indicators of an effective specification.

INTRODUCTION Before embarking on this chapter a word of explanation should be given about the quotation which heads this chapter. 'In dreams begins responsibility', a quote from W.B. Yeats, was the title Stocking (1987) chose for the book published as a tribute to Tom Evans, a past director of the King's Fund College. The quotation was a favourite of his which he frequently used to illustrate the point that managers, as leaders with far reaching visions for change, also had the responsibility for enabling the change to occur, if these visions were not simply to remain idle dreams.

In researching the literature as background to the work on this chapter and reflecting on the pace of change in the NHS heralded in by the three White Papers' *Promoting Better Health, Working for Patients* and *Caring for People* (Department of Health, 1987, 1989a, 1989b), the quotation seemed entirely apt. This chapter focuses on the part that contracts and contract specifications have to play in the managed competition introduced by the reforms. Thus if the three White Papers referred to earlier were the vision for change, then effective purchasing and effective contracting processes were part of the 'toolkit' that would make it happen.

The Department of Health (1989c) in its early guidance, *Contracts for Health Services, Operational Principles*, identified the key characteristics of contracts for healthcare services. These were emphasized by Ham (1991), and included the following:

◆ The nature and level of the service to be provided.
◆ The price to be paid and the duration of the contract.
◆ The appropriateness of treatment and care.
◆ The achievement of the optimum clinical outcome.
◆ All clinically recognized procedures to minimize complications.
◆ An attitude which treats people with dignity and as individuals.
◆ An environment conducive to patients' safety, reassurance and contentment.
◆ Speedy response to patients' needs.
◆ The involvement of patients in their own care.

The Department of Health (1989c) guidance also referred to other measures of quality that would be applied (adherence to professional codes of practice) and to the provision of systems to assure quality.

How much has been achieved since the original guidance was published? Much of the literature published since then, which attempts to evaluate progress made in implementing the NHS reforms, uses as one criterion for this evaluation the progress made in the types of contract used, i.e. the move away from simple block contracts towards more sophisticated types of contracts (Appelby *et al*. 1993). These concerns centre more on the issues of cost, price, and activity for each contract and on levels of activity that move between different providers and contracts, than on issues of quality.

Opit (1993) argues that although the inclusion of quality indicators into the contract was encouraged using parameters such as waiting times and length of stay, general practitioner fundholders were more demanding in that they attempted to include criteria which were of greater advantage to their own patients. Opit (1993) goes on to argue that commissioners are dependent on the provider for information, and only the provider can capture information about the quality of the services they are providing. This obviously makes systematic comparisons between different providers and different services more problematic.

All these issues would indicate that purchasing remains in its infancy. Kerr *et al*. (1993) stated that

> the purchaser provider system may have gone 'beyond the end of the beginning' but it is still at an early stage of development.

The NHS is now poised at another crossroads in its development. In April 1996 new health authorities will be taking over the responsibilities now undertaken by the separate health authorities and family health services authorities; recent executive letters, *Developing NHS Purchasing and General Practitioner Fundholding* EL(94)79 and *Developing NHS Fundholding Towards a Primary Care Led NHS*, map out proposals for greater responsibility for general practitioners in purchasing and for a greater focus on primary care. This inevitably will mean that newer strategies for purchasing and contracting will need to be developed.

Against this ever moving background of change, this chapter outlines the role, purpose and responsibility that contract specifications have in the current NHS.

THE PURPOSE OF A CONTRACT SPECIFICATION

The main purpose of a contract specification is to act as an enabling mechanism for the establishment of contracts which will meet the health needs of the population to be served.

In fulfilling that purpose the specification has a number of functions including the following:

♦ To provide a framework for the contractual relationship between commissioner and provider.
♦ To define the service(s) to be commissioned.
♦ To inform providers of commissioner requirements.
♦ To facilitate market testing of healthcare services.

In this chapter the term 'contract specification' is used to refer to the document that sets out the requirements for a certain service or specialty e.g. paediatrics, gynaecology, district nursing services, etc. The matters specified within it are therefore particular to that service or specialty, and will reflect the commissioner's special expectations as opposed to the general requirements of a provider. It is therefore important that the specialty specification is read in conjunction with the 'General Terms and Conditions of Contract' which details conditions and standards relating to all services to be provided within contract, such as the need to adhere to Patient's Charter standards.

Before the process of contract negotiation can begin, it is therefore essential that the commissioner has clearly defined the range, type and quantity of service that he wishes to purchase.

The commissioner should also specify the expectations he has in relation to the quality of the service to be delivered. Finally, the commissioner should establish in the specification how the ensuing contract will be structured and monitored.

The specification which contains these ingredients will enable the commissioner to assess how a provider is performing by measuring his outputs against the requirements specified.

Culyer *et al.* (1990) identifies the problems in the lack of information which prevent a comparison on performance between providers. He states:

For the government to know whether the output is appropriate, or whether suppliers performance is adequate, requires sufficient information about performance for a judgement to be reached.

The contract specification when properly constructed provides a tool to enable such judgements to be made.

One of the key tasks of a commissioning authority is to identify providers who will be both effective in terms of their ability to deliver a service which will meet the health needs of a population, and efficient in terms of their use of the resources available, i.e. market testing. A commissioner may decide to undertake the process of market testing for a number of reasons including:

♦ Dissatisfaction with performance of provider(s).
♦ The wish to test capability of providers to offer a new service.
♦ The need to test the competitiveness of providers in terms of price and quality of services.

In order to fulfil this task the commissioner has firstly to be able to state unambiguously what service he is wishing to purchase, what level of activity will be required, and what expectations he has in terms of quality of service delivery. The contract specification is the document which contains all this information, and which should accompany any invitation to potential providers to submit a tender for future service provision.

The specification therefore serves the purpose for the commissioner of providing a vehicle for the translation of his purchasing intentions into specific service requirements.

For the potential service provider involved in the process of market testing, the specification serves the following main purposes:

♦ It enables the provider to prepare a tender identifying the level and type of resources he will require in order to provide the service in both quantitative and qualitative terms.
♦ It enables the provider to construct a price for the delivery of the service.
♦ It enables the provider to decide whether or not this is a service which he is capable of providing and wishes to provide.

Most health authorities have fairly formal procedures for receiving and opening tenders. Once the tenders have been opened the commissioner is able to evaluate their content by matching the requirements detailed in the specification with the proposals from each of the potential providers. The task of evaluation gives another opportunity for collaboration between commissioners and interested parties. For example, some health authorities have convened panels consisting of people such as general practitioner representatives, Community Health Council members, and user representatives to contribute to the evaluation of tender sub-missions.

The specification is a tool that the panel will need to use in identifying a preferred provider and in making a recommendation to the commissioner on the awarding of a contract.

Culyer *et al.* (1990) reiterate that the outcome of market testing needs to be that the commissioner has information that is:

> *sufficient to be able to act either to enforce contractual terms, or to be reasonably confident that switching their custom to other suppliers will improve matters from their perspective.*

The contract specification is an essential part of that process of market testing.

THE PROCESS IN PREPARING A SPECIFICATION It is important to recognize that the preparation of a specification is not a task that occurs in isolation from other activities but is one of the key parts of the commissioning cycle shown in Figure 5.1, which draws on key aspects of the commissioning cycle overlaid with details of the service specification review.

When writing a specification, the commissioner needs to seek advice and have a body of knowledge on a number of matters which will inform its content. Examples of where such advice and knowledge is needed include:

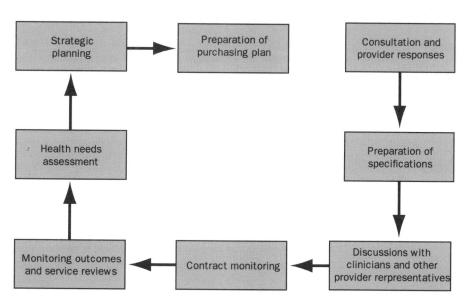

Figure 5.1
The commissioning cycle

- The health needs of the local population.
- The merits of different services, different methods of service delivery and differing priorities.
- The ways in which the pattern of services might be altered to improve the overall health of the population.
- The acceptability of services to users in terms of both the range and quality of services provided.

Sources from which such advice and knowledge accrues include an individual commissioner's own experience and training, local morbidity and mortality information, Department of Health guidance, Audit Commission Reports, policy documents, etc.

In addition it is important that commissioners make use of national guidance such as Effectiveness Bulletins and pay heed to research and development strategy.

Regular dialogue also needs to take place in both formal and informal settings including:

- Multi-agency service planning teams.
- Service user forums.
- Meetings with Community Health Councils.
- Meetings with clinicians.
- Contract review meetings with providers.

Responsibility for the preparation of a specification rests clearly with the commissioner, but it is a task which should be shared with a range of individuals including service providers, their clinicians, other professional advisers and service users.

NHSME (1991) refers to the work of a DHA Project Team reviewing service specifications and states that:

> *Specifications should be shared, being constructed in collaboration with providers and their clinical staff; and also with General Practitioners, Family Health Services Authorities and Local Authorities, to establish common views.*

In other words it is not sufficient to consult with others once a specification has been written, but the work of preparing the specification should be the result of collaboration between a not insignificant number of individuals and interests.

NHSME (1991) also referred to recently published guidance included in EL(90)221, *Involving Professional Staff in Drawing Up NHS Contracts*, which reiterated this principle and reported further on the work of the DHA Project Team, stating that:

> *Professional advice (both local and independent) is likely to figure prominently in the development of service specifications with a vision of how the resident population's health needs may be met – relative merits of different service alternatives (e.g. hospital versus community care, targeting of non-acute services for best value for money and max-*

imum impact), and interfaces between health and other services.

In May 1993 in a speech on 'Purchasing for Health' Dr Brian Mawhinney the then Health Minister stated that:

realism in contracts can be achieved only if they take into account doctors' views on clinical need and practice, workload planning, and medical developments.

Thus, if one accepts the premise that a range of individuals and interests should be involved in the provision of advice to commissioners and in the construction of specifications, one challenge for those commissioners is how to achieve that involvement in the most effective way. The second challenge is presented by the receipt of conflicting advice, for example, in the area of relative priorities of different needs or services, and in suggesting how limited resources might be used in the most appropriate manner.

Commissioners have to face up to both of these challenges and have to find the most effective way of meeting them. Commissioners would be failing in their responsibilities if they avoided involving others because the task was too difficult or ran the risk of receiving conflicting advice.

STRUCTURE OF A CONTRACT SPECIFICATION

It is not intended in this chapter to suggest a model specification, and it is indeed questionable as to whether one such model exists. However, throughout this section of the chapter the text is accompanied by extracts from a service specification for paediatric services and one for general surgery, which it is hoped will illustrate the points being made.

The structure of a specification may vary according to the particular service being commissioned, or in the light of local circumstances. However, one structure for a contract specification is suggested which the authors have applied and have found to be helpful. In that structure the headings for the various sections of the document are as follows:

♦ Service definition
♦ Performance requirements
  – Activity levels
  – Quality standards
♦ Monitoring information
♦ Forward look

Service definition

The Oxford Dictionary describes the word 'definition' in the following terms:

1. A statement of the precise nature of a thing.
2. Making or being distinct, clearness of outline.

In the service definition of a specification the commissioner should state in a precise way the nature of the service he is wishing to purchase. It is also vital that in order to be able to assess whether he is capable of providing the service, and to identify the costs associated with such provision, the provider has a distinct, clear outline of what is required.

The specification should clearly state the range and type of services to be provided and should identify the group of patients to be served. Services covered in one specification will on many occasions link with or be dependent upon other services. Therefore it is important that attention is drawn to any other complementary specifications.

Decisions as to what to include in the service definition should be informed by discussions with service providers, including clinicians, with other agencies (such as Education and Social Services in the case of children's services), with voluntary organizations, with service users and carers.

In deciding what to include within the definition, the phrase 'clearness of outline' is important. The definition should not be a detailed breakdown of each component of the service, specifying for example how many beds, or how many outpatient clinics should be provided. There is no need for the definition to make reference to how the service should be provided, it is more concerned with what should be provided. The skill in writing the definition is in striking the right balance between giving sufficient information to the provider to understand what is required, and leaving him with the freedom to decide how it should be provided. In writing the specification the author must bear in mind who will be reading it: to provide a detailed definition of what is meant by a paediatric service is likely to be a source of irritation to a consultant paediatrician.

Reference should also be made to any services that are to be excluded from the specification.

The example shown in Box 5.1 for a paediatric service suggests what might be included in a service definition as a 'clear outline' of a commissioner's requirements.

A second example of a service definition which takes a slightly different approach to the paediatric specification is the one shown in Box 5.2 for general surgery.

Performance requirements

Activity levels

The specification should state the level of activity that the commissioner requires from the provider, making clear the contract currency to be used for measuring that activity, e.g. finished consultant episodes, bed days, attendances, referrals, face to face contacts, etc. Following the completion of contract negotiations the agreed unit costs, and the total cost for the activity specified should also be shown under this heading.

Box 5.1
Service definition:
paediatric services

The provider is required to:

♦ Provide inpatient, day patient, outpatient, and Accident and Emergency hospital services for children. Services should be extended to those up to the age of 19 where continuing care by the children's service is more appropriate. Outpatient services should include access to specialist clinics such as diabetic clinics.

♦ Provide an integrated service for children with disabilities, and/or special needs, which in many cases will be multifaceted and will require a multidisciplinary approach.

NB: This specification should be read in conjunction with the specifications for community health services for children, child protection services, audiology services, orthoptics and speech therapy services.

One of the issues that needs to be addressed by commissioners is the selection of the most appropriate currency for the service being specified. In purchasing hospital inpatient services a decision will need to be taken as to whether measuring activity on the basis of finished consultant episodes or bed days will give a more accurate picture of the activity being undertaken. In specifying for maternity services is it more appropriate to ask for activity to be measured on the basis of the number of women delivered rather than on finished consultant episodes?

In community health services there has been a debate for some time as to the most effective way of measuring activity. The common practice of using face to face contacts as the contract currency has been called into question because there can be such variation between one contact and another in terms of the amount of time each one takes and the quality of care delivered.

Some commissioners and providers are therefore looking at the development of packages of care as a means of measuring activity. While such packages may give a clearer description of the care being delivered, there needs to be a clear definition of the activities included to enable commissioners to make judgements with regard to value for money and to make comparisons between providers possible.

The importance of definition applies not only to packages of care, but to whatever contract currency is used to avoid ambiguity about the level of activity required, to ensure that activity is costed correctly and again to enable comparisons between providers to be made.

Box 5.2
Service definition:
general surgery

To provide to the population a service to assess, diagnose, treat, ameliorate, repair and rehabilitate, through invasive and non-invasive procedures, bodily defects resulting from congenital abnormality, local or systemic disease or injury.

To minimize impact of morbidity and incidence of disability by providing an easily accessed network of appropriately trained practitioners in suitably equipped facilities.

This contract excludes:

vasectomy (subject to a separate contract)

The following procedures are to be provided only in exceptional circumstances and each case must be approved on an individual basis by the appropriate Consultant in Public Health Medicine:

liposuction
augmentation of breast
cosmetic superficial venous surgery (OPCS code L85, L86, L87)
removal of tattoos
reconstruction of breast (except following mastectomy)
cosmetic rhinoplasty
plastic excision of abdominal wall/other sites
circumcision for non-medical purposes
cosmetic operations on nipple
cosmetic excision of redundant skin of eyelid
reversal of sterilization

The management of elective demand should be organized in such a way that the needs of the clinically urgent cases are met first and the needs of those patients who will wait over 12 months by 31 March are met secondly. Only when these two requirements are satisfied will other patients be treated under this specification. This specification must be read in conjunction with the 'General Terms and Conditions of Contract' which details conditions and standards relating to all services to be provided within contract.

Box 5.3 indicates the level of service required for the residents of different localities.

Quality standards

The requirements upon providers in terms of the quality of their performance should be specific, rather than general, statements of good practice, for example, the requirement that:

Patients should be treated with dignity and afforded privacy

Box 5.3
Service levels

	Cost per case £	Locality One		Locality Two		Locality Three		Locality Four		Total	
		Act	Cost	Act	Cost	Act	Cost	Act	Cost	Act	Cost
Inpatients – elective											
Inpatients – non-elective											
Day cases											
Ward attenders											

while very valid in terms of indicating good patient care is too broad to allow for effective monitoring of performance. An alternative might be:

> *The provider should have in place a written operational policy which covers the arrangements for ensuring that patients are afforded privacy throughout their stay in hospital. The policy should deal with the arrangements for privacy at the time of reception and when receiving treatment. It should also address the use of accommodation at ward level. A copy of the policy should be submitted to the commissioners at the start of the contract period.*

In the above statement a specific requirement is placed upon a provider, namely to have a written operational policy in place, and a date is given for the submission of that policy. When considering what to include under the heading of 'Quality Standards', the importance of being able to monitor whatever is specified should be borne in mind. The inclusion of monitoring dates within the specification assists in the task of contract monitoring and helps to ensure that this section of the document does not become simply a list of good intentions.

The other factor to be borne in mind is that the requirements placed upon providers should be realistic. It is obviously important that targets should be set which providers need to strive towards, but it is also important that those targets are achievable.

There is no point stating, for example, that a provider should reduce the waiting time for an outpatient appointment to four weeks within a twelve month period if the current waiting time is twenty weeks. In this example it is more sensible to set interim targets which are realistic and which avoid firstly inevitable failure, and secondly a loss of credibility of the specification.

It is important that the specifications also make reference to the expectations of providers in terms of Patient's Charter standards. Local standards specified by the commissioners should not conflict with any national standards but should rather be complementary to them.

Boxes 5.4 and 5.5 illustrate the types of topics that might be included under the heading of 'Quality Standards', again using the examples of paediatrics and general surgery.

Box 5.4
Paediatric services

In addition to the specific issues detailed below, it is expected that providers will adhere to the National Association for the Welfare of Children in Hospital (NAWCH) guidelines on the care of children in hospital.

1. Providers will be required to adhere to a Children's Charter which incorporates the principles contained within the Patient's Charter, but which also takes account of the following:
   - a recognition of the special needs of children in terms of providing them with information about their treatment and/or their stay in hospital, the need to prepare them for admission to hospital, and where appropriate, surgery, and an appreciation of the possible implications of their special vulnerability.
   - the importance of involving parents in the care of their children.
   - the need for the care of children to be provided by appropriately trained staff.
   - the need to avoid undertaking surgery during the evenings or at night except in the most exceptional circumstances.
   - the need to ensure the smooth transition, wherever appropriate, from children's to adult services to ensure an effective continuation of care.

Providers will be required to submit a report on the monitoring arrangements for their Children's Charter to the commissioners by Month Six of the contract period.

2. A written operational policy should be in place which covers the arrangements for the admission of a child to hospital, both on the day of admission, and where possible, prior to that day. The policy should also cover arrangements for the reception of day cases and ward

attenders. A copy of the current operational policy should be forwarded to the commissioners by Month Three of the contract period.

3. Providers should ensure that no child waits longer than one week for an urgent OPD appointment, and should set a target of four weeks for a non-urgent appointment. It is expected that very urgent cases would be seen as ward attenders.

4. A written operational policy should be in place covering the arrangements surrounding the death of a child in hospital. It is expected that the policy will cover issues such as the arrangements for the immediate support of the bereaved parents, together with support for other children on the ward and their relatives, and support for all ward staff where felt necessary. A copy of the current operational policy should be submitted to the commissioners by Month Six of the contract period.

5. Providers are required to report on a quarterly basis on the audit activities that have been undertaken. The reports, in addition to summarizing the outcomes of particular audits, should also indicate the topics to be addressed during the next three months, and should report on progress being made towards the establishment of clinical audit.

There is value in specifying quality standards which mirror a provider's own quality strategy, both in terms of recognizing the specification as a shared document, and in reflecting the provider's own objectives in offering a quality service.

Monitoring information   When considering what to include under this heading, thought should be given to the information that is required by the commissioner to enable him to monitor that particular contract (Box 5.6).

The specification should give clear details of the information needed, the format in which it should be presented, and the frequency with which it should be submitted. Requirements on minimum data sets (MDS) and coding should also be highlighted within this section of the specification.

The provider should have the capability of collecting the information requested, and the commissioner should be able to justify why any particular item of information is required and demonstrate how it has been used. Commissioners can be rightly criticized if they ask providers for information which they do not make use of, or which does not contribute to, the delivery or development of healthcare services.

Box 5.5
Surgical services

These procedures should normally be undertaken on a day case basis. A percentage day case level is indicated for the following procedures.

	%
Repair umbilical, para-umbilical and epigastric hernia	x
Repair femoral hernia	x
Repair inguinal hernia	x
Laparoscopy	x
Varicose veins stripping or ligation	x
Anal stretch	x
Haemorrhoidectomy	x
Excision breast lumps	x
Operations on duct of breast	x

Agreed protocol with Breast Screening Service for admission of patients with positive results within 14 days or less.

All Consultants should participate in the National Confidential Enquiry into Perioperative Deaths (NCEPOD).

The commissioner is committed to the development of minimally invasive techniques and expects joint management of appropriate patients with the radiological department.

Within vascular angiography the following targets should be reached:

♦ x angiograms

♦ y angioplasties

Box 5.6
Monitoring information

Information required for contract monitoring (monthly)

1. Inpatient FCEs
   – elective
   – non-elective

2. Day cases

3. Ward attenders

Other information required for commissioning purposes (quarterly)

1. Report on waiting times for outpatient appointments

2. Summary of complaints received and action taken

Some of the information requested will be required for monitoring the provider's performance in terms of activity undertaken, and financial management, whilst other information will be related to the quality of the provider's performance, for example a summary of complaints received and action taken.

Forward look The final section included in the suggested structure is not concerned with the current contract. Instead it deals with issues that the commissioners would like to address with the provider during the contract period, with a view to possible changes in future contracts.

For example, the commissioner may want to explore with a provider changes to the contract currency used for a particular service. It may be, for example, that the commissioner wishes to contract for certain community health services on the basis of packages of care rather than face-to-face contacts.

Other issues that might be included under the heading of 'Forward Look' are given in the example of a contract specification in Box 5.7.

Box 5.7
Forward look

> During the period of the contract the commissioners will wish to discuss the following issues with the provider:
>
> 1. A review of child and adolescent mental health services in conjunction with other service providers.
>
> 2. The feasibility of bringing about a further shift in emphasis of provision from secondary to primary care in order to avoid inappropriate hospitalization.
>
> 3. The possible further development of specialized paediatric nurses to provide support for children at home.
>
> 4. The scope for further integration of children's services in the delivery of care.

PITFALLS TO AVOID WHEN PREPARING A CONTRACT SPECIFICATION When preparing a specification, commissioners need to be careful to avoid a number of pitfalls and they need to find the balance between certain conflicting factors. Examples of those factors and pitfalls are:

◆ Realism versus idealism.
◆ Over-specification versus generalization.
◆ Lack of collaboration in preparation.
◆ Lack of local sensitivity.

Realism versus idealism   It is important to set targets that whilst challenging are nevertheless achievable. The importance of realism throughout the process of preparing a specification is a strength that should be recognized whether it be in specifying activity levels, quality standards or monitoring requirements.

There is little to be gained in the commissioner 'flexing his muscles' in preparing such a demanding specification that either potential providers decide not to offer a service, or the contract inevitably fails and has to be renegotiated.

It is right that the commissioner has a vision as to how services should be delivered in the future, and of the changes that should be brought about to improve the health of the population. That vision, however, needs to be tempered with an appreciation of the different constraints placed upon providers, and an understanding of what is achievable within the resources available.

The need to find the right balance between realism and idealism is another factor that supports the argument for collaboration between commissioners, service providers and service users in the preparation of specifications. It is through collaboration that a view can be formed as to the capabilities of a particular provider, and an understanding can be gained of any special local circumstances which might have implications for a provider.

The skill of the commissioner lies in his ability to decide where the balance rests, and in being able to judge the extent to which a provider can be challenged by means of the specification to move towards the realization of the commissioner's vision.

Over-specification versus generalization   The commissioner also needs to be able to find the balance between being on the one hand too specific and prescriptive, and on the other hand being too vague or abstruse.

An illustration of being too specific would be a specification which detailed how a receptionist in an Accident and Emergency Department should address patients on their arrival, or one which detailed how the day-to-day running of a Radiology Department should be managed.

The danger in over-specifying is that the commissioner begins to move from the role of deciding *what* is to be provided in terms of activity and quality, and instead starts to become involved in *how* it is provided, which as an operational issue is the responsibility of the provider.

A further risk in being over-specific is that it restricts opportunities for innovative thinking on the part of the provider. As a result, opportunities for fresh and exciting developments in service delivery within the contract may be lost.

There have been instances when some providers have asked commissioners for very detailed specifications to include, for example, requirements in terms of staffing levels in a particular area, or the mix of skills in that area. It is suggested that the inclusion of such a level of detail in a specification should be the exception rather than the rule as it runs the risk of not only commissioner involvement in operational matters, but also of discouraging providers from finding innovative and more efficient ways of delivering services.

The consequence of being too vague in terms of the requirements laid out in a specification is likely to be one of ambiguity as to the expectations of the commissioner.

An illustration of vagueness would be a specification which stated that:

The provider is expected to liaise with general practitioners in connection with discharge arrangements for patients.

No indication is given in this statement as to the purpose of such liaisons, or the timescale within which they should occur.

Unclear requirements lead to ambiguity, which provides the potential for misunderstandings between commissioners and providers, misleading or poor tender submissions, and poor contract decisions. This in turn means that the commissioner will be hampered in his ability to make choices and decisions between different service developments and different providers referred to earlier when discussing market testing.

Earlier in this chapter, reference was made to one of the purposes of a specification being to provide a framework for the contractual relationship between commissioner and provider. In order to fulfil that purpose, the correct balance needs to be struck between over-prescription which could stifle the relationship, and a vagueness which could make it ineffectual.

Lack of collaboration

The importance of the preparation of contract specifications being a collaborative exercise has already been highlighted.

The effectiveness of such collaboration will be minimized if it only happens once a year at the time when the specification is written.

The contents of that specification should be the result of a continuing dialogue between commissioners, service providers, service users, the voluntary sector and other professional advisers. Failure to give sufficient weight to this activity will reduce the value and, it is suggested, the appropriateness of the specification.

Lack of local sensitivity

If a specification is to be credible it is important that it reflects local needs and circumstances. There is a danger in writing a single specification for more than one provider in that some of the requirements may be irrelevant, or inappropriate, and therefore the validity of the specification is called into question.

For example, the requirement:

... to have a written protocol for the use of a water birth pool

may be relevant to one maternity provider where such a facility exists, but is a nonsense to another provider where there is no such facility.

A requirement to:

reduce outpatient waiting times for routine appointments to eight weeks

is inappropriate for a provider where the maximum wait is already down to six weeks.

Again, the way in which a commissioner can ensure that specifications are sensitive to local issues and circumstances is to recognize the previously stated principle that specifications should be the result of collaboration. NHSME (1991) stated that specifications should be:

shared, being constructed in collaboration with providers and their clinical staff

together with users and other agencies.

INDICATORS OF A GOOD CONTRACT SPECIFICATION

In a speech given in May 1993 on the subject of 'Purchasing for Health', Dr Brian Mawhinney identified seven imperatives for effective contracting:

♦ Better working between purchasers and providers.
♦ Involvement of doctors in the contracting process.
♦ Involvement of nurses.
♦ Realism about activity and the impact of change.
♦ Ensuring contracts are appropriate.
♦ Robust information on activity and prices.
♦ Effective monitoring arrangements.

Reference has already been made to the essential part that the specification plays in the contracting process. The effectiveness of any specification can, it is suggested, be judged by the extent to which it supports the seven imperatives identified by Dr Mawhinney.

It is important that commissioners routinely evaluate each of their contract specifications in order to assess whether they do contribute to improved relationships with providers, whether they are the result of involvement by doctors, nurses and other professions, whether they contain realistic expectations and whether they support efficient contract management.

It is also important to recognize an evolutionary process in the development of specifications. When the role of commissioning began to emerge in 1991, specifications were largely descriptions of current services, indicating levels of activity and standards being achieved. Specifications should now be focused on the range and quantity of services needed and the quality of services to be provided in order to meet identified health needs and achieve health gain in the population served.

SUMMARY

In concluding this discussion, six indicators of a good specification have been identified and are listed below. A specification is one that fulfils its purpose if it:

♦ Confirms the strategic direction and purchasing intentions of the commissioning authority.

♦ Enables market testing to be undertaken so allowing commissioners to make decisions with regard to their future purchasing intentions.

♦ Is the result of collaboration with a range of people and organizations including providers, particularly clinicians, general practitioners, other agencies such as Social Services, and service users.

♦ Places realistic expectations upon providers in terms of both the quantity and quality of the service to be delivered.

♦ Results in a robust contract which is appropriate to the identified needs of the population to be served, and which achieves the optimum clinical outcome.

♦ Allows the commissioner to effectively monitor the performance of a provider by identifying benchmarks against which outputs can be measured.

At the beginning of this chapter reference was made to the need to turn dreams or visions into realities. In the current NHS the vehicle for bringing that transition about is the process of commissioning. The tools that the commissioner has available to him in carrying out that process are the contract specification and the contract itself. The challenge for the commissioner is in ensuring that the tools are fit for the purpose, and that he has the skills to use them effectively.

FURTHER
QUESTIONS

The following questions identify some issues from this chapter which you may wish to consider or discuss further with your colleagues.

♦ How collaboratively are specifications for your services developed? What is your own involvement in drawing up the service specification?

♦ Are the quality indicators in your specifications measuring the right things or are they just measuring the things which are easy to measure?

♦ How are service users, particularly patients and clients, involved in setting service specifications? How do we know that we are specifying the right things for them?

♦ Do service specifications have sufficient tolerances and triggers to reflect the variations which occur in real life clinical practice?

♦ How will we manage drawing up service specifications as the NHS moves into primary care led purchasing?

REFERENCES Appleby, J., Smith, P., Ranade, W., Little, V. and Robinson, R. (1993), Competition and the NHS: monitoring the market. In Tilley, I. (Ed.) *Managing the Internal Market*. Paul Chapman Publishing.

Culyer, A. and Posnett, J. (1990), Hospital Behaviour and Competition. In Culyer, A., Maynard, A. and Posnett, J. (Eds) *Competition in Health Care, Reforming the NHS*. Macmillan Press.

Department of Health (1987), *Promoting Better Health*. London: HMSO.

Department of Health (1989a), *Caring for People*. London: HMSO.

Department of Health (1989b), *Working for Patients*. London: HMSO.

Department of Health (1989c), *Contracts for Health Services, Operational Principles*. London: HMSO.

Ham, C. (1991), *The New National Health Service, Organisation and Management*. Oxford Radcliffe Medical Press.

Kerr, R., Liddell, A. and Spry, C. (1993), *Towards an Effective NHS: A Personal Contribution to the Debate*. Office for Public Management.

Mawhinney, B. (1990), Purchasing for Health. A speech reported in *Managing Contracts, Further Good Practice and Innovation* (1994), NHS Executive Purchasing Unit.

NHS (1991), *Professional Advice for Purchasers (A DHA Project Discussion Paper)*. London: DOH.

Opit, L. (1993), Commissioning: an appraisal of a new role. In Tilley, I. (Ed.) *Managing the Internal Market*. Paul Chapman Publishing.

Stocking, B. (Ed.) (1987), *In Dreams Begin Responsibility. A Tribute to Tome Evans*. London: King's Fund College.

NEGOTIATING A CONTRACT

Michael Faulkner

OBJECTIVES

◆ To explain why contracts are negotiated in the NHS.

◆ To assist the reader in preparing for and carrying out contract negotiations.

◆ To outline other approaches for reconciling differences.

INTRODUCTION As earlier chapters in this book have indicated, a contract is an *agreement* between two parties: a commissioning agency and an NHS Trust, an NHS Trust and a pharmaceutical company, a GP and the FHSA. This chapter covers the process which is normally used to arrive at such an agreement – the process of *negotiation*.

There are alternatives to negotiation. At its simplest, if there is already full agreement between the two parties, all that is required is a simple drafting exercise to make sure that the formal agreement document correctly reflects the understanding between the two parties.

Similarly, if a supplier has been awarded a contract as a result of a tendering exercise with an absolutely fixed specification, then no negotiation is required. The supplier simply undertakes to fulfil the contract as specified. Negotiation is neither required nor possible because the contract is effectively being let on a 'take it or leave it' basis.

Finally, if a negotiation fails and no agreement can be reached by the two parties meeting together agreement can be reached through a process of *arbitration*. Arbitration involves a third party in hearing the evidence from both sides and then determining what would be a fair agreement. Arbitration may be *binding* or not. Binding arbitration is when both sides agree in advance to accept the decision of the arbiter. A form of arbitration sometimes used in pay negotiations is called *pendulum arbitration*. In this case, the arbiter will find completely for one side or the other on the merits of the case presented.

Arbitration is, in fact, the process used in the NHS where purchaser and provider are unable to reach agreement over a contract. The regional health authority or regional office of the NHS Executive has reserve powers to arbitrate and to impose a solution on both parties. A case study highlighting the arbitration process is given at the end of this chapter.

NEGOTIATION   These alternatives serve to emphasize two key points about negotiation:

♦ Negotiation is only necessary when the two sides have *different* views of what the contract should say.
♦ Negotiation is only possible when both sides have some *power* – something to bargain with.

Reconciling   At the start of the contract negotiation process, if we asked both
conflicting   parties privately what they would really like the contract to say, we
positions   would probably get two 'wish' lists which conflicted with each other. We might get something like the lists shown below.

The commissioning agency wish list

1. We would like to spend much less on hospital care so that we can invest in primary care.
2. We would like all waiting lists to at least meet the Patient's Charter standards.
3. We would like all emergency admissions to be found a bed immediately without delays in A & E.
4. We would like patient satisfaction to improve substantially.
5. We would like to pay a fixed amount of money to the Trust to cover all emergency and elective admissions.
6. We would like improved information to enable us to monitor quality of care more thoroughly.

The Anywhere Hospital NHS Trust wish list

1. We would like to increase our prices so that we can reduce current pressures on our nursing staff.
2. We would like our purchaser to fund more elective episodes of care to enable us to get our waiting lists down and keep them down.
3. We would like to increase our prices so that we can improve things for our patients. We know they are dissatisfied with some aspects of the quality of care which we provide but we need more resources to fix the problems.
4. We would like to know exactly how much money we have coming in so that we can set our budgets appropriately.
5. We would like to be paid according to the amount and type of work which we actually do.

6. We would like to reduce the amount of information which we have to provide to purchasers.
7. We would like to introduce a new outreach nursing service for patients who have had day surgery. This would enable us to treat more patients on a day care basis.

A quick glance at these two lists shows us that we are some way from a perfect meeting of minds. In fact, it is difficult to imagine how any kind of agreement could possibly be reached on the basis of these two wish lists.

We might also notice a number of other features of the two lists:

1. Within each list there are *conflicts* between items on the list. The purchaser wants to spend less money but get more and better care. The provider would like guaranteed funding but also to be paid according to the amount and type of work actually done.
2. Each party would like to avoid any financial *risks*. The purchaser would like the provider to guarantee an overall cost. The provider would like the purchaser to undertake to pay for the amount of work actually done.
3. There are some *shared goals*. Both parties would like to address issues to do with waiting lists and patient satisfaction. Both have a concern about monitoring quality but very different approaches to the problem.

Negotiation is a process which is often used to enable two parties to reach agreement when their starting point is one of *disagreement*. The process is shown in Figure 6.1.

Figure 6.1
Reaching agreement

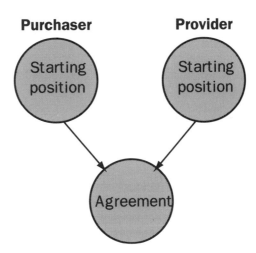

In the negotiation process, neither party is going to get exactly what they want. They are going have to make compromises and sacrifices in order to reach agreement. The issue which negotiation addresses is: ' how much compromise and sacrifice should I make?'

More specifically, negotiation allows people to answer questions like:

◆ Could I have got a better deal in this situation?
◆ What would have happened if I had pushed a bit harder?
◆ Have they compromised as much as I have?

Negotiation is a method for *testing* out the *fairness* of a particular set of sacrifices and compromises.

In a successful negotiation, *both* parties should come away feeling:

◆ This is an agreement which, whilst not ideal, is one we can live with.
◆ We made some reasonable compromises and sacrifices.
◆ They made some reasonable compromises and sacrifices.
◆ They did not abuse their position and neither did we.
◆ We will be able to have a sensible negotiation again next time.

Negotiation is sometimes described as a *win:win* situation. Both parties have to feel that they did all right in the negotiation process.

Why negotiations fail

Negotiations sometimes fail because:

◆ One party is unwilling to compromise at all or both parties are unwilling to compromise at all.
◆ One party takes advantage of the situation to demand that the other party do all the compromising.
◆ One party makes an agreement which they cannot deliver.

What happens when negotiations fail?

Negotiations can fail at three points:

Immediate failure

The parties just cannot or do not reach agreement. This may be characterized by a dramatic walk-out or by a sense of mutual failure. Either way, the consequence is either that business cannot be done at all or that some other form of agreement making has to take place. This is a lose:lose situation. It is worth noting that this situation can arise through no fault of the negotiators. It may be that there is no basis for agreement. Party A wants something which Party B cannot provide. Negotiation, no matter how skilled or patient, cannot reconcile the irreconcilable.

Failure on delivery

An agreement has been made but it was unrealistic. One party has agreed to something which they cannot deliver. Typical examples in the NHS are sub-contractors bidding too low a price, or Trusts signing up to provide information which their systems will not support. Again, the outcome is lose : lose. The failure on delivery may not occur quickly. If, for example, a commissioning agency negotiates a price which is so low that the provider has no money available to invest in maintenance or training, the provider may go into a cycle of decline which means it is no longer able to meet the purchaser's requirements. This might take a few years but the ultimate result is still lose : lose. In negotiating commercial contracts, an over-aggressive and short-sighted negotiator may put a good supplier out of business. Again, the result is lose : lose.

Failure of relationship

Few negotiations are 'one-offs'. More usually, they are part of a continuing relationship and the parties may well want to do business year after year. This is nearly always the case in NHS commissioner provider situations. Sometimes, one party will have a particularly strong negotiating position – perhaps the provider has just lost another contract or perhaps a competing supplier cannot provide the service this year. There is an overwhelming temptation to exploit this temporary advantage and to adopt a 'take it or leave it' attitude. The inevitable consequence of yielding to this temptation is that, when the balance of power changes, the other party will seek to take advantage of its negotiating position. Negotiators have to take particular care over how much they exploit temporary differences in negotiating power. Remember that win : lose will normally be followed by lose : win.

A successful negotiation A successful negotiation leads to a win : win outcome. What might the outcomes be for a negotiation between an NHS commissioning agency and an NHS Trust:

1. The NHS commissioner has purchased enough care of good quality to meet the priority healthcare needs of its population.
2. The NHS commissioner has paid a price which it can afford from its budget without having to cut back on other important services or key investments.
3. The NHS commissioner has got a *share* of any productivity gains which the provider may have achieved.
4. The NHS commissioner has got a price which is *competitive*. They are not paying 'over the odds' without good reason.
5. Risk is shared reasonably between the commissioner and the Trust. If there is a sudden change in healthcare needs, the commissioning agency will have to change their plans but the Trust will also deal with some of the effects.
6. The Trust can afford to provide the volume and quality of services required with the income which it will receive.
7. The Trust can cover its fixed costs.

8. The Trust has a share of its own productivity gains.
9. The Trust may be able to introduce some of the new services that it would like to.

These are the concrete items which go into the contract. There are some other important outcomes of a successful negotiation.

1. Each party has respect for the other.
2. Each party has a better understanding of the position of the other.
3. Each party has negotiated a contract which will be supported within their own organizations.

The last item raises an important point about negotiation. Most negotiators are carrying on two negotiations at the same time. Each is negotiating with their 'opponent' but each is also handling a negotiation within their own organization.

A Trust's negotiator is not just negotiating with the commissioning agency. He or she is also negotiating with colleagues and with senior management within the Trust. Similarly, in a commissioning agency, the commissioning manager may be negotiating internally with Finance, Public Health, other commissioning managers and so on.

The most frustrating thing for any negotiator is to conclude a long and difficult agreement with a supplier or purchaser and to return to his or her own organization only to be asked 'Is this the best you could do?'

The following sections which deal with the practicalities of preparation for negotiation and with the negotiation process itself should help to avoid this thankless position.

Is negotiation just a game?

To some extent, negotiation is a game but it is a game with a very important purpose. Only by pushing the other party and testing out what is really possible and impossible can we be sure we have got the best possible deal. Similarly, only by being pushed and tested can the other party be sure that we have really given them the best possible deal that we could.

Negotiators have some shared goals and some conflicting ones. Only by playing the negotiation game can we resolve the conflicting goals and get on with the important business of addressing the shared goals.

It is also true that the negotiation game can actually make things different and better for patients. Sometimes we do not know what we really can achieve until we are pushed very hard to do it. Change is not something which comes easily to big organizations and we may need a tough negotiation to give us the impetus to make change happen.

Many skilled and experienced negotiators would say that the most difficult negotiation is with people who are not very good at it. This is for a number of reasons. Inexperienced negotiators may fall into any of the traps outlined in the section on why negotiations fail. They may not know when to compromise and when not to and they exploit real or imagined advantages inappropriately.

The most common problem, though, in dealing with inexperienced negotiators is making sure that they do not sign a deal which they cannot deliver. The contract is just a piece of paper – it is the reality which matters. Negotiators have a responsibility to ensure that their opposite numbers do not give too much away. For example, it is in nobody's interest to get a very good price only to find that you have to top up funding half way through the year. Similarly, it is in nobody's interest to allow a good supplier to go out of business simply because they quoted an unrealistic price.

Summary of key points about negotiation

1. Negotiation is the process through which two parties reach an agreement which is not ideal for either but with which both can live.
2. Negotiation involves 'playing a game' to make sure that the best possible deal has been agreed.
3. Negotiations are rarely one-off events; they usually have to be seen in the context of a continuing relationship.
4. Negotiators are usually conducting two negotiations in parallel – one external and one internal.
5. A successful negotiation is one in which both parties feel they have won – the objective is a win:win solution.

And a final comment on negotiation from a very experienced trade union officer.

We start off some way apart and I know we are going to have to walk towards each other. My objective is to make them take bigger steps than I do!

PREPARING FOR NEGOTIATION

Good preparation is the key to good negotiation. The first step in preparation is to think through very carefully what your own *negotiating position* is. A convenient way of doing this is to set out your negotiating objectives under the following headings:

Must haves

These are the minimum objectives which you must achieve if agreement is to be reached. If you fail to achieve *any* of your must have objectives, you cannot reach agreement – you must allow the negotiation to fail.

Some examples of 'must haves';

♦ Prices high enough to cover your fixed and variable costs.
♦ Prices which you can afford to pay.
♦ Clinical practices which your clinicians will support.
♦ Minimum standards required by the government.

Some 'must haves' might be in the form of *must not have*:

♦ Information requirements which your systems will not support.
♦ Quality requirements which you cannot meet.

Intend to haves   Intend to have objectives are ones which are important to you and which you aim to achieve. They are not, however, so fundamental that failure to agree one would cause the negotiation to fail. If you were unable to secure agreement to *any* of your intend to haves, you would probably feel that it was a pretty poor negotiation. Similarly, if you achieved *all* of them, you have been extremely skilful (or lucky).

You will fight hard to get your 'intend to haves' but, at the end of the day, you are prepared to surrender some of these in order to reach an agreement which is acceptable to both sides.

Some examples of 'intend to haves':

♦ A price reduction of 5% for cruciate ligament repairs.
♦ Replacing monthly quality reports by quarterly ones.
♦ Funding for an outreach asthma nurse.
♦ Provider accepts up to 10% cases over contracted level without extra payment instead of the current 5%.

Like to haves   Your 'like to haves' are a bit like the pawns in a game of chess. They are quite valuable but they are there to be sacrificed in order to achieve some more important goal. A skilled negotiator will be able to trade a like to have in exchange for an intend to have.

Some examples of 'like to haves':

♦ Purchaser agrees to 50% funding of training programme for nurse practitioners in A & E.
♦ Pilot diabetic outreach service.
♦ Patient information leaflets available in additional languages.

Again, some 'intend to haves' and 'like to haves' might be expressed as *not* having.

♦ We intend not to have to seek prior approval for cosmetic procedures.
♦ We would like not to have to guarantee discharge summaries within 48 hours.

Drawing up your negotiating position under these headings involves intensive internal consultation, discussion and negotiation. There is no point going to an external negotiation with a set of objectives which is not supported by your organization or by your clinical colleagues. You will simply end up negotiating a contract which you cannot deliver.

It is very important to have *as few* 'must haves' as possible. 'Must haves' are, by definition, *non-negotiable*. The more you have, the less flexible your negotiating position and the more difficult it is to reach an acceptable agreement. Be very tight with your definition of 'must haves'. They are the things that will cause you to walk away from the negotiation – the things that lead to a lose:lose situation.

In your preparatory internal negotiations, you will probably need to work quite hard to persuade your colleagues that certain things they think are absolutely vital are not really things that should cause the negotiation to break down. Persuade them that things which are very important are *'intend to haves'* – you will fight hard for them but, if one of these is the only thing getting in the way of an excellent agreement, it may have to be sacrificed.

Understanding their negotiating position

Once you have prepared and agreed your own negotiating position, the next step is to try to understand the negotiating position of your opposite numbers. You can do this in exactly the same way and under exactly the same headings.

Spend some time first of all thinking about their *'must haves'* – the things they absolutely have to get agreement on. In the NHS, you will have some clues about these from government statements, purchasing strategies and Trust Business Plans and Strategic Direction documents. If a relationship and a contract already exists, you are quite likely to have good insights into the goals and problems of the other side.

Analysing the two negotiating positions

Once you have developed your own negotiating position in terms of 'must haves', 'intend to haves' and 'like to haves' and speculated about the position of your opposite numbers, you can start to do some analysis of the two positions. Questions which you can usefully address include:

1. Where is there common ground between the two positions?
2. Where are there real conflicts?
3. Which of their 'must haves' will give us serious problems and how can we meet their essential requirements. Remember that if you are right in predicting one of their 'must haves', you have to find a way of meeting it, otherwise the negotiation will fail.
4. Which of their 'intend to haves' would be easy for you to offer and which ones would be difficult?
5. What items in the two lists could be linked together?
   Example: You would like to reduce readmissions. We would like an outreach nurse attached to the day surgery unit.

Developing your arguments

Negotiation has elements of game playing, but it is much more than that. You will have to *argue* persuasively and cogently for the objectives you care about. For example, if you are a purchaser looking for a price reduction you might need to demonstrate:

1. Their prices are higher than other providers.
2. You could purchase the service elsewhere.

3. You need the money because of reductions in your purchasing power.

To present these arguments properly, you will need good information. You need to be able to persuade the provider that you are very serious about going elsewhere if they cannot meet your requirements.

Similarly, if you are a Trust, you may be arguing for a reduction in information requirements. You will need to be able to show:

1. The current information is not really helpful.
2. It is expensive to collect and, therefore, takes funds away from patient care.
3. You have an alternative proposal which meets their needs but which is better for you.

A typical area of negotiation in NHS purchaser/provider contracts is that of waiting lists. Short waiting lists are, on the face of it, a common goal between purchaser and provider. However, the provider will need to argue for enough funding to clear any backlog and then to maintain the waiting list at the new level. The purchaser may well need to argue that the waiting lists are being badly managed rather than additional funding being required.

Whichever case you are arguing, you need to have the facts and figures at your finger tips and you need to be sure that the data you are presenting cannot reasonably be challenged by the other side.

Preparing your counter arguments

As part of your preparation, you should also be trying to anticipate the arguments which will be advanced by the other side and preparing your counter arguments.

In the waiting list example above, if you are the provider you will want to demonstrate:

♦ You *are* managing the waiting list properly.
♦ It has been 'cleaned up'.
♦ The inflow of new patients is such that the list will keep growing or stay at its current level unless additional cases can be funded.
♦ You have done your bit by reducing length of stay, reducing cancellations and so on.

Sometimes, the process of preparing for negotiations will actually make you do things better. For example, if you have not cleaned up your waiting list, managed it properly or done anything about cancellations it would be a good idea to do so before you get into negotiations. It is very unsettling to go in with what you think is a good case only to have it come apart in your hands.

Setting up your infrastructure

In the nature of the negotiating process, you need to be able to answer questions quickly and accurately. The kinds of questions which may come your way are:

1. How many extra sessions would you need?
2. What would that cost?
3. Suppose we increased the volume, by how much would you be able to reduce the cost per case?

Well ahead of the actual negotiations you need to have in place ways of answering similar questions. You will need very good dossiers of relevant information and you will also probably find it helpful to have some simple *spreadsheets* which enable you to look at the effects of volumes on prices, activity levels on waiting lists and so on.

You also want to have available a *support team* who can research answers for you quickly and accurately.

As earlier sections of this book have indicated, NHS contracting takes place in accordance with a nationally prescribed timetable and a fairly tight one at that. You should *never* guess at answers to important questions about price, capacity, quality and so on. You do, however, need to be sure that you can get good answers within (say) 24 hours.

Selecting and organizing your negotiating team

Who should negotiate is a vexed question in many NHS Trusts. If the contracts department undertake negotiations in isolation, there is a substantial risk that the clinicians will not support the contract which is agreed or will spend the next year complaining about it.

If each clinical director goes off and does it, a good deal of valuable medical time may be taken away from patient care. It is also very likely that each clinical director will argue strongly from the point of view of his or her service without thinking about the implications for the Trust as a whole.

For example, if the clinical director for orthopaedics persuades the purchaser to put much more money into that service, a consequence may be that some other service becomes unviable. This might prejudice the ability of the Trust as a whole to provide a comprehensive range of services or it might mean that the Trust is left with some highly specialized facility which it can neither sell nor use for any other purpose.

The real answer is that it normally does not matter too much who actually does the face-to-face negotiations provided that:

1. The negotiating position has been very clearly agreed with everyone who is affected by the contract.
2. The negotiator is skilled in negotiation.
3. The negotiator is clear about what he or she can and cannot agree to without referring back.

If arguments have to be advanced which require in-depth technical knowledge then someone with that knowledge should be on the negotiating team – at least for that part of the negotiation.

The minimum size for a negotiating team is two: one person to do the talking and one person to do the listening. The person doing the listening should normally be the negotiating team leader. To this core of two can be added:

♦ Someone to take notes.
♦ Someone to do sums.
♦ Subject matter experts as necessary.

In reality, clinical directors do not often get actively involved in all contract negotiations. Involvement is usually limited to the negotiation about the clinical aspects of their directorate rather than prices.

Many clinical directors rely on their business managers to attend negotiation meetings on their behalf. The business manager will have an overview of the directorate and will be aware of all the clinicians' wishes. They will, therefore, be able to bring a 'corporate' view of the directorate's requirements to the negotiation table. Furthermore, the business manager should be aware of the wishes and aspirations of other directorates and so can ensure that contracts negotiated for their directorate do not conflict with others.

It should also be remembered that whoever undertakes negotiations may not only agree contracts with one or two health authorities, but may also be required to agree contracts with numerous GP fundholders. In some areas there may be as many as thirty different GP fundholding practices and a process of negotiation will have to be undertaken with each one.

Negotiations often take place at the GP's practice rather than at the hospital and so it is impractical to expect a clinical director to negotiate every contract.

Even though GP fundholder contracts are relatively small in terms of activity and income, if there are a large number of fundholders in an area they can, together, represent a significant amount of a Trust's income. Each fund may have different needs in terms of information and quality requirements and, therefore, each contract will require the same preparation for negotiation as large health authority contracts.

How senior should the team be?

In most cases, it is sensible to keep the chief executive and other very senior people in reserve. They may need to be wheeled in at an appropriate point to help to resolve particularly difficult sticking points.

The team should be sufficiently senior to be able to take decisions flexibly within the context of the negotiating brief. Nobody enjoys negotiating with someone who is not empowered to make agreements.

Training the team   Negotiating is a particular skill and most people need to learn it. Formal training and, above all, practice in negotiating really does make a difference.

Ideally, negotiating teams should be trained to work together as teams. As a minimum, they need to understand that they are there as a *representative team*. They are not free agents who can say what they like, talk over each other and argue amongst themselves.

Within the negotiating team there should be very clearly defined *roles and rules*. The key roles are:

◆ Speaker – the person who presents the arguments and responds to questions and arguments from the other side.
◆ Leader – the person who manages the negotiating team, updates the team's view of the other side's negotiating position and works out the team's tactics.
◆ Note taker – the person who records agreements which have been made and propositions which have been put forward.
◆ Expert – the person who presents particular technical arguments.

The minimum rules which are helpful include:

◆ Nobody speaks except the speaker or an expert.
◆ Nobody agrees to anything unless the speaker has been instructed by the leader to do so.
◆ Nobody argues with anyone else in their own team or interrupts them or talks over them.
◆ Anyone in the team can ask the leader for a recess.

These points are dealt with in greater detail in the section on managing the negotiation process.

Preparing for negotiation – summary
◆ Planning is the key to successful negotiation.
◆ Prepare *your* negotiating position under the headings:
  – Must have
  – Intend to have
  – Like to have
◆ Make sure that your negotiating position reflects the views of the senior management of the organization and the people who will have to deliver the contract.
◆ Anticipate *their* negotiating position under the same headings using sources of published information and your own knowledge and insights.
◆ Analyse both negotiating positions looking for:
  – Common ground.
  – Points of conflict.
  – Items which could be linked.
◆ Prepare your arguments and counter arguments making sure that you are using facts and figures which will not be disputed.

- ◆ Fix anything which is likely to undermine your negotiating position.
- ◆ Set up your infrastructure in terms of:
  - – Information dossiers.
  - – Spreadsheets.
  - – Support team.
- ◆ Select your negotiating team.
- ◆ Train your negotiating team.
- ◆ *Rehearse* your negotiating team.

STAGES IN THE NEGOTIATION PROCESS

Negotiation normally takes place in a face-to-face meeting or, more frequently, in a series of face-to-face meetings. The negotiation process moves through a number of stages:

Arguing

Each side will present the arguments for its case and will support these with relevant facts and figures. While one side is presenting its arguments, the other side will, if it is wise, listen carefully, interrupting only to ask clarifying questions. The 'listening team' should also try to take good notes.

Once one side has finished presenting its arguments, it is often useful for the 'listening team' to summarize back the key points of the arguments which have been presented to them and give the 'presenting team' an opportunity to clarify or correct their understanding of the arguments which have been presented.

It is not appropriate to respond or react to arguments at this stage.

In presenting arguments, you will be trying to give the impression that *everything* for which you are asking is essential, reasonable and worthwhile.

Challenging arguments

Each side will now set out to argue against the case which has been presented to them. They may challenge the data which has been presented or, more commonly, the interpretation of that data. They will advance *counterarguments* – why such and such is impossible, or unnecessary or pointless.

Although individual negotiators have their own personal styles, the argument and challenging phases should normally be conducted in a quiet, rational and civilized manner. There is very little place in negotiations for shouting and ranting.

What you are trying to achieve is a thorough testing and exploration of the other side's position – what are their sticking points and where might concessions be possible.

Signalling

By the end of the argument and challenge phases, each side knows about the other side's 'wish list'. They can probably see that there is some distance between the two positions and that someone is going to have to move. We now need to provide some clues about what might be negotiable and what might not. This involves sending some *signals* to the other side. As negotiation has some aspects of game playing, we do not send completely honest signals. We signal in a way which is designed to persuade the other side that any concessions we may make are very valuable and difficult for us. We are trying to convince them that:

Our 'must haves' are 'must haves'.
Our 'intend to haves' are also 'must haves'.
Our 'like to haves' are 'intend to haves'.

In essence, we are trying to inflate the currency of our negotiation.

How do we signal?   Signals are usually sent in the way in which we express things and in the tone we use. If for example, we wanted to signal that one of our 'like to haves' is an 'intend to have' we might say something like:

> *We consider it very important to train nurse practitioners and, as we have explained, we cannot fund this completely from our own resources. We believe that 50 50 would be equitable. We understand that your own budget is very tight. What contribution would you think is reasonable from you?*

This statement does two things. It signals to them that the 50% funding is something on which we are prepared to negotiate. It may also trap them into putting an offer on the table more quickly than they should. An unwary negotiator might respond.

> *We think 50% is far too high – we might consider 25%.*

If somebody does make an offer inadvertently, 'pick it up and put it in your pocket'; you have got something for nothing. Continuing the dialogue above, you might respond.

> *We are very pleased that you accept the principle of joint funding of the training. Obviously we are some way apart on the split. Quite honestly we think 50 50 is fair and reasonable but perhaps we can come back to the detail later on.*

As the teams exchange signals, each side can update its view of the other side's negotiating position. As we receive signals, we start to form a better view of their musts, intends and likes.

Sooner or later, we are going to have to send signals which indicate which of our intend to haves are negotiable. This might be expressed as follows:

> *Simplifying quality reporting is of critical importance to us for the reasons which we have explained. We also under-stand your concerns on this issue. We think our proposals*

will work very well and meet your needs but perhaps we can explore other ways of tackling the problem.

This signals a possible area for negotiation.

Objectives which are really non-negotiable or which you wish them to go on thinking are non-negotiable have to be restated very clearly and the arguments reiterated.

We cannot maintain the required standard of service at the current price. Without the 5% increase which we have asked for we cannot reach agreement on this issue. It is the absolute minimum. The real figure would be nearer to 20% but we know that would present real difficulty. This is the very best we can do.

Negotiating teams should not respond to or comment on these signals. They should just listen to them and interpret the signals which are being sent. Responding too early will lead into the trap illustrated by the nurse practitioner training example shown above.

Bargaining   The signalling stage provides information, not always reliable, about the other side's negotiating position. The next step is bargaining. Bargaining is a process of exchange – trading concession for concession. The skilled negotiator will be able to secure high value concessions from the other side in exchange for low value concessions on his or her part. Of course, value is subjective. A concession which you might make could be of very high value to the other side but not really too difficult for you. You must make them *believe* that they have extracted a concession which you regard as very valuable otherwise they will not think they have got the best possible deal.

Bargains are always presented as *possible bargains*:

You have asked us to do x. This is very difficult for us but we might possibly be able to do it if you would agree to do y.

The skilled negotiator will try to make sure that x is one of our like to have items and that y is one of their intend to haves.

The response from the other side might be:

I am afraid that y is not possible for us. We might, however, be able to move a little on z if you are prepared to commit to x.

This process of putting *possible bargains* and counter bargains on the table goes on until both sides feel that they have an understanding of what the shape of the final agreement might look like. We can also get a better idea of what the 'must haves' of the other side are by trying to include them in possible bargains. If we keep getting a firm 'no', we become more and more confident that they are really non-negotiable items.

It is worth noting that, in the bargaining process, bargains need not relate linked items. It is quite possible to say that in exchange for some concession on price, we will offer some concession on introducing a new service.

It is also important to remember that you should get a price for every concession. Even if there is something which you are perfectly willing to agree to, use it as a bargaining counter – do not give it away, without getting something in return.

Using recesses   Negotiating teams should not try to make decisions 'on the run'. It is perfectly reasonable to ask for recesses from time to time. These are opportunities for the negotiating team to meet in private, to review their negotiating position and tactics and to prepare for the next stage of negotiation.

Remember that the speaker in your team should only be putting forward proposals or making agreements which you, as a team, have agreed upon.

Structuring an   Once the bargaining process has gone on for some time, we can
agreement   start to test out what an agreement might look like. Essentially, this consists of *summarizsing* the potential bargains which seemed to get a favourable response from both sides. A summary might look something like:

> *We are very pleased that you are prepared to accept our proposed price increase provided that we are able to reduce the readmission rate to x%.*
>
> *We also seem to be in agreement that we will establish a joint working party to develop a simplified quality reporting system.*
>
> *You have also asked us to bear the costs of the Day Surgery Outreach Service. This is extremely difficult for us but we think that we may have found a way of doing it at least on a pilot basis. This would be conditional on your agreement to fund all of the training for nurse practitioners.*

The other side will then need to comment on your summary and a further bargaining stage may need to take place.

This process of testing agreement goes on until a real agreement emerges.

A note on tactics   During the negotiating process, a pressure builds up to reach agreement. The two sides are moving towards each other from apparently very different starting positions and both sides start to want to make a deal. A tactic which you may wish to employ is to put something back on the table just when agreement looks very close.

I believe that we are very close to an excellent agreement now and both of us have, I think, tried to meet the needs of the other. I think the only thing which divides us now is something which is probably not very important to you but is critical for us. If you could just agree to x, I think we have a deal.

Often, this tactic will work. However, there is some risk that it will unstitch the agreement and start the bargaining process off again. So, it must be used with care.

Documenting the agreement

Once agreement has been reached, it has to be carefully documented either in the form of a draft contract or a memorandum of understanding. It is best for the agreement to be drafted jointly. If both sides have notetakers in their teams, they should be asked to get together and agree a joint document.

As with any agreement, the draft should be clear and unambiguous. It is never appropriate to try to make changes at the documentation stage. It should be a record of what has been agreed rather than being an extra stage of the negotiation process.

The negotiation process – summary

1. Negotiation usually takes place through one or more face-to-face meetings.
2. Negotiation goes through a number of phases although not always strictly one after another. The key phases are:
   - Presenting arguments.
   - Challenging and presenting counter arguments.
   - Sending signals about your negotiating position.
   - Putting possible bargains on the table.
   - Structuring an agreement
   - Documenting the agreement.
3. Decisions should be made during recesses, not during negotiations.
4. When bargaining, try to exchange something of low value for something of high value but encourage the other side to believe that they have secured a very valuable concession from you.
5. Be very careful not to make an agreement through inadvertence.
6. Document the agreement carefully. Do not use the documentation stage to reopen negotiations.
7. Stay cool, think before you speak and treat the other side with courtesy and respect at all times.
8. As the other side's position becomes clearer to you, try to think of creative ways of meeting their needs without compromising your own position. Successful negotiation requires both flexibility and creativity.

TRAINING AND OTHER RESOURCES

Spreadsheets

If you work in a Trust or commissioning agency, your finance department or information department should be able to set up a computer model using a spreadsheet package such as Lotus or Excel to support your negotiations.

A company called Personnel Development Projects provides a specialist service building computer models to support contracting and business planning in the NHS. They also provide comprehensive training for individual negotiators and for negotiating teams. Their address is:

Personnel Development Projects
27, Eastgate
Whittlesey
Peterborough
PE7 1 SE
Telephone 01733 350215

Training

In addition to the organization mentioned above, training in negotiation skills is available from The Industrial Society and from the Institute of Management, the addresses of which are given below.

The Industrial Society
3 Carlton House Terrace
London
SW17 5DG
0171 839 4300

The Institute of Management
Management House
Cottingham Road
Corby
Northamptonshire
NN 17 1TT
01536 204222

CASE STUDY – ARBITRATION

The Any NHS Trust was seeking to introduce new 'exclusions' from their forthcoming contracts for what they considered to be high-cost, low volume activity. These were mainly in highly specialized areas whose directorates had overspent their budgets during the previous contract year.

For the Midland Health Authority the projected total cost of these new exclusions was significantly higher than the value of their remaining contract activity. Being excluded from the contract, the proposed 'exclusions' would be charged at the Trust's ECR (extra-contractual referral) price. Therefore, the authority would face an uncertain charge for these services during the contract year.

The health authority, who were not the Trust's main purchaser, wanted to reduce the financial risk surrounding the proposal and asked that all activity be kept within a contract. They were willing to consider a 'cost and volume' arrangement to help minimize risk for the Trust but insisted on a very low marginal price if projected levels of activity increased during the year. The authority was not willing to give what they saw as an open-ended cheque to the Trust to pay for the 'exclusions' and rejected the Trust's proposals at a contract negotiation meeting.

The Trust would also not move from its position and stated that if the purchaser would not accept its list of exclusions then there could be no contract. All activity would, therefore, be subject to the higher ECR tariff prices.

Both parties, inevitably, failed to meet the regional timetable for agreeing contracts and were, therefore, automatically deemed to be in dispute. The case was referred to the regional office for arbitration.

Both the Trust and health authority's chief executives were severely criticized by the regional office, as the failure to agree a contract was regarded as a management failing on both sides.

FURTHER QUESTIONS

The following questions identify some issues from this chapter which you may wish to consider or discuss further.

♦ What methods, other than negotiation, could be used to reach agreement between an NHS provider and an NHS purchaser?

♦ What arrangements for conducting negotiations would be most appropriate in your organization?

♦ What training do you think people in your organization would find helpful?

♦ What work needs to be done to make sure that negotiating teams have the right support and infrastructure?

CHAPTER 7

MANAGING A CONTRACT

Kim Hodgson

Kim Hodgson

OBJECTIVES

♦ To demonstrate that contract management involves joint problem-solving between the parties concerned.

♦ To show how effective monitoring can help to anticipate problems before they become crises.

♦ To suggest ways of monitoring the key elements of contracts in the NHS.

INTRODUCTION Elsewhere in this book, we have emphazised the importance of viewing contractual relationships between purchasers and providers as essentially *collaborative*. Successful contracting is about achieving win:win conclusions – contracts which meet the needs of both purchaser and provider.

This is true of all contractual situations but particularly so in the context of the NHS in which, essentially, purchasers and providers are on the same side. If either purchaser or provider loses, so does the patient or prospective patient.

The same collaborative principle which applies to specifying and negotiating contracts applies equally to the *management* of contracts. If a contract is going wrong it is in the interests of both parties to:

♦ Identify the problem before it becomes a crisis.
♦ Agree appropriate actions to solve the problem.
♦ Implement those actions.
♦ Review the outcome to ensure that the problem has been resolved satisfactorily.

It is also very much in the interests of both parties, once the issue has been dealt with, to review what has happened and to *learn* how to avoid similar problems occurring in the future. In our experience, the learning process happens far too little. The consequence is that the same problems recur year after year.

A truism of contract management in the NHS and elsewhere is that some contracts are significantly easier to manage than others. The skill with which the contract has been negotiated has a major effect on the way in which that contract can be managed and on how problems are identified and resolved.

As we have indicated elsewhere in this book, a contract for services is a contract which specifies things which will happen in the *future*. In this sense it is different from a contract to purchase something like a car or a house which has already been made. If a contract is concerned with the future, it is sensible, in drawing up that contract, to try to anticipate some of the problems which may arise and to agree in advance how they will be handled. Where this has not been done, the people attempting to manage the contract are put in the position of trying to develop solutions in a hurry and, very possibly, whilst in the middle of trying to solve an immediate real-world problem.

Every contract should, therefore, have built into it clear and simple procedures for *monitoring* the contract and for *resolving problems*.

MONITORING A CONTRACT

Monitoring is a process which is undertaken both by purchasers and providers. In the case of purchasers, they are monitoring to ensure that they are getting the quantity and quality of services for which they are paying. In the case of providers, they are monitoring to ensure that they are delivering what they have contracted to deliver and that they are consuming resources in the way in which they expected to consume resources.

At the moment, in the NHS, there is a significant degree of duplication of monitoring between purchasers and providers. Such duplication is very wasteful of scarce resources. Purchasers should not monitor contract compliance in detail themselves but should concentrate on getting providers to establish effective internal monitoring systems. If the purchaser can have confidence that the provider is monitoring the quantity and quality of service provided, then little more should be necessary than to review summary reports and to carry out the occasional spot check.

The only reason for monitoring is to provide early warning of things not happening as expected. It performs the same function as the instruments in a car or on an anaesthetic machine. Just like well designed instrumentation, contract monitoring should be designed to give us precisely the information which is needed and to filter out information which will merely serve to distract attention. To pursue the analogy one stage further, far too many contracts have 'dashboards' full of irrelevant dials and gauges which tell clinicians and managers little of value but which take their minds off what they really do need to know.

Monitoring is something which has to be *designed* into the contract from the start. Just like good instrumentation, good monitoring processes will:

◆ Measure the right things.
◆ Be calibrated properly.
◆ Tell us when we need to be concerned.

A key principle of effective and efficient monitoring is that of *exception reporting*. Clinicians and managers do not want to know everything which has happened. They only want to know about those things which are out of line with what they want and expect to happen. They do *not* need to be told about all the things which are going according to plan, they *do* need to be told about the exceptions – things which are not going as expected.

This implies that there is a clear view of what constitutes an exception. Clinicians and managers probably do not want to know about every patient who had to wait 30 seconds past his or her scheduled appointment time. They may well be interested in knowing how many had to wait more than 30 minutes. The information which is received will depend on how an exception is defined.

This could be expressed in a contractual clause in terms such as:

The number of patients who are seen by the doctor more than 30 minutes after the time of their appointment will be reported on a monthly basis. The report will indicate the name of the clinic and the total number of patients waiting more than 30 minutes.

The reader may also wish to note that this clause specifies quite tightly what constitutes being seen on time.

An argument could be made for reporting for how much longer patients have been waiting. For example, what proportion have been waiting 40 minutes, 50 minutes and so on. In practice, this may simply serve to distract attention from the real issue that no-one should have to wait more than 30 minutes past their scheduled appointment time.

There are three aspects which are useful to measure in the monitoring of a contract:

◆ Is the *quality* of service what was expected?
◆ Is the *quantity* of service what was expected?
◆ Is the *consumption of resources* what was expected?

Monitoring quality   Quality, in essence, is a very simple concept – does the product or service do what it is meant to do? If so, it is of good quality, if not, it is of inadequate quality.

The acid test of quality is the extent to which the consumer of the product or service is satisfied with it. If he or she is not satisfied, the product or service is not of adequate quality. If the consumer was able to exercise a choice, they would not buy that product or service again because they are not satisfied with it.

Any contract therefore, should impose an obligation on the provider to demonstrate that an overwhelming majority of the consumers of their service are satisfied with it. It is not necessary for the purchaser to specify how this should be measured, merely to specify that it should be measured in a way which they find convincing and comprehensive. This leaves the provider free to find the most economical and convenient way of measuring the satisfaction of their consumers.

An appropriate contractual clause might be:

The provider shall demonstrate that they have in place an adequate system for measuring the satisfaction of consumers with their services and that they shall report immediately any instances of consumers being dissatisfied together with the action which they propose to remove the cause of dissatisfaction.

Increasingly, national systems of *accreditation* are coming into play which should reduce the need for every provider to demonstrate their quality management systems and for every purchaser to check those systems. Under an accreditation scheme such as those operated by the British Standards Institute (BSI) and the King's Fund, a provider is audited by the awarding institution to ensure that it comes up to agreed standards. A purchaser is then entitled to rely on the award of accreditation by the auditing organization. Reputable organizations such as BSI and the King's Fund will carry out regular and ad hoc audits to ensure that the accredited organization is still living up to the required standards in practice.

In the case of the NHS, there is a need to identify who is meant by 'consumers'. The term certainly includes patients and their families and nearly always mean GPs. In some cases, it may include people like teachers or community groups.

Clinicians will sometimes argue that it is not always possible to satisfy patients and their families. Their expectations may be unrealistic and beyond the limits of what is clinically possible. Obviously this is true. It is equally true that part of the role and skill of the clinician is to help the patient and his or her family members to arrive at a realistic expectation of what can be achieved. To the extent that clinicians fail to do this, the quality of service is defective. Where a defect is found, clinicians and managers can then try to find better ways of preventing that defect.

A practical example is that of pain management following day surgery. Patients are often given or allowed to have quite unrealistic expectations of the amount of pain which they might experience and, as a result, are dissatisfied with the pain control with which they are provided. Once they are informed properly that they are very likely to suffer quite severe discomfort, and will probably not be able to play football in the afternoon after their operation, their level of dissatisfaction decreases dramatically.

With the exception of waiting list indicators, standards set out in the Patient's Charter can quite easily be incorporated into a patient satisfaction monitoring process. The Patient's Charter, after all, does no more than to educate people about what they should reasonably expect from the service.

In most cases a fairly simple Patient Satisfaction Report, ideally complemented by something to be completed by relatives, could be used routinely to collect the key information which would tell us the extent to which patients and their relatives are satisfied with the services provided and which, more importantly, will direct attention to areas which require further work.

If patient satisfaction is to be a key quality indicator, it is important that clinicians and managers measure not just satisfaction with the *process* of healthcare delivery but also with the *outcome* or benefit achieved. It is nice to know that everyone thought their nurses were wonderfully kind. It would be useful to know that patients also felt that their health care *helped* them in some way.

The satisfaction of patients and their families is a necessary component of quality monitoring but is it a sufficient one? Not quite. Let us take the example of a motor car again. Car manufacturers rely on the judgements of customers to determine the success of their products. If customers like them, they will buy them; if not, they will not. In addition, however, the government imposes quite stringent standards in terms of safety and environmental impact. These exist over and above the satisfaction or otherwise which individual consumers express through their buying decisions and can be thought of as representing the wider interests of society as a whole.

In the same way, in a health service, there may need to be a few additional measures to be sure of the quality of the service which is provided. These should, however, be the things which individual patients and their families are unlikely to reflect in making their judgements about the quality of service.

Some of these standards will be analogous to the regulations affecting motor car manufacture. For example, there are statutory or quasi-statutory regulations regarding safe practice in health care, the qualifications of staff and the carrying out of particular procedures such as securing informed consent.

Again these could be reflected in a very simple contractual clause such as:

The provider shall demonstrate that they have in place systems and processes to ensure full compliance with all statutory and quasi-statutory regulations relevant to the service being provided.

The onus is on the provider to demonstrate that they are assuring their own quality. They are free to find the most convenient and economical way of doing so.

In some cases, additional quality indicators may be required. These might include postoperative infection rates, perinatal mortality and so on. The key is to agree as few indicators as are necessary rather than as many as are possible.

Purchasers will wish to specify compliance with national waiting time standards as part of their contracts. Again though, the provider should be asked to propose how these should be measured and reported.

Purchasers need to accept that measurement has a cost. The more the provider is asked to measure, the less resource will be available for delivering care.

Monitoring quantity

♦ Monitoring quantity should be a relatively straightforward process although NHS information systems often seem to struggle with the task. The essential information likely to be needed about the amount of care delivered will include:

♦ Type of care – outpatient, day case, inpatient, community visit etc.

♦ Type of patient – diagnosis and/or procedure.

♦ Circumstances of care – emergency admission, planned admission etc.

♦ Source of referral – GP, postcode, self-referral etc.

♦ Contract under which care has been provided.

There may be certain aspects of quantity which clinicians and managers particularly want to measure. For example, they may wish to monitor the ethnic composition of the people receiving their service to find out whether or not they are achieving equity of access or to help to tailor services to specific health or cultural needs.

They may be interested in monitoring the age and gender distribution of people using services to help with planning and tailoring services. The recent debate over mixed-sex wards is a good example of where it would be useful to know about the composition of customers by gender. Planning specialist services for adolescents might be an example of where age-related information would be helpful.

On the whole, this kind of information should be produced reasonably easily by existing information systems. What is useful, though, is to have it presented in a form which allows senior managers and clinicians in purchasers or providers to spot deviations from the expected trend quickly and easily. Often this will suggest displaying information in the form of graphs and charts rather than as huge computer printouts.

A particularly useful form of monitoring chart is one which shows the actual year to date figures cumulatively against an expected curve. The use of cumulative figures helps to even out random peaks and troughs in workload.

An example of a cumulative activity chart is shown in Figure 7.1.

Such charts can be made even more helpful by plotting a trend line on them as more data becomes available. Most computer spreadsheets have facilities for plotting trends and your information department should be able to provide the necessary technical assistance.

Monitoring activity routinely may also provide helpful information about *seasonality* – that is, are there patterns across the year in the flow of activity. Where such patterns do occur, they provide an opportunity for providers to match their resources more closely to the flow of work. In practice, very few providers make a serious attempt to do this and, therefore, miss out on an opportunity to use their resources efficiently.

A final point which should be made about information in relation to quantity of activity is that this is largely how the government through the NHSE tends to measure the performance of the NHS and its constituent organizations such as NHS Trusts. Quite clearly, such information is almost totally meaningless if it is divorced from information about clinical outcomes, the mix of patients receiving care and patient satisfaction. However, any monitoring system needs to take account of the requirement to comply with national data collection and reporting requirements. These are often expressed as *Minimum data sets* – the minimum information which an organization is required to supply. This topic is dealt with more fully on the chapter concerned with contracting and information.

Figure 7.1
Cumulative activity
chart

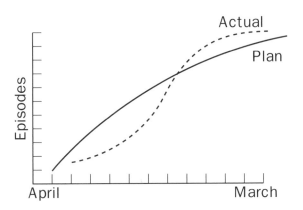

Monitoring resource consumption

Monitoring quality and quantity tells us whether the contract is being delivered. Clinicians and managers also need to know that they are delivering it within the resources available and they need to have early warning if they are starting to consume more resources than planned.

In a perfect world, it should be possible to monitor resource utilization simply by looking at monthly budget statements. In practice, this does not work very well for the following reasons:

♦ Not all of the resources which are used appear on budget sheets.
♦ There may be significant delays in reporting expenditure.
♦ There are often significant errors in reporting.

Many NHS managers will have had the experience of thinking things were going well only to receive a very unpleasant surprise when something finally made its way through to their budget statement.

A reasonable alternative is to monitor directly the major resources which a particular type of service uses.

In most services, the cost of staff will be a major ingredient in the total cost mix. This includes not only the normal costs of established staff but also overtime payments and the use of agency and locum staff.

In some services other costs will be of particular importance such as the cost of medications, or blood products or prostheses or pathology tests.

It is advisable for managers and clinicians to monitor such major costs themselves as they are *incurred*. Monitoring incurred costs is similar to using your cheque stubs rather than your bank statement to assess your current financial standing. As soon as you have taken a decision to spend money, assume that it has actually been paid and update your records accordingly. This will involve a certain amount of extra work but it will protect you from the vagaries of NHS accounting systems and shelter you from unpleasant surprises.

As with measuring activity, it if often useful to keep a *cumulative expenditure chart* to show you where you are compared with where you expected to be.

USING MONITORING INFORMATION

As indicated earlier, the purpose of monitoring is to provide early warning that things are not turning out as expected, in particular, that they are not turning out as the contract specified.

As soon as there is an indication from monitoring information that something unexpected may be happening, clinicians and managers should be implementing an action plan which will always follow the format shown in Box 7.1.

Box 7.1
Action Plan

1. What is causing the deviation or variance which has been observed?
2. What is a short-term 'blip' or a longer-term trend?
3. What action do we need to take to address the immediate effects?
4. What action do we need to take to address the underlying cause?
5. What are the implications for contracts next time round?
6. What are the implications for how we manage our contracts and our resources?

CAUSES OF QUALITY PROBLEMS   Most quality problems are caused by members of staff not behaving as they are meant to. A systematic approach to monitoring the satisfaction of patients, families and GPs will very quickly highlight areas in which people are doing what they are supposed to do. To say that problems are nearly always caused by people not doing what they are supposed to do is not necessarily to attribute blame to the individual members of staff involved.

Problems may be caused, for example, by unrealistic staffing levels on a ward, by an insensitive vacancy freeze which addresses a short-term financial problem but which may cause a long-term quality problem.

Problems may even be caused by lack of consultation between two departments. Physiotherapy changes its internal rotation system for reasons which make perfect sense to them but, in doing so, they cause major quality problems on the orthopaedics ward.

Three important points need to be made about addressing quality problems:

1. The chief executive should be personally involved in monitoring quality. This is partly to send the right kind of messages to the organization and partly because quality problems can often only be resolved properly through the actions of more than one service or department.

   The quality of care which a patient experiences is, typically, the end result of a long chain of actions and processes. The breakdown in the quality chain could have occurred at any point in the chain.

   In terms of sending the right messages to the organization, it is very easy for front line staff to get the impression that top management is only concerned with the financial performance of the organization and that quality of care will always be sacrificed in the interests of financial results. However unjust this belief may be, in our experience it is one which is very often held within NHS Trusts. It is sensible, therefore, for chief executives to be very visibly concerned with quality and not only when something dramatic happens.

2. It is important to avoid a *blame culture*. The purpose of monitoring quality is to identify ways in which *the organization as a whole* is failing its users and to do something about it. Members of staff should be encouraged to see information from patients, families and GPs as an important resource which will help them to create the kind of organization of which they can be proud to be members. If they see that such information is actually used to punish people, instead of putting their energies into resolving problems, they will put those energies into the much less useful and possibly dangerous task of not being caught.

   Naturally, if a member of staff is wilfully working in a way which is harmful or discourteous to patients, families or GPs then this needs to be dealt with very firmly. On the whole, though, people should see feedback from patients, families and GPs as information which can be used by the whole organization to make things better.

3. It is also important to communicate *good news*. Although from a contract management point of view, clinicians and managers are interested in the exceptions, in things going wrong, members of staff also need to be told about all the things which are going *right*. All the surveys carried out within the NHS demonstrate that the vast majority of our users are very satisfied with the quality of care which they receive. It is important that information about how satisfied most users are should be communicated alongside any information about how things could be done better.

CAUSES OF QUANTITY PROBLEMS

In contrast with quality problems, many quantity problems arise from causes outside the provider unit. For example, it only takes quite slight shifts in the type of patient being treated, the number of emergencies or the severity of conditions to throw quite a large spanner in the works.

Provider units tend to have very little control over the nature of the patients for whom they are caring – they do what is needed for whoever needs it.

These sorts of problems are essentially mutual problems for purchaser and provider. Neither has the capacity to predict exactly how many of what kind of patient will turn up. Accordingly, they need to be solved on a mutual and collaborative basis.

Many contracts will have built in to them two important devices for dealing with the unpredictability of patient flows: trigger mechanisms and internal adjustments.

Trigger mechanisms

These come into operation if the number of cases of a particular type are significantly greater or lower than anticipated in the contract. If the number of cases is greater than the trigger level, the provider is entitled to go back to the purchaser to seek additional resources. Such additional resources may, of course, be released by cutting back the contract in some other area of work and the provider needs to be sure that they can easily move resources from one area to another. It is not satisfactory if an ENT surgeon is under-employed while the Trust has to fund an additional locum orthopaedic surgeon.

Wherever a trigger mechanism is negotiated, it would be prudent for the provider unit to draw up a detailed contingency plan and to model its effects so that, should the trigger take effect, an appropriate course of action can be taken smoothly and efficiently.

Internal adjustments

Internal adjustments allow the provider to offset over-performance in one area against under-performance in another. This sort of arrangement needs to be handled with care and within pre-set limits or there is some danger of patterns of service being seriously distorted and underlying problems failing to be addressed. However, with these caveats, internal adjustment clauses in a contract can be pragmatic and sensible ways of dealing with the uncertainties of patient flows.

If there is a problem with quantity of work which cannot be addressed by either of these mechanisms, purchaser and provider will have to get together to reach a shared understanding of the problem and to agree upon a course of action. This will be very much easier if the problem is detected at an early stage and if purchaser and provider work very hard throughout the year at building and maintaining a relationship of mutual trust and respect and open communication channels.

Crucially, the purchaser needs to understand that providers cannot just absorb large quantities of unplanned and unfunded work and that they are under a legal obligation to 'balance their books'. Similarly, the provider needs to understand that purchasers cannot just 'magic up' large amounts of new money. Purchasers also need to understand that, even if fewer patient are being cared for than anticipated, there may not be huge savings for the provider because of the large element of relatively fixed costs in most providers' financial structures.

An element of compromise will normally be required on both sides. The provider will probably have to absorb some of the problem by being more efficient. The purchaser may well have to absorb some of the problem by cutting back on a different area of health care or delaying some cherished scheme.

One final point to make about monitoring quantity is that of *data quality*. Many of us have come to rely very heavily on information generated by computer systems. There is an adage in the computing world called the GIGO principle. GIGO stands for garbage in and garbage out and reflects the proposition that the data coming out of a computer system will, at best, be no better than the data going in. If patients are not correctly coded in terms of diagnosis, source of referral and postcode, extremely misleading statistics can be generated.

As a cautionary tale, I worked recently with a very experienced clinical manager whose computer reports were telling her that her service was under-performing against contract. As a result, she put extraordinary efforts into moving patients as rapidly as possible through her service. I asked her why, if activity levels were down, it seemed so busy. A check through the figures revealed a simple computer error. Instead of running 25% below her target, she was actually running 25% above and moving upwards ever faster. The point of the story is that if your information system is telling you one thing and your eyes are telling you something different, check the figures before you do anything dramatic.

CAUSES OF RESOURCE PROBLEMS

Resource problems can arise both within and outside the provider unit. Probably the most common cause of resource problems is a 'knock-on' effect from changes in patient flows. Quite often, a vicious circle can arise as shown in Box 7.2.

Box 7.2.
Changes in patient flows

1. We admit more patients than we anticipated.
2. Less urgent (less ill) patients are delayed.
3. We have a higher proportion of iller patients.
4. They stay longer and require more resources.
5. We have less capacity than we anticipated.
6. Go back to step 2.

When this vicious circle takes a hold, waiting lists increase and costs go up.

There is also a secondary cycle which sets in (Box 7.3).

This sort of problem has to be identified and resolved at a very early stage or it will get worse very quickly. Once it has been established that there is a significant change in the mix of patients presenting, an action plan has to be agreed between purchaser and provider to stop the situation going out of control. If there is uncertainty about whether this is just a blip or a long-term trend, it is always safer to assume that it is a trend. If the trend then tails off,

Box 7.3.
The secondary cycle

1. Patients are more ill.
2. Staff are under more pressure.
3. Absence increases.
4. Staff are under even more pressure.
5. Agency budgets get over-spent.
6. Vacant posts are frozen.
7. Staff are under yet more pressure.
8. And so on and so on.

the two parties can congratulate themselves and their staff that they have dealt effectively with the situation and then put things back to normal. The action plan would be similar to that for a trigger arrangement. Resources would be diverted from one area to the area which is having to cope with increased demand.

While handling the situation, it is also important to try to understand the causes. Sometimes, there will just be a change in the pattern of illness for no reason that can be easily understood. Sometimes though, there will be a simple explanation, such as changes in the referral practices of GPs, and these may be susceptible to influence on the part of the purchaser or the provider. Changes in the practice of one provider can cause changes in patient flows at a neighbouring provider unit. For example, long waiting times in one Accident and Emergency Department can cause patients to move to another less busy one.

Resource problems can also arise from causes within the provider unit. Typical causes include:

♦ Discharge procedures not working properly leading to increased lengths of stay.
♦ Changes in the practice of individual clinicians which impact on costs such as pharmacy, imaging, pathology or prostheses.
♦ Absence running higher than anticipated leading to extra costs in terms of locums and agency staff.

The best way to prevent these problems is to have a systematic approach to the management of clinical practice. Most organizations which make products or deliver services have a *specification* which spells out how that product is to be made or that service delivered. It would be unusual to say to members of staff in any other organization 'just do it how you feel'.

Although matters are more complex and complicated in health care because of the differences between patients and because elements of clinical practice are not really proven or do not command a consensus, there are approaches to the management of clinical practice which can be useful both in managing resources and in ensuring uniform standards of care.

An approach which seems quite sensible is that of the *integrated care pathway* or *anticipated recovery path*. In this model, clinicians and others from all the disciplines involved agree what a typical programme of care for a patient of a particular type would be like. They might specify, for example, what inputs would be provided by each discipline at various stages of the patient's treatment and they would agree when they would expect a patient to be discharged.

When a real patient is treated, *variances* from the anticipated programme are recorded and analysed. In this way, we start to find out about why we use different amounts of resource for different patients. Sometimes the approach will highlight where there are failings in administrative systems – we did not discharge patients when we planned to because we did not book the home-help, the taxi, the community nurse. Sometimes we did not do it because the registrar was not empowered to discharge patients and the consultant did not do a ward round on Friday afternoons.

The use of a process such as integrated care pathways not only gives us early warning of over-use of resources but helps us to see exactly *where* the problem is coming from.

SUMMARY

Successful contract management starts before the contract is negotiated and extends beyond the period of the contract into a process of contract review and learning.

Contracts can be made significantly easier to manage if:

♦ Clinicians and managers have made sure that the contracts are realistic and deliverable.
♦ Both sides have given thought to what could go wrong and made provision for dealing with such circumstances should they arise.
♦ Flexibility has been built in to deal with minor fluctuations.
♦ A clear and simple procedure has been agreed in advance for shared problem solving.

Contracts need to be understood by all the staff who are engaged in delivering them. They need to know what has been agreed and why.

Monitoring involves designing instrumentation which will tell us about:

♦ Quality.
♦ Quantity.
♦ Resources.

Monitoring systems should be as clear and simple as possible. They should rely on exception reporting – telling us when things are not turning out as anticipated.

The key to quality monitoring is the satisfaction expressed by patients, families and GPs. This should be routinely monitored using simple feedback forms.

Purchasers should not specify how quality should be monitored. It is more appropriate to allow the provider to propose their own quality monitoring system provided that it meets the purchasers' basic requirements.

Chief executives should be personally involved in monitoring quality and the rest of the organization should know that this is the case.

Computer systems should be able to provide the information which is needed about quantity of services or activity. It will often be helpful to present information in the form of graphs and charts rather than numbers.

Information coming from computer systems is entirely dependent on data quality (remember GIGO). If it looks wrong, it probably is wrong.

Managers and clinicians should keep their own records of resource utilization unless and until they are completely confident that the information they receive from other sources is accurate and up-to-date.

Provider units should be encouraged to establish sensible systems such as integrated care pathways for managing clinical practice.

Purchasers and providers should be talking to each other all the time. If channels of communication are open and mutual trust and respect has been built up, problems with contracts can usually be solved reasonably easily. If not, they probably cannot be solved without a great deal of bitterness and game-playing.

FURTHER QUESTIONS

The following questions identify some issues from this chapter which you may wish to consider or discuss further with your colleagues.

♦ To what extent do your contracts have:
  - Arrangements such as triggers for dealing with fluctuations in anticipated activity?
  - Clear and simple arrangements for mutual problem-solving?

♦ Does there need to be a detailed quality specification or could the provider propose a comprehensive and reliable quality assurance system?

♦ To what extent is your chief executive seen to be playing the leading role in quality assurance?

♦ How confident are you in the information which you receive about your resources?

♦ What systems do you have in place for managing clinical processes?

♦ What systems do you have in place for monitoring your performance against your contracts?

♦ How do you learn from this year's contract performance so that you can write a better one next year?

FURTHER READING

♦ Koch, H. (1992), *Implementing and Sustaining Total Quality Management in Healthcare*, Longman.

This book is written in clear simple language in a sensible format and provides a sound introduction to the whole field of quality management.

♦ Ovetveit, J. (1992), *Health Service Quality: An Introduction to Quality Methods for Health Services*, Blackwell, Oxford.

This book opens up some the debates about quality assurance in health care. It provides very good explanations of key terms and ideas and also offers a practical framework for introducing modern quality assurance approaches within the NHS.

INFORMATION TO SUPPORT CONTRACTING

CHAPTER 8

Lin Horley

OBJECTIVES

- ◆ To outline how information is used throughout the contracting process.

- ◆ To investigate the emergence of HISS (Hospital Information Support System) systems for acute providers and their counterparts within community services and their role in supporting the contracting process.

- ◆ To discuss the use of information systems by purchasers and their role in helping to establish population health needs.

- ◆ To show the relation of information systems to contracting currency and indicate how developments such as HRGs (Health Related Groups) are likely to impact upon information which supports contracting.

- ◆ To identify the likely impact of the National NHS Information Management and Technology (IM & T) Strategy on the contracting process.

- ◆ To look at the likely impact of GP-led purchasing on information systems.

INTRODUCTION Recent changes in the overall structure, management and funding of the health care system have invoked a major shift towards dependency on information technology. Effective flows of data exchange between purchasers of healthcare services and providers of those services in the acute and community sector are needed to support the new requirements and the contracting process. There is now an information revolution occurring in all healthcare organizations, with information becoming a key resource for managers and clinicians. Information is crucial in order to identify people's healthcare needs. Translating those needs into services, setting business plans, and regulating organizational performance against set targets is the only way to monitor whether improvements are being made.

Following the government NHS reforms, introduced by the White Paper *Working for Patients* (Department of Health, 1989), a heavy demand was placed upon those who provide services to patients to ensure that such services can be 'billed' or included within a certain contract, providing a 'spell of care' for a patient. The concept is that the funding follows the patient, thus improving the quality of care through a more competitive environment. As an outcome, acute and community care providers are quickly developing more aggressive marketing strategies. This involves examining ways of effectively restructuring their specialties and supporting services to be successful in this new purchaser/provider world.

INFORMATION AND THE CONTRACTING PROCESS

Exactly what is a 'purchaser' and indeed a 'provider' in the contracting context?.

A *Purchaser* can be the district health authority, a GP fundholder, or an NHS Trust who is 'buying' a service from another provider of care.

Providers are GPs or hospitals which are: NHS hospital Trusts which now have the autonomy to manage their own funds, DMUs (directly managed units) which are still supported by regional funds, community Trusts, or other services provided by community providers.

There are now 419 acute NHS Trusts and over 2000 GP fundholding practices.

The principles of contracting

In essence, the basic principles of contracting within the NHS are simple:

♦ Purchasers and providers may enter into a contract which lays down the scope and level of healthcare provision expected during an agreed period for an agreed amount of funding.
♦ Where no contract exists, the provider charges the relevant purchaser for each 'episode of care' undertaken on an individual basis.

A contract between two NHS parties is not legally binding. However, it serves to define the services procured by the purchaser, the cost of those services, and the standard of service to be delivered by the provider.

In order for the contracting process to work effectively it is necessary that *relevant information* flows between providers and purchasers. *Relevant information* is defined as any information required by purchasers before they will transfer funds to providers.

At present this concentrates mainly on '*contract minimum data sets*' (CMDS), the contents of which are nationally defined. By far the largest areas of service covered by these are:

1. Waiting lists.
2. Admitted patient care.
3. Outpatient services.

However, services such as physiotherapy, radiology, pathology and A & E are increasingly being separately identified and monitored as part of the contracting process.

The sheer volumes of data needed to support this process, and the timescales imposed by the invoicing cycle, mean that electronic storage and transmission methods have to be exploited as far as possible.

In general, providers have operational systems from which contract information is extracted as a by-product of the day-to-day activities carried out. This data is then processed to identify the service that has been provided and the purchaser who is responsible for funding that particular service. Data must then flow to the appropriate purchaser within agreed timescales and agreed levels of completeness in order that the purchaser will release funds to the provider.

Types of contract Contracts between purchasers and providers of care can be in several forms:

1. A 'block' contract is the simplest of contract whereby a 'chunk' of activity covering a composite of specialties (and procedures) is drawn up, based on agreed assumptions about volume and costs. Penalties are imposed for over- and under-performance and in such cases money may subsequently be withdrawn or added at a previously agreed marginal rate.
2. A 'cost and volume' contract identifies the level of expected activity. The purchaser will pay approximately 80% of the contract value until this ceiling is reached, at which point payment of the remaining 20% is triggered and any activity over the ceiling is then paid at an agreed marginal cost.
3. A 'cost per case contract' is where money is not committed in advance by the purchaser. The purchaser pays agreed costs for each case as the episode of care for the patient occurs.
4. An 'ECR' or extra contractual referral is where the episode of care falls outside any existing agreement, and is negotiated on an individual basis between the purchaser and provider. The cost of care attracts a higher rate to cover the extra administration effort involved.

At the outset of the contracting process fairly simple 'block' contracts were set up between providers and purchasers of health care. An example of a block contract might be for instance a DHA buying a specialty-based service from a provider with anything within that specialty being included within the block contract.

These contracts are now becoming increasingly complex and difficult to track. The block contract which may just cover a hip replacement and one or two outpatient appointments sounds relatively easy to trace through any system. However, the hip operations may have been negotiated on a sliding scale basis. This would mean that as more operations are purchased, the cost of each operation would be reduced accordingly. Economies of scale are brought to the fore in this instance, whereas if only one or two were purchased a 'normal' standard cost would be assumed.

Contract minimum data sets

Unfortunately information systems have been somewhat slower to develop than the requirement for the CMDS. The CMDS is the minimum amount of information that can be supplied by providers in order to bill the purchaser for a spell of care for a patient. This CMDS consists of the demographics of the patient including their district of residence, the GP with whom they are registered, and the clinical data, i.e. diagnosis and procedure for their period of stay in hospital. Examples of acute and community CMDSs are shown in Appendices 1 to 3.

Purchasers require the CMDS information within six weeks of the patient's discharge from hospital, otherwise payment can be refused. This is why it is in the provider's interest to supply the information as quickly as possible.

This may sound quite simple and easy to follow. There are, however, some fundamental problems for providers in their identification of which contract the patient should be attached to, or whether they should be an ECR.

Providers need to establish the contractual status of a patient at the very start of the care process via the means of a quick look-up procedure which will identify the patient's district of residence (DOR) and their GP, showing whether or not that GP holds fundholding status. It is on the basis of data gathered at this stage that an invoice can be raised for agreement with the purchaser according to the reason for treatment at the hospital. It must be noted that during the evolution of the reforms most providers did not have competent information systems in place that could track these relatively simple CMDS requirements.

Initially a patient may be admitted for a particular problem which is included within the block contract. Difficulties can arise should additional complications be diagnosed which are not directly covered by the original contract. This necessitates further collaboration with the purchaser before the extra treatment or operation can be carried out. Agreement is invariably reached by means of a telephone call to the purchaser, be it the GP or other health authority.

Coding An essential element to the whole contracting process is the need
methodologies for cohesive coding systems to code both clinical diagnoses and
operative procedures. ICD-9 is the International Classification of
Diseases used world wide; version 10 was released in 1995. OPCS-4
is the Office of Population Census and Surveys classification of
Operative Procedures. Although both of these are relatively useful
to provide the basic coding needed for epidemiology and contracting, they have often been criticized for not having enough detail for
clinical research and analysis.

Dr James Read therefore has developed the READ classification
of coding which covers a much wider realm and a recent addition
has been PAM (Professions Allied to Medicine). Dr Read, a GP,
originally developed the codes specifically for primary health care,
covering the range of diagnoses and procedures particular to GPs.
However, he has since expanded the READ codes to enable them to
become a standard way of recording and exchanging clinical data
throughout information systems within the NHS. READ codes
became Crown Copyright in April 1990, and Dr Read is now the
Director of the NHS Centre for Coding and Classification within the
NHS Executive.

It is important throughout the contracting process that coding
methodologies are both consistent and timely. Coded clinical
information is vital to determine the exact diagnoses for the
patient, both principal and secondary, and any procedures which
have been undertaken. In order that a provider can charge a
purchaser for a finished consultant episode (FCE), the clinical
information has to be completely coded within six weeks of the
patient's discharge from the hospital.

Conclusion One of the key elements supporting the whole contracting process
is effective IT systems that *support* the information flows in a
timely, accurate and convenient manner. GPs need to have a clear
picture of hospital waiting times for the first outpatient appointments and admission for their patients. They also need to be able to
track their referrals throughout the course of treatment, and to
have access to pathology and radiology test results. Very few
hospitals can provide direct links. However, with the evolution of
the NHS-Wide Networking programme (as outlined later in this
chapter) this should soon become more viable technically and
financially.

Many providers are becoming increasingly ambitious about the
way they are defining their 'products' for contracting. Unfortunately they often forget that whilst they can define the service, the
information has to be collected in order to charge for the product.
Information systems in the NHS are still generally way behind the
business needs for contracting but are slowly being developed.

THE EMERGENCE
OF HISS AND CISP

Hospital
Information
Support Systems
(HISS)

Due to the extra demands for contracting information, hospitals have been reviewing their IT strategies with the knowledge that current systems do not meet the internal market requirements. Management systems commonly used such as Patient Administration Systems (PAS) were designed to meet statutory information requirements, but could not support contracting. These systems have quickly become dated as the need for operational on-line tracking of contract identification has become a necessity.

In December 1992, the NHS Management Executive launched its national Information Management and Technology (IM & T) Strategy. The strategy was geared, among other key programmes, to aid hospitals in the development of HISS and recommended that the way ahead should be for hospitals to implement fully integrated systems which would provide a cornerstone to support both the internal market and clinical information needs. A schematic of the IM & T conceptual HISS is shown in Figure 8.1 The Department of Health (DoH) set up a HISS Central Team (HCT) to assist sites with HISS procurements and implementations. The HCT offer guidance through a programme of supporting procurement consortia,

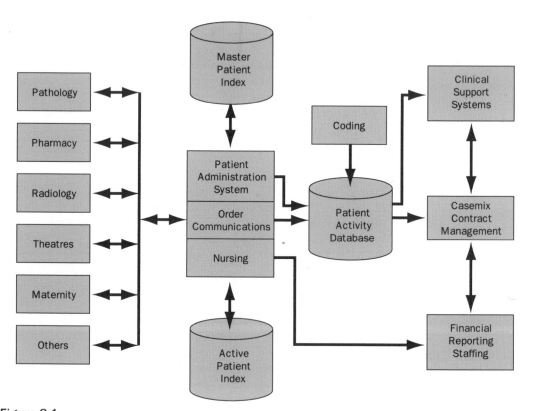

Figure 8.1
The IM & T Strategy's conceptual HISS
Source: Thomas *et al.* (1994), with permission from *The Health Service Journal*

negotiating framework agreements with suppliers, strategic consultancy, producing guidelines and providing training.

DoH funding for Three hospital sites were selected by the Department of Health as
HISS sites pilots to be centrally funded for HISS. They were Darlington Memorial, City Hospital Nottingham and Greenwich District Hospital. These sites were considered to be 'greenfield' sites meaning they did not have many information systems in place. The first sites now have the Patient Administration System (PAS), the Order Communication System (OCS) and some departmental systems implemented.

There has been an inordinate amount of negative publicity surrounding HISS, and varied reports on the large sums of money which have been invested in these initial systems. The 'big bang' approach adopted (replacing all systems with an integrated database) at the three pilot sites is now being reviewed and a more incremental strategy recommended. Whichever way HISS is viewed, the overall concept is valid, although to date HISS sites have tended to concentrate more on the implementation process than on the documented realization of benefits. HISS systems have now been implemented in over 40 NHS hospitals.

If implemented well, with a full benefits analysis and realization programme, a HISS can improve communications throughout, thus enhancing quality of care for patients.

One of the key success factors to any HISS is that data is only entered once and that duplication currently carried out manually and on disparate systems should largely be eliminated. Many sites have PAS, but not many of those sites run the system on a real-time basis whereby data is entered as and when the event occurs. Many of the admission/discharge and transfer (ADT) transactions are undertaken by clerical staff who only work in office hours. These duties are rarely seen to be ones that it would be beneficial for nursing staff to undertake in the absence of the clerical staff. Data is often 'lost' when a patient is admitted and discharged during this period and provider sites are therefore unable to recoup the funding for those patients.

Order OCS (a central component of HISS) is an electronic ordering system
Communications where tests can be ordered directly to departments such as
Systems (OCS) radiology, and pathology, and the subsequent results reported back. It is the OCS which brings the discipline of real time bed management and compels staff to enter the ADT information before they have the benefit of placing a group of requests on a patient, i.e. you cannot place an order for a patient who is not registered and admitted on the system in a known location. This brings about major benefits to clinical staff who are looking for available beds for emergency patients, where they can now see at a glance the up-to-date bed picture. Similarly, the Nursing Care

Planning Systems, historically directed at nursing staff, are now adopting a multidisciplinary focus with therapy departments and clinicians sharing the facility.

The success of OCS relies on effective interfaces with departmental systems such as pathology, radiology, pharmacy, theatres and A & E. The ability to order all tests and requests from one source is vital if clinicians and other healthcare professionals are to view the system as a useful tool.

Many things can impact on efficiency, in particular scheduling patient care effectively. Hospitals that become competent at managing the whole scheduling process will reduce their costs and therefore be better placed to contract for services. Availability of theatre time, booking investigative procedures such as radiology, pre-admission clinics and even transport to deliver the patient, can all play a part in the variance of length of stay between acute providers. Hospital Information Support Systems can help address some of these issues, but not many hospitals have thought through or implemented a unit-wide scheduling system.

Contracting is brought to the fore with HISS. The facility to track contracts and ECRs should be built in to the front-end as part of the PAS process. The discipline of real-time, once-only data entry for demographic and clinical information improves the capture of the CMDS. HISS systems should support in a very flexible way the algorithms necessary to assign a contract identifier once certain data is entered for a patient. As an example if a patient presents with a letter from a GP for a surgical outpatient appointment in preparation for a repair of an inguinal hernia, HISS would need to:

1. Analyse whether or not the GP is fundholding.
2. Look at the post-code and match a district of residence (check if a contract is held with the DHA if the GP was not a fundholder).
3. Look at the procedure which would need to be checked against those payable by GPFHs (if the GP was a fundholder).

From all of the above it would then need to assign a potential contract identifier, which could well be subject to change according to the circumstance.

It is important to be able to identify at a very early stage in the process why the patient has been booked to come in to hospital. This necessitates user friendly encoding systems that give easy look up facilities for diagnoses and operative procedures. This should allow codes to be assigned easily to patients who are placed on the waiting list, through to those who have been admitted and treated as inpatients or day cases.

Contracts are now being geared more towards cost and volume (rather than block) by offering a complete 'care package' of treatment. To clarify this, a particular scenario might be where a patient is referred for a range of treatment including: an initial consultative outpatient appointment, a radiology request, a period of inpatient treatment inclusive of an operative procedure, and two follow-up outpatient appointments. The enabler in this would be HISS, which should offer providers the ability to track all this care, attaching it to a particular contract identifier.

A fundamental issue for most providers who are procuring and implementing HISS is that most of the software emanated from the USA. There is a need therefore to anglicize the system to meet NHS requirements and the complexities of contracting makes this process quite difficult. If it always consisted of an 'either or' algorithm it would be easy to address, but it is more multifarious than this. The system has to identify: the DOR, the GP and whether or not the GP is fundholding, the procedure (and whether or not it is a payable fundholding procedure) and the method of admission. From all of this information a specific contract identifier has to be assigned.

Clinical care protocols are a further area for consideration. Purchasers are placing increasing pressure on providers to use protocols in order to lessen the variance across acute services in differing treatment methods. Care protocols are seen as the way to improve the quality of care, and demonstrate that the purchaser is receiving the full value for the costs incurred. Most specialties have protocols and guidelines within the department but these are often in paper form and difficult to access. HIS systems of the future will need to be developed to support all the diverse types of protocols, from those which cover the ordering of tests, through to the more complex aspects of treating conditions such as asthma. This will require more 'intelligent', knowledge based systems.

Many HISS suppliers are now firmly established within the NHS and are working with providers to help them develop the systems further in order to meet the increasing demands of contracting. The HISS Central Team have recently compiled a catalogue (NHS Executive, 1995) which details 24 suppliers who conform to the basic requirements for a HISS. It also offers information about the implementation process for 18 provider sites.

Community Information Systems A project to support the community providers in developing their systems was set up by the Information Management Group (IMG). One of the key deliverables of the project called CISP (Community Information Systems for Providers) is to help commissioners of care sustain contracting and costing for non-acute services. Other deliverables include:

♦ Identifying shared community and GP functions and information to support the development of integrated primary healthcare teams
♦ Sharing information with other providers to support the provision of seamless collaborative care.

Other key elements are to enable the establishment of protocols in liaison with healthcare commissioners so that more sophisticated contractual agreements can be met.

Current community systems have mainly been designed to collect statutory information such as contacts between healthcare professionals and patients. They were not operationally focused. Therefore data is usually fed into the system retrospectively. The systems did not give the ability to share data across differing disciplines and lacked a ubiquitous set of terms to describe clearly the work undertaken.

As Trusts have evolved there has generally been a split between acute and community providers. This could be seen as a negative aspect of the new world, mainly because it has encouraged acute and community providers to procure separate systems which will undoubtedly require interfaces. In order to provide collaborative care for patients, the clinical record should be as seamless as possible. Historically, interfaces have been difficult to develop, particularly bi-directional interfaces (where data flows both ways) which would be mandatory for the 'seamless' approach. Interfaces such as these are both expensive and technically complicated to develop. This is often because systems are written in differing computer languages and reside on diverse and sometimes proprietary hardware platforms.

At present community systems are commonly unable to provide the framework required to support the care packages which are evolving as the methodology best able to supply information for the contracting process. Care packages are packages of collaborative care aimed at providing an indicator of the resources required, quantifying the quality, and measuring the outcome of patient treatment. They will also provide the opportunity to support written protocols of clinical practice including costs.

A typical care package may include: a care programme, i.e. for leg ulcer management; the care objective (curative); the projected outcome; a protocol summary (including skill mix required; frequency of treatment; duration and location of treatment); costing; qualifying factors; and finally quality standards.

Within the contracting framework this information is essential in order to: agree prices; for the community teams to assess potential demands for their catchment areas; to agree with commissioners of health care the contractual arrangements; to provide annual accounts; to negotiate contracts; to account for services provided and to invoice for them; and finally to provide statutory information for DoH.

If community and acute unit systems are linked, in both the short and the longer term, it will enhance the contracting process and improve the quality of care by supplying immediate information flows across the services.

Overall, HIS systems and their counterparts in community services can only enhance the contracting process by improving the capture of data as and when the event happens. It is the only way to eliminate much of the paperwork currently being passed back and forth between purchaser and provider to support the contracting mechanisms.

INFORMATION SYSTEMS USED BY PURCHASERS

To ensure value for money, one of the key objectives of the purchaser role is to initiate improvements in the quality of care of patients through the contracting process. Purchasers want to set standards which affect their patients such as waiting times for outpatient appointments, inpatient care and other related procedures such as radiology requests. They also wish to monitor outcomes but this data is currently almost non-existent. As an alternative they are likely to view information on readmission rates, and the reason for the readmission. From this data purchasers can identify if there are potential quality issues, such as post-operative complications, which can sometimes result from patients being discharged too soon, or from wound infections. This information can be obtained through the CMDS, and whilst there is still no agreed definition of 'readmission', unplanned finished consultant episodes (FCEs) occurring soon after a previous spell of care can be used as an indicator for assessment of the complications.

Effective provision of information is vital to purchasers if they are going to use it to make decisions about how to contract for improved health for the community. A national review of purchaser IM & T needs has recently been undertaken by the NHS Executive, the results of which have yet to be published. There is also a project to help purchasers develop their information systems called DISP (Developing Information Systems for Purchasers – IM & T NHS Executive). One of its main objectives is to encourage improvements in the use of data and information systems.

Purchasers not only need to know about the quality of care but also whether it is relevant to need; i.e. whether the service provision is based on the *real* healthcare needs of the population. For instance, there may well be over-provision of one type of service and yet gaps in others. They also need to know if the services are delivered as efficiently as possible within the resources available to the provider.

Some acute providers supply CMDS information to purchasers via their regional clearing houses. The regional clearing house databases were set up specifically to serve as a distribution source for purchaser information needs. Data from PAS, DIS (District Information System), and Casemix databases, are fed via a simple 'flat file' format through to the clearing house for the purchasers to access. The flat file developed by Northern Region (hence its name Northern Flat File (NFF)) is used by six regional health authorities.

Other acute providers send their CMDS data direct to the purchaser on disk, or sometimes over a network.

Data from the regional clearing houses is fed through to the Mersey Inter-Regional Clearing House. This was set up for purchasers to access episodes which cross regional boundaries. It is a national service and its utilization across purchaser and provider is both varied and on a voluntary basis.

There is now a plan, however, to develop a NHS-Wide Clearing Service (NWCS); the NHS Executive has recently approved the business case for the project. Transfer of data via the service will be in the form of EDIFACT (Electronic Data Interchange For Administration, Commerce and Transport) based messages taken from provider systems and input into purchaser databases. (A key facilitator for this project will be the NHS-Wide Networking Programme described later in the chapter.)

CMDS data will be received over the network from providers and converted via EDIFACT using X.400 messaging standards into a form suitable for recipient purchaser systems. The NWCS has been designed to replace the utilities currently provided by regional health authorities, which will cease to exist as of April 1996.

GP PURCHASING – IMPLICATIONS FOR INFORMATION SYSTEM REQUIREMENTS

Approximately 85% of GP practices are now computerized using differing software packages such as VAMP, EMIS and many other systems. Most of these were initially designed as costing packages to support administration and, more recently, fundholding. Now needs are expanding, GPs are looking towards not only receiving information (e.g. on inpatient waiting times, discharge summaries etc.) from the acute and community systems, but taking the results/reports into their own software packages avoiding rekeying of data. In order to monitor the care provided, its quality, and the subsequent expenditure involved, GPs want to observe the progress of a patient through the secondary and tertiary process. This will allow them the facility to ensure that their patients have received the treatment which the provider was contracted to supply. They need easy access to look at hospital waiting times for inpatient and outpatient care, to have an immediate discharge summary, to view and retrieve results and reports, and to book outpatient appointments. Some acute sites are now looking at linking their GPs into their systems and providing them with the modem links and PCs.

As GPs take more of a lead in purchasing care for their patients, the design and development of systems to support fundholding will clearly need to improve. A study was commissioned by the NHS Executive Information Management Group (IMG) in two regions, Wessex and Yorkshire. The study was undertaken by management consultants (Hoskyns Group plc, 1993) and looked at the quality of data flowing between NHS organizations about GP fundholder purchased patient care.

The main objectives of the project were to:

♦ Establish the causes of poor quality data to enable them to be addressed.
♦ Identify good management practice which can be shared more widely.
♦ Promote a better understanding of the information needed about GP fundholder purchased care.

The study was completed in October 1993 and identified the main 'events' in the patient care process about which information is needed by the organizations with an interest in GP fundholder purchased patient care. The results of the study were reported to regions during December 1993 and identified some major problems in certain areas such as the linking of referrals to invoices. For example a referral number is generated from the GPFH system so that the treatment for a patient can be tracked and attached to the appropriate invoice. Unfortunately these referral numbers cannot often be used by acute provider systems, which therefore does not allow them to use it when communicating with the practice. Other problems identified included variances in administrative procedures between providers and the fundholding practices further complicating the contracting process.

The impact of GP fundholding has led to the appointment of practice managers to manage both the funding and services of the practice. Often the practice manager is a qualified accountant and IT specialist. GPs have also taken the initiative on training, and registered on various management and IT courses. Receptionists and practice nurses have had quickly to become conversant with information technology and the new processes involved with fundholding.

GP purchasing   GPFHs can currently only purchase a limited range of services and may not set up a contract of over one year's duration because they are assessed on an annual budgetary basis. At present they purchase care under short-term, cost and volume, block, or cost per case contracts. The services for which they can contract include: inpatient, day case, outpatient, direct access, domiciliary and community. They can also purchase care from the private sector or provide services themselves. Any patient whose cost of care will exceed £5000 will not be paid by the fundholder but be passed on, via the FHSA, to the DHA for payment.

In some instances where specialist services are required and in order to increase influence, GPFHs may group together to form a consortium. This often happens where services are limited and negotiations carried out by one practice may not be the optimal route. The largest practice usually acts as the lead purchaser and the overall number involved with the consortium will increase the possibility of reducing cost and risk.

GPFHs do not pay for maternity or medical services although this will change in the future as there is a move towards 'super funds' where GPs have even more autonomy over purchasing. A recent Executive Letter (EL(94)79) from DoH described three new types of fundholding: the first called *community fundholding* aimed at small practices not yet ready to take the full fundholding commitment, the second *standard fundholding* which is an expansion of the current scheme, and thirdly *total purchasing* where GPs purchase all hospital and community care for their patients.

Overall the main impact this will have on information systems is to increase the need for integration, giving the GPs access to acute and community systems in order for them to take relevant data into their own databases enabling the complete picture of health care for a particular patient. Most acute providers are still having difficulties in supplying the GPFH information in a timely way. Often this is due to the IT systems being out of date; many of the PAS systems have been in use for over ten years and do not supply the relevant data required for fundholding. It can also arise, however, from lack of training and understanding on behalf of the provider staff who are responsible for capturing the fundholding information.

Eighty-five per cent of GP practices are now computerized with systems which play a major role in coping with the demands of contracting. A new system to accredit GP systems to nationally agreed standards was implemented in April 1994. These standards, known as Requirements for Accreditation, will mean that GPs can be sure that if their systems are compliant, they will be capable of integration with other IT systems across the NHS.

Timely and accurate data flows are an essential element for enabling fundholders to manage their activities. To date this has largely been complicated by the disparity of systems used by providers and the fundholders themselves, and lack of network infrastructure.

HRGS AND THEIR ROLE IN SUPPORTING THE CONTRACTING PROCESS

Healthcare Resource Groups (HRGs), originally designed as a resource management tool, are now being used to inform the contracting process. An HRG may be defined as: 'a group of inpatient episodes which are likely to absorb comparable amounts of health care resource'. They are delineated by the diagnoses and procedures for which patients have been treated during their stay in hospital.

HRGs are based on data extracted directly from the CMDS which all hospitals are legally obliged to supply in order to complete the inpatient summary of activity. ICD-9/10 (International Classification of Diseases V.9 and V.10, which was released in 1995) and OPCS-4 (Office of Population Census and Surveys V.4) are the diagnostic and procedural codes used to feed HRGs. READ codes are also becoming widely used across both provider and GP systems. Written by Dr James Read, the codes map to ICD-9 (V2) and ICD-10 (V3). These codes all meet standard national classifications used throughout the NHS, therefore negating the need for additional data. The Generic Grouping algorithm for HRGs as identified by the IMG, is shown in Figure 8.2.

The recent launch of Version 2 of HRGs was delivered at an event sponsored by the National Casemix Office. Here the talks focused on the internal market and how important HRGs are in support of the market framework. The only way to improve, and indeed monitor, the effectiveness of services is to be able to compare like with like. Comparison of length of stay for instance has been a guide to measuring efficiency. Generally acute hospitals are becoming more efficient by treating more patients with the same resources. Length of stay for most specialties has reduced and there has been a marked increase in day surgery.

HRGs will be a vital component to the contracting process. Contracts are devised mainly on a 'block' basis at present but there is a drive to move towards contracting on cost and volume. Purchasers and providers are not currently required to contract in costed HRGs, but the NHS Executive expects them to demonstrate that HRG costs have been used to direct the monitoring and development of contracts.

The implementation timetable set by the Executive requires acute providers to cost HRGs in at least one specialty during 1994/95. This speciality can be selected from orthopaedics, ophthalmology or gynaecology. From this exercise comparative cost data will be extracted to inform the 1995/96 contracts. A further 'roll-out' programme to inform the 1997/98 contracting process will involve costed HRGs covering all major specialties.

One of the main problems to date which has limited the operation of the internal market has been an inconsistency in the way purchasers and providers have defined their services. Examples of these inconsistencies (taken from the National Steering Group on Costing (NSGC, 1992) which conducted a survey in 1992 of purchaser and providers) are:

♦ Inconsistencies in product definition.
♦ Different costing methodologies.
♦ Inaccurate counting of activity.
♦ Differing units of measuring of activity.

HRGs are being developed to try and iron out these inconsistencies and ensure a less variable approach to the contracting process and make costing more precise.

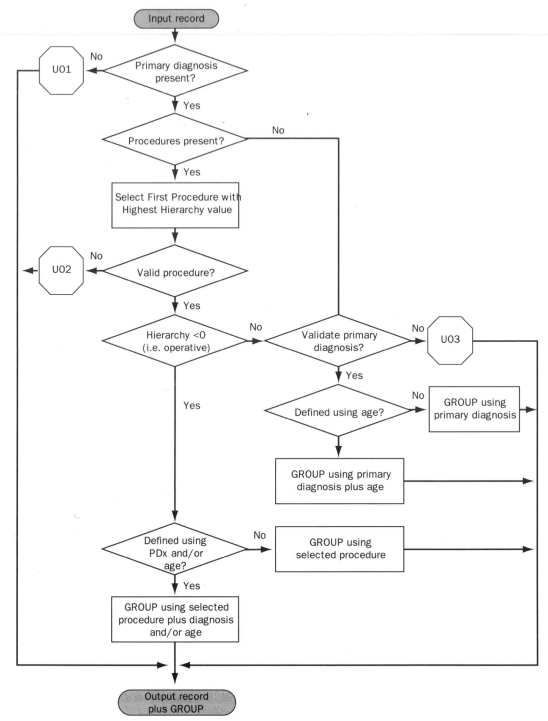

Figure 8.2
Generic grouping algorithm – a summary
Source: Information Management Group : NHS (1994), with permission

THE NATIONAL   The NHS Executive's IM & T Strategy (1992) formed a structure for
IM & T STRATEGY   gaining the maximum benefit from information management and
technology investments. Two major projects evolved from the
Strategy, the NHS-Wide Networking programme and the new NHS
number, both of which are key to improving information management in the NHS.

NHS-Wide   One of the essential elements of IM & T strategy is the NHS-Wide
Networking   Networking Programme. This ambitious programme has been
Programme   developed to provide a simple and cost effective way of sending
data to and from anywhere within the NHS. A caveat to this was
that the information must be not only accurate, but also secure and
confidential. The network must also be designed in such a way that
it not only supports the needs of today, but is flexible enough to
address the future data exchange needs as far as these can be
predicted.

   The transfer of patient data through a whole period of care, from
general practitioner, to acute provider and to community, should
eventually be possible via the NHS Network even though information systems may be different in each case at local level. Confidentiality will be a critical issue to ensure that the data is safe and not
passed inappropriately into the wrong hands. The infrastructure is
therefore being built in such a way as to ensure data security.

   One of the early benefits to acute providers will be the ability to
transfer pathology requests/results, radiology requests/reports,
discharge summaries, and letters, directly to GP practices. In some
cases they will be able to import this information directly into their
systems (which is currently the most desired method of transferring the data, and would be the most efficient), the so-called 'end-
to-end' approach. GPs will have access to provider and community
systems, giving them the opportunity to refer patients directly by
booking outpatient appointments, sending letters electronically,
viewing waiting times, and to look at any activity which is taking
place whilst their patients undergo treatment.

   This will become a vital foundation to the contracting process,
eliminating much of the paperwork and improving the efficiency of
data exchange overall. Contract minimum data set information will
become available on line, eliminating the need for continual
checking and (often) misunderstandings between purchasers and
providers.

   A briefing paper has recently been published by the Information
Management Group (NHS Executive, 1994) which offers further
information on the NHS-Wide Networking Programme.

NHS number   In support of more effective data exchange within acute provider,
primary, and community units, the DoH has proposed a new
common single identifier for the NHS. The number will be a
unique personal identifier, which will be in a suitable format for

modern information systems. It will be all numeric, comprising ten digits (the last being a check digit), and was due for issue during 1995. This is now likely to be delayed. Further information on the format and substance of the number can be obtained from a fact sheet issued by the IMG (1993).

It is planned for this number to be rolled out slowly across the NHS, giving the opportunity to rationalize all the diverse numbering systems currently being used for patient identification. One of the key problems with present disparate information systems used by acute providers, is that patients are often given a separate number for the Accident and Emergency (A & E) department, another on the Patient Administration System (PAS) and sometimes yet another on the pathology systems. In many cases these systems are unable to interface, creating more ground for confusion and ambiguities when trying to amalgamate contracting information.

It is clearly going to take time for this unique number to be adopted and implemented across information systems. In the first instance the proposal is to provide the data on disk so that it can be loaded onto acute and community systems. However, the matching for this may be fuzzy; for instance if you are going to match by surname, forename, date of birth etc., there are obviously going to be some discrepancies between the two sources of data. A way forward would be that patients themselves should be informed of their new number, without having to ask for it. This would help facilitate the distribution and provide the necessary match when they present for treatment.

Once fully implemented the NHS number should provide the key to the exchange of data across the NHS-wide network, and be the unique patient identifier for contracting for health care across the nation. This personal reference will help support the tracking of patients through GP, purchaser, acute provider and community services helping to work towards an Electronic Patient Record.

Electronic Patient Record

In the long term it is the aim of the NHS to build an Electronic Patient Record that can be shared across the entire care process. This will be available on a 'need to know' basis giving better quality of treatment for patients by providing all relevant information wherever the patient presents. With the advent of 'multimedia', doctors and nursing staff fully exploiting information technology (IT), the NHS-Wide Network, and the NHS number, the electronic medical record may not be too far away. The obvious benefits of this simplicity of communication are that instantaneous data exchange will enable the contract process to be performed 'dynamically' as and when information is entered into the systems. This is the vision of both purchasers and providers who are burdened with an excess of bureaucratic paperwork and information systems which are often not interfaced let alone integrated.

SUMMARY

In every niche of the new NHS market people are striving to develop systems which will support the contracting process. In the main the contracting mechanism has moved forward rapidly and the development of the information systems needed to underpin the process have not kept pace. In the acute provider world HISS suppliers are still trying to understand the NHS and the marketing requirements of today. They have yet to look forward to the complex changes tomorrow may bring.

In the community, systems are still relatively simple and have yet to be developed fully to support care packages which will feed necessary data for the contracting process.

GP software companies are now beginning to think through the best process for linking to acute sites and extracting pathology/radiology information to put into their patient record. They have not yet really begun to look at directly relating more detailed patient based information to 'link' the full CMDS. The NHS-Wide Networking Programme will facilitate this. However, there are still many issues to be addressed.

How data will be exchanged, the format, and the standards required is just one key area to be examined. Electronic data interchange (EDI) is a system of telecommunications protocols developed by the IT industry defining how messages should be coded and formatted for exchange through computer systems. EDIFACT is a standard which has been developed by the United Nations. EDIFACT has been designed to define messages; each message requires a protocol which ultimately has to be accepted and agreed by the UN. Unfortunately both the volume, and the eclectic nature of messages required to be exchanged within the NHS for CMDSs presents a formidable challenge. The NHS-Wide Clearing House (once developed), facilitated by the NHS-Wide Networking Programme, should answer some of these key issues.

CONCLUSION

So where does all of this lead to and where will the whole information process be in ten years time? In short, the answer is we do not know at this stage. It is probable, however, that information systems and data flows will become more flexible, more integrated, and that the contracting process will probably become increasingly complex as systems permit. Software suppliers, for all of the disparate systems, are having to wake up and conform to set standards which will expedite the flow of information throughout health care.

It is certainly apparent that to date there has been no clear prescription for supporting the flow of contracting data. Therefore many differing practices have evolved which are slowly being reconciled.

The purchaser/provider scenario has evolved and grown and has subsequently overtaken the technology which is able to support it.

The NHS has historically been criticized for being dilatory in its IT strategy. However, this is a time for change and the requirements of contracting have clearly overtaken technology – which is now struggling to 'catch up'.

FURTHER QUESTIONS

Listed below are areas you may wish to consider if they are relevant to your particular practice:

♦ *Information and how it is used throughout the contracting process.*

From the provider perspective: If you are setting contracts related to particular 'products' which you wish to delineate specifically, think carefully in the first instance as to how your information systems will support the process. Is the product clearly identifiable, if not will you have to implement a paper based procedure in order to track related cases? Many providers are losing funds because they are not able to track and invoice complicated product definitions.

♦ *The emergence of HISS for acute providers and CISP for community services.*

The DoH is becoming increasingly stringent about business cases for systems such as HISS and CISP. Benefits, and how you might realize those benefits (both cash and non cash-releasing), will need to be carefully thought through. If this is not tackled business cases are likely to be rejected at the first hurdle. Going through the process will help identify:

- How you will implement the system.
- Any problems which might be encountered.
- How to increase awareness as you involve staff from each discipline.

♦ *Information systems used by purchasers and their role in helping to establish population health needs.*

Looking at the *real* healthcare needs of the population requires quality information with little variance in how it is compiled. Perhaps the only way to reduce variance in data capture is to prompt providers to be more ambitious in the application of care protocols. These will of course require 'knowledge' based information systems to support their application. However, such systems are still in an 'embryonic' state in this country.

♦ *GP purchasing – implications of information system requirements.*

Is your main provider able to link the referral number you generate to the invoice raised? Are you able to access results and take them into your own database? Do you receive clinical discharge summaries electronically? All these and more are now becoming technically viable.

♦ *HRGs and their role in supporting the contracting process.*

Standard coding procedures to support HRGs are vital; are you clear about the path toward ICD-10, or support for READ which is now a national standard? How good are your encoding systems, do you have quick, easy look-up procedures?

Providers should be preparing for using HRGs as 'products' from April 1995 in at least two of the following specialties: trauma and orthopaedics, gynaecology, and ophthalmology.

♦ *The National IM & T Strategy*

The Strategy offers much toward the contracting process in terms of communicating and linking events nationally which should also move toward informing the 'Health of the Nation'.

FURTHER READING

♦ STEP, Standards Enforcement in Procurement Guide for Managers, NHS Executive IMG, ref E5101.

♦ The Electronic Data Interchange Process An Overview, NHS Executive IMG ref: E5127.

♦ GP System Accreditation, General Medical Practice Computer System Requirements for Accreditation V2, April 94, NHS Executive IMG ref: B2090.

♦ HRG V2. National Statistics, NHS Executive ref: G7028.

REFERENCES

Hoskyns Group plc (1993), *Data Quality Initiative Phase II, GP Fundholding, Findings of Scoping Study.* NHS Executive:

Department of Health (1989), *Working for Patients.* London.

Department of Health (1993), Information Management Group, Lynne Bennett, *New NHS Number Format and Use.*

Information Management Group: NHS Executive (1993), *POISE – Procurement of Information Systems Effectively.*

Information Management Group: NHS Executive (1994), NHS-wide networking and acute units: a briefing.

Information Management Group: NHS (1994), *What are Version 2 Health Care Resource Groups?* December.

National Steering Group on Costing (NSEC) (1992), *Survey of Purchasers and Providers.*

NHS Executive: Department Of Health (1992), *IM&T Strategy Overview*.
NHS Executive: HISS Central Team (1994), *Distribution of HISS Catalogue*.
Thomas, R. *et al*. (1994), *Health Service Journal* 28 July: 25.

APPENDIX 1:
INDIVIDUAL
PATIENT BASED
CMDS

Field	Length	Validation	Format	Comment
Purchaser ID	5	Valid code	A/N	
Provider ID	5	Valid Code	A/N	
Contract serial number	6		N	May be less than six characters long
Sequence number	8		N	Sequence number for each provider submitting CMDSs so that an audit trail can be produced
Record Status	2	0 through 5	N	0 – New programme of care 1 – Completed programme of care 2 – Closed programme of care 3 – Update or correction for active programme of care 4 – Cont. of programme at end of period (Month, Quarter or Year End) 5 – Deleted record, where an error has occurred. Enables the CMDS to be sent at the beginning and end of a programme and allows amendments as well as an end of year audit of caseload
Care objective	2	11 through 18 or 99	N	11(H) – Assessment 12(E) – Enabling Children 13(C) – Curative Care 14(R) – Rehabilitation 15(M) – Maintenance Care 16(S) – Supportive Care 17(P) – Palliative and Bereavement Care 18(A) – Anticipatory Care 99(X) – Not Applicable
Care Programme identifier	3	Classification Attached	N	
Staff Group Profession		1 through 22	1 or 2	characters long
Discharge Reason	2	1 through 11	N	1 or 2 characters long

Field	Length	Validation	Format	Comment
Patient Surname	35		A	May be less than 35 characters long
Patient Forename	35		A	May be less than 35 characters long
Postcode of usual address	7	Valid postcode for purchaser	A/N	Sometimes recorded in 8 character format
Local Patient Identifier Ethnic origin	10	Valid code	A/N	May be less, or more than 10 characters. When the NHS number is fully implemented this can be deleted
NHS Number	17		A/N	To be changed to a ten digit numeric field in due course
Birth Date	8	CCYYMMDD	Date	
Sex	1	1 through 3	N	1(M) – Male 2(F) – Female 3 – Other
Code of GP Practice (Registered)	6	Valid code	A/N	
Code of General Practitioner (Referring)	8	Valid code	A/N	
Code of General Practitioner Practice (Referring)	6	Valid code	A/N	
Source of Referral	2	1 through 33	N	
Start Date	8	CCYYMMDD	Date	
End Date	8	CCYYMMDD	Date	

APPENDIX 2:
GROUP BASED
PROGRAMMES
CMDS

This will require a different record format as follows:

Field	Length	Validation	Format	Comment
Purchaser ID	5	Valid code	A/N	
Provider ID	5	Valid Code	A/N	
Contract serial number	6		N	May be less than six characters long
Sequence number	8		N	To enable an audit trail to be produced for each provider
Record Status	2	0 through 5	N	0 – New programme of care 1 – Completed programme of care 2 – Closed programme of care 3 – Update or correction for active programme of care 4 – Cont. of programme at end of period (Month, Quarter or Year End) 5 – Deleted record, where an error has occurred. Enables the CMDS to be sent at the beginning and end of a programme and allows amendments as well as an end of year audit of caseload
Care Objective	2	11 through 18 or 99	N	11(H) – Assessment 12(E) – Enabling Children 13(C) – Curative Care 14(R) – Rehabilitation 15(M) – Maintenance Care 16(S) – Supportive Care 17(P) – Palliative and Bereavement Care 18(A) – Anticipatory Care 99(X) – Not Applicable
Care Programme Identifier	3		N	
Start Date	8	YYYYMMDD	Date	
End Date	8	YYYYMMDD	Date	
Number of programme sessions held	3	1 through 99	N	
Total number of attendances or visits at programme sessions	3	1 through 99	N	

APPENDIX 3:
PROVIDER CMDS

Month: May 1995
Provider: RQM00
Produced: 22-JUN-95

Extra-Contractual Referrals for Payment: DHA

Ref. No. \ECR\IP\9596\- - - - - - - - \01

Contract: RQM00....

Personal Details
- - - - - - - - -

Postcode:

DOB:
Sex:

Registered GP:

Episode Details
- - - - - - - - -
Patient No:
Clinical Directorate:
Specialty:
Consultant Code:
Consultant Name:
Episode Start:
Episode End:
Patient Classification:
Method of Admission:
Source of Admission:
Method of Discharge:
Discharge Dest:

Clinical Details
- - - - - - - - -

Diagnoses:
Operations:

Product Details
- - - - - - - - -

Product Code:
Description:
Price:

ECR Authorisation Number: _____ Tertiary referral: YES/NO
Private and Confidential

SECTION III

CONTRACTING ISSUES

"VISIBLE PALPITATIONS IN NECK, RAPID EYE MOVEMENT, TREMBLING OF RIGHT HAND ~ NOT SURE ABOUT THE SMALL PRINT, ARE YOU!"

THE LEGAL AND POLICY FRAMEWORK

CHAPTER 9

Richard Long

OBJECTIVES

- ♦ To explain the main principles of English contract law, which apply to all contracts between NHS bodies and private ones.

- ♦ To discuss the extent to which the above principles apply to NHS contracts, to explain the NHS contracting environment and to list and comment on the current guidance on NHS contracts.

INTRODUCTION

Contract is one of the areas of law in which a little learning, far from being dangerous, will be repaid many times. All clinical directors and business managers should understand the basic principles involved.

LEGAL CONTRACTS

One important distinction needs to be made at the outset between contracts enforceable at law (most contracts between private individuals and commercial organizations fall into the category) and NHS contracts (contracts between NHS bodies). The latter are not enforceable at law, but are arbitrated on in the event of a dispute by civil servants of the NHS Executive. NHS contracts are discussed in greater detail later: the following section deals with English contract law as it applies outside the NHS, which NHS managers have to consider when contracting with non Health Service bodies. Current, topical applications of contract law include the Private Finance Initiative and contracting out of non clinical services. Contrary to beliefs in some NHS quarters, there is nothing special or mysterious about the contracting aspects of these processes: they are simply applications of contracting as used for all transactions in the private sector as well as for all existing purchases of goods and services from the private sector.

FORMATION OF A CONTRACT

All business transactions are based on contracts. This term applies to any legally enforceable agreement between two or more parties, whether or not it is in writing. There is a commonly held belief, in business as well as in the NHS, that a verbal agreement or an exchange of letters amounts to no more than a negotiable understanding, rendered into something enforceable only after the intercession of two firms of solicitors, numerous pages of text ('the legal stuff') a quantity of non-standard size high quality paper and the application of a closely guarded metal seal to a red plastic wafer. In fact none of these steps are necessary to the formation of a legally binding contract. All that is required is:

♦ *an offer* (oral or written) on certain (defined) terms (to provide goods or services or to pay for them if provided)
♦ *acceptance* (oral or written again) of the offer (which must be unconditional).

The offer and acceptance together comprise *agreement*.

♦ *consideration* (payment which must not predate the agreement)
♦ *an intention to create legal relations* (which is presumed between commercial parties).

It follows that there are numerous traps for the unwary or the uneducated:

The unwanted baby?

It is an easy matter to create a contract when you do not intend to or fail to create a contract when you do. Remember that most contracts need not be in writing. (The Statute of Frauds 1677 established exceptions, some of which still exist, most notably for contracts involving land). If you order a box of bandages from a supplier and they agree to supply on their usual terms and price, a contract is formed. The problem with an oral contract is providing evidence that it was ever formed, and if so on what terms.

A contract consists of its terms. If you fail to set out unambiguous terms, there may be no contract, or the terms which are ambiguous may be unenforceable. The rule of ambiguity, which can work both ways, is that ambiguous terms are construed against whoever drafted them. This is often useful when looking for ways to avoid unpleasant terms which you have not bothered to read before entering into a contract with a supplier. However, be extremely careful if you are proposing the terms.

It must be clear who are the parties to a contract

They must be the parties who will perform the obligations in the contract. For instance if the supplier is Ninebob Copiers Limited, it is no use the contract stating 'Ninebob Maintenance Limited will maintain the copier free of charge' unless the second company is also a party to the contract.

TERMS: THE CONTENTS OF THE CONTRACT A contract consists of its terms. There are two sorts of terms: conditions and warranties. The main difference between the two is that breach of a condition, being more important, entitles the victim to treat the contract as repudiated by the other party. Breach of warranty entitles him only to claim damages.

Visible terms The technical name for these is 'express' terms. These are the terms which can be read in the contract document. They may include terms written in appendices, annexes and schedules together with plans and diagrams. If it is not clear whether a document attached to the contract is intended to be part of it, then trouble is likely. The contents of documents merely referred to in the contract may be express terms of it, whereas the contents of documents clipped to the contract, but not referred to in it, may not become part of the contract (particularly if they become separated from the main contract document). It is therefore good practice for any of these to be annexed to the contract document itself, and for the annexes to be scheduled in the contract, to avoid surprises.

Invisible terms The technical term for these is 'implied terms'. These are terms which no amount of reading of the contract documents will discover; they are terms which the law has decided belong in your contract, whether you wanted them there or not. Originally they were terms necessary in order to bring the contract into line with the intention of the parties. For instance if a contract failed to mention the price of goods to be sold, there is an implied term that the buyer must pay a reasonable price. In 1926 Lord Justice MacKinnon formulated the immortal 'officious bystander' rule as a test for when the court should imply a term into the contract: that is 'if, while the parties were making their bargain, an officious bystander were to suggest some express provision for it in their agreement, they would testily suppress him with a comment "Oh, of course!"' This remains the test for whether a term should be implied, or read, into a contract.

More recently terms have been implied into contracts by statute, and these are now the more important category of implied term:

♦ *Sale of Goods Act 1979 as amended by the Sale and Supply of Goods Act 1994*: Perhaps the most important example is the Sale of Goods Act 1979 (now amended), which implies conditions, amongst others, that goods shall be of satisfactory (previously merchantable) quality and reasonably fit for the purpose for which they are being bought.

♦ *Supply of Goods and Services Act 1982* which extends the provisions of the 1979 Act and obliges the provider of services to do so with reasonable skill and care and within a reasonable time if no time limit is mentioned.

♦ *Unfair Contract Terms Act 1979* which limits the ability of the party proposing the contract to impose very one-sided terms, especially in a sale to a consumer. In particular, it limits the ability of a party to exclude liability for possible risks.

♦ *Misrepresentation*: A misrepresentation is an untrue statement made by one party to the other which induced the latter to enter into the contract. It is not a term of the contract. A misrepresentation of fact, depending on whether it is fraudulent, negligent or innocent, may entitle the other party to cancel the contract or claim damages.

Other problems The following problems can also lead to the contract being cancelled or damages claimed:

♦ Mistake as to the party or subject matter of the contract.

♦ Illegal contracts (executed despite a law forbidding them, such as an illegal gambling contract).

♦ A contract entered into by infants (under 18) or by a person without the mental capacity to understand the contract (a significant exception in health service work).

ENFORCEMENT When the parties who entered into the contract fall out, one or
AND REMEDIES more will go to the contract document to see if the outrageous conduct of the other amounts to a breach of the contract. If it does, and assuming a compromise cannot be negotiated, the answer will not always be to sue for damages. The remedies available include the following, depending on the nature of the breach, although at this stage qualified legal advice should be sought in all cases where the loss involved is significant to either party.

Rescission
The contract is treated as though it had never existed. This will usually be applied when it is possible to return to the original position by, for instance, returning goods bought.

Damages
This is the most common remedy in cases where financial compensation is appropriate.

Specific performance
This is comparatively rare, but, in some cases, the court will order the party in breach to do what they originally promised.

Injunction

This is a decree by the court ordering a person to do or not to do a certain act (other than simply performing the contract). Although difficult and expensive to obtain, it is common for people to apply for injunctions in cases where the court may still prevent the thing happening they particularly fear, and for which damages after the event will be a poor compensation.

Time limits

The Limitation Act 1980 provides that most contracts can be enforced for up to six years after the alleged breach. A deed, in practice a type of contract which was traditionally sealed, but need no longer be, may be enforced for up to 12 years. In the case of a minor, or other person under a disability, time starts to run only when the person comes of age or the disability is removed.

The courts   While it is possible to bring an action in person rather than using a solicitor, in practice no-one without unlimited free time, patience and a perverse liking for pointless bureaucracy should attempt it. With the arguable exception of 'small claims', court procedure is so bewilderingly complicated that few lawyers claim to understand it completely. Law and officially sanctioned procedure is supplemented by 'practice directions' and local rules invented and enforced by court administrators. Major reforms in court procedure are believed to be underway, and this is to be welcomed. For those unlucky enough to go to court the main categories are as follows:

The High Court

High Court centres are located in London and many provincial towns and cities. Actions in excess of £50 000 should be started in the High Court. Actions in excess of £25 000 may be. The Court may decide to transfer your action from High Court to County Court, or from one centre to another, if it is for any reason expedient to do so.

The County Court

County Court offices are in many of the same places with additional offices in small provincial towns. Although County Court procedure was originally designed to be more user friendly than in the High Court, few would make this claim for it today. Although different, it is equally complex. In provincial centres cases technically 'in the High Court' are held in the same room, before the same District Judge, as cases 'in the County Court'. The rules, procedures and etiquette are, however, different. Even lawyers sometimes confuse which court they are in, having perhaps spent most of the day in the same room, while transferring their attentions from the County Court to the High Court and back again.

Small Claims

There is no Small Claims Court. In fact this is merely a means of commencing small scale actions in the County Court using simpler procedures. The guidelines as to what constitutes a 'small claim' are currently under review. Legal representation is strongly discouraged and costs (other than expenses) are not awarded to the winning party. If an NHS organization or commercial company is sued using the small claims procedures, it cannot really win. If it fights the action, it will cost a great deal of management time. If it does not, it has no option but to pay the claim.

OTHER PROCEDURES

Assignment

A legal doctrine known as 'privity of contract' enforces the common sense principle that only parties to the contract may have rights and obligations under it. If A contracts with B, C might be justifiably surprised to discover he had either rights or obligations under that contract. However, this can result in anomalies. If A contracts with B and includes a term that B should pay £1000 to C, C cannot sue B to enforce this term. Only A can do this. Again, if A contracts with B, but then sells his business to C, C, as the new owner of the business, may need to enforce A's rights against B. For this reason a person who is entitled to the benefit of a contract may transfer that benefit to another person: this transaction is known as assignment. Whereas a contract usually amounts to an agreement to do something, an assignment is the actual doing of it, or deed. For this reason, and for other technical reasons, the document effecting the assignment is usually a deed. However, only rights or benefits of a contract can be assigned. The burden or obligations cannot.

Agency

Agency is the relationship which arises when one person is authorized to act as the representative of another person. Sometimes an agent is authorized to make a contract with a third party on behalf of the person authorizing the agent, who is known as the principal. An agent's authority may arise in different ways: it may actually have been given by the principal, either expressly or by implication of law ('actual' authority). Authority to act as agent may be considered to exist where circumstances make it appear to others that the agent has authority. For instance a director of a company will normally be taken to have authority to act for the company, unless the company takes active steps to inform others that he does not. There are other forms of authority.

A general rule of agency is that an agent makes a contract on behalf of the principal and accepts no benefit or liability under it. The principal can sue or be sued under the contract. The agent cannot. The principal and agent may themselves have a contract under which they may sue each other, but this is another matter. There are exceptions to the general rule which may make an agent liable under or entitled to the benefit of a contract. If the responsibility of an agent becomes an issue, it would be important to take legal advice.

FORMALITIES

Enforcement

If you wish to enforce the terms of a contract against a party to it, it must be signed by that party. For this reason it is usual for there to be two copies of every contract, signed by both (or all) parties, each keeping a copy.

Evidence

It is vital to keep a copy of a contract and, if it refers to published terms not contained in the contract itself, to ensure that you have a copy of these terms (preferably before you sign the contract).

Execution

Contracts must be signed by people having actual or ostensible authority to do so. It is safest when dealing with companies to insist that a director of the company signs. It is good practice for your own organization to insist on the same procedure.

When is a contract not a contract?

When it is headed with the words 'subject to contract' indicating that the terms are only proposed, and not finally agreed. This is a useful convention to enable you to negotiate the outline of a contract in correspondence without being held prematurely to an initial proposal before you are completely happy with all the terms. The use of these words at the head of any letter will enable you to use it in negotiations. The words 'without prejudice' are used in correspondence on a contentious matter, indicating that anything you may suggest is without prejudice, if agreement cannot be reached, to your existing right to sue, without being held to any compromise or admission you may have suggested or made during negotiations.

Property law

One area where the above common law rules do not apply is in property (land and buildings). Property law is a large and complex branch of commercial law. One important difference is that property contracts do have to be in writing. Another is that far-reaching and expensive rights can easily be created unintentionally. For instance any company or business partnership (e.g. a GP practice) which is allowed to occupy NHS premises in return for payment of any kind is likely to acquire security of tenure. While it may be possible to bring pressure, perhaps through the local FHSA, to undo this, it will, at least, be a headache.

NHS RULES REGARDING THE USE OF LEGAL CONTRACTS

Guidance is regularly issued by the NHS Executive regarding contracting with the private sector, particularly in the area of facilities and non clinical support services. One of the most important areas here, on account of the large sums of money being spent, is the guidance issued on capital projects, HSE(94)31, and two codes operated mainly by the Facilities and Estates departments of NHS Trusts and health authorities: CONCODE and ESTATECODE.

CONCODE is defined in the publication itself as 'a code of procedure for building and engineering contracts in the NHS. ..... (it) contains a mixture of policy and guidance for those involved with works contracts and consultant commissions.' It is amended regularly.

ESTATECODE is 'for all managers in Trusts and Health Authorities who have a responsibility for the estate at a strategic or operational level....Its aim is to make all health service managers appreciate the cost of owning and running the estate'. It includes a good deal of advice for managers handling contracts with the private sector.

Other guidance recently issued in this area includes:

♦ *Energy efficiency in the low energy hospitals* EPL(94)26.
♦ *Energy efficiency in the NHS: Energy efficiency office good practice programme* EPL(94)29.
♦ *Risk Management in the NHS* EL(93)111. This deals with the important policy area of insurance as well as other methods of managing and limiting the financial and other consequences of operational risk.
♦ *The management of the estate in the NHS: Fire code Policy and principles – Directions from the Secretary of State* EL(94)29.
♦ *Contracting out finance related functions* FDL(94)31.

NHS CONTRACTS The 1990 Act defines an NHS contract (in section 4(1)) as 'an arrangement under which one health service body ("the Acquirer") arranges for the provision to it by another health service body ("the Provider") of goods or services which it reasonably requires for the provision of its functions'. It goes on to define 'health service body' predictably, except that non-fundholding GP practices are not included. The section then states

> *Whether or not an arrangement which constitutes an NHS contract would, apart from this sub-section, be a contract in law, it shall not be regarded for any purpose as giving rise to contractual rights or liabilities, but if any dispute arises with respect to such an arrangement, either party may refer the matter to the Secretary of State for determination*

In other words NHS contracts are not enforceable in law.

In practice it seems that the NHS does not intend taxpayers' money to be spent by Trusts and health authorities on lawyers and courts, but believes that the NHS Executive will be able to arbitrate on contentious matters more cheaply and more efficiently. This may be so, although caution should be exercised. The courts do not like to have their functions limited in this way and have already decided that certain contracts, if they appear to be legally enforce-able, may be taken to court, even though they are between two health service bodies. It seems likely that the annual contracts between providers and purchasers, and service level agreements between Trusts, will continue to enjoy this exemption. However, legal advice should be sought where there is any doubt.

Disputes and arbitration/ conciliation.

This does not mean that the basic rules of contract law can be ignored with NHS contracts. Although it is unclear what criteria the NHS Executive will use to resolve disputes, it seems likely, in the absence of further clarification, that it will use rules approximating to the law of contract. It may, however, modify this by using its discretion to exclude contract terms it considers unreasonable or which contravene relevant guidance.

Some guidance as to the procedure to be followed in the event of a dispute is offered by the Annex to *Market Management* 1995/1996 ('Conciliation and Arbitration'). However, this does not offer criteria for interpretation in the event of a disagreement about the meaning or intention of a contractual term or about the action to be taken in case of an event unforeseen by the contract. A number of 'tests' are set down such as 'Have both parties adhered to the key milestone dates in the contracting cycle?' and 'Has the provider notified the purchaser of price structure changes by the required date exemplifying the effect?' The implication of this is that breach of any of these procedural guidelines will be regarded as a breach of an implied term of the contract by the offending party. Arbitration on the point will presumably go against the party in breach (assuming that can be established). The guidance states (several times) that disputes should be resolved locally where possible, though by what process or criteria it remains unhelpfully silent.

ARBITRATION

The NHS and Community Care Act 1990 provides for the Secretary of State for Health to arbitrate on disputes between NHS bodies. In practice, for all except the most difficult disputes, responsibility for arbitration would be delegated to a manager or committee at the appropriate level at the NHS Executive regional office. As has been said, the guidance Trusts have received to date strongly recom-mends that disputes should be resolved locally where possible. In practice this discourages Trusts from referring disputes upwards and puts pressure on managers to compromise even at the risk of losing income rather than acquire the reputation of a troublemaker. At this level disputes are likely to be between

◆ Trusts and purchasers.
◆ Trusts and fundholders.
◆ Trusts and Trusts.

In the case of a dispute between two Trusts, managers will attempt to resolve matters without talking to the purchaser. However, in the other two cases the purchaser is involved to start with.

As with contractual disputes in the commercial sector, tactics for resolution are affected as much by the economic or political weight wielded by each party as by the persuasiveness of their arguments. In any dispute with a health authority as purchaser, a Trust will be batting uphill: health authorities are more than just purchasers. They are in many people's eyes, and perhaps in reality, a superior headquarters in the NHS 'chain of command'. Even on the commercial model, the health authority purchaser is the customer and consequently right (at least as often as possible). Disputes on contracts with purchasers are not of the same nature as disputes on contracts in the commercial sector. Purchasers rarely default on their contractual obligations. Arbitration is not initiated to enforce contractual terms that either party is trying to avoid.

Arbitration will almost always be because the contract has not, for all sorts of unavoidable reasons, been performed to the letter: there has been an element of over- or under-performance, or both, or it turns out that there was a misunderstanding about some aspect of provision which the contract did not adequately deal with. In these cases local experience suggests that the procedure works as follows:

1. One party (usually the Trust) writes to the other (usually the purchaser) explaining the problem from their point of view and asks how the purchaser wishes to deal with the problem.
2. Some time may be spent in correspondence while the Trust seeks to clarify the issue and the purchaser seeks to avoid any additional expenditure.
3. A meeting may be called formally to look at ways of resolving the problem. The meeting is unlikely to be facilitated by any independent person acting as arbitrator or conciliator, although this is possible. Both parties will tend to work towards a practical solution in the knowledge that savings will have to be made from provision somewhere.
4. In the unlikely event that the problem cannot be resolved between purchaser and provider, it may be referred to the NHS Executive regional office.

Some regions hold 'market days'. These are not true contract dispute resolution forums. Instead they are likely to be, depending on how developed the purchasing is in the area in question, an opportunity for further negotiation of contracts or a 'complaints session' by providers before contracts have actually been signed. These will usually be attended by all purchasers and providers in the region.

To say that arbitration on NHS contracts is a procedure as yet undeveloped would be a considerable understatement. Presumably regional officers charged with carrying it out will use their common sense, no doubt all that is required in many cases, and their knowledge, perhaps unconscious, of the principles of English law in others.

NHS CONTRACTS: HISTORY   Contractual relationships have always existed in the Health Services. Before the National Health Service Act 1946 many hospitals now run by the state under the NHS were under private, charitable or local authority managements. Many of these were therefore effectively in the private sector. GPs, as providers, were and have remained in the private sector: the 1946 Act did not nationalize GP services as it did hospital services. Once hospitals were owned and managed by the state, it would not have been possible for them to sue each other. Legal action would have had to be commenced by the Secretary of State, acting for the Crown, against himself. This would be contrary to the legal (and perhaps common sense) principle that the Crown cannot sue itself. This principle governs all contracts between government departments including health authorities acting in the name of the Secretary of State for Health.

What was, before the Health Service reforms of the 1990s, impossible continues to be undesirable after the reforms. The principle that the Crown cannot sue itself is not a bar to litigation between NHS Trusts, or between NHS Trusts and health authorities, since NHS Trusts are not bodies of the Crown. NHS Trusts are independent (though heavily regulated) corporate bodies, which would technically be able to sue each other were it not for Section 4 (1) of the 1990 Act quoted above. Even in the event that an NHS Trust were to consider suing another over some matter not covered by the 1990 Act, the relevant NHS regional office could be relied upon to intervene.

However, parts of the NHS, most notably general practitioners but also dentists, opticians and others, have continued to operate as private providers under contract to the NHS. The details of these arrangements are outside the scope of this chapter but the precedent of bodies contracting to health authorities to provide services and contracting with suppliers in the private sector is one which NHS Trusts are following. An important difference is that NHS Trusts, although technically independent, are tied to the NHS by more than contracts: their boards are appointed by and accountable to the Secretary of State for Health. In the case of GPs, FHSAs have acted for the Secretary of State in the past to employ GPs as providers. FHSAs have managed contracts with GPs and acted to resolve disputes by arbitration. The parallel with NHS Trusts is sufficiently close that the merger of FHSAs with health authorities purchasing from Trusts is to proceed during 1995.

GPs as purchasers are in a new and different situation. These are the general practitioner fundholders (GPFHs or fundholders) to whom money is allocated by the Secretary of State for Health for the GP practice concerned to spend on behalf of its patients with other providers. GP fundholders therefore now contract (as purchasers) with NHS Trusts (as providers) for those services which the Secretary of State has designated to be purchased by the fund. Not all fundholders have identical arrangements nor do fundholders act as purchasers for all services. However, during 1995, the range of services to be so purchased is to be extended, the number of fundholding practices to be increased and certain practices which have made a success of fundholding are to be given much wider purchasing responsibilities. All of these arrangements are of course NHS contracts.

The future of purchasing in the NHS
Some aspects of the Health Service reforms have taken root and now command widespread, and possibly all party, support. The principle of the purchaser/provider split, which is the reason for having NHS contracts, is cautiously accepted by opposition parties. It is therefore unlikely that NHS Trusts would, following a change of government, be dismantled. However, the composition of boards, the number of Trusts (and therefore managers) and the already qualified independence of Trusts might well be changed in the future in response to calls for greater public accountability. The principle and operation of GP fundholding policy remains more controversial; this area of NHS contracting could well face changes in the future.

NHS CONTRACTS: PROCEDURES
The key difference between NHS contracts and those in the private sector is not their content or the rules for adjudicating on them, but the market environment in which each type is formed. The ordinary English law of contract assumes a free market and leaves the parties in the main to negotiate the best terms they can, given their respective negotiating strengths and weaknesses. It follows that properly advised contracting parties need no further incentive to ensure that contract terms are as far as possible clear and unambiguous: to do otherwise would leave them exposed in the event of a dispute.

By contrast, in the NHS, the market is heavily managed: the national structure of the NHS largely determines who will contract with whom and the executive lays down the form which contracts should take. Guidance (contracting timetable and signing off): EL(94)55 states, for instance, that 'all contracts must be agreed between NHS purchasers and providers by 15th March, 1995 ... and signed by 31st March'. Such an instruction would be nonsensical in a free market, but makes perfect sense in the managed NHS where purchasing decisions are made first and contract terms negotiated later. In this environment there is no incentive for providers to accept terms that are not to their liking: the purchasing decision has already been made and the price already set. The contract that follows would not last five minutes in a court of law: the only imperative is that it is signed by 31 March. Both the parties know, that in the event of a dispute, the terms in the contract may be set aside by the NHS Executive to achieve a practical solution.

NHS CONTRACTS: DEVELOPMENT

In the absence of a fully formed market incentive, the NHS over the last few years has sought to influence the terms of contracts by specifying more sophisticated and less ambiguous pricing mechanisms and by issuing guidance on purchasing policy in all areas. The following is a summary of the significant current guidance (taking the most recent first, up to the end of 1994):

♦ *1995–96 Contracting Review: Handbook* EL(94)88: This useful letter summarises 'all significant guidance for contracting in the current cycle'. The other letters mentioned are quoted in it.
♦ *Developing NHS Purchasing and GP Fundholding* EL(94)79: This letter concentrates on primary care led purchasing and aims to 'make it essential that local arrangements are in place to ensure that GPs (fundholder and non-fundholder) contribute to the contracting and wider purchasing process'.
♦ *Improving the Effectiveness of the NHS* EL(94)74: This emphasizes the importance of contracting for cost-effective services. This is to be done by using clinical outcome specifications and audit criteria.
♦ *Priorities and Planning Guidance for the NHS* 1995-96. This sets out the timetable and 'six key milestone dates to which all purchasers and providers are required to adhere'. As mentioned above all contracts must be signed by 31 March.
♦ *Clinical Audit: 1994/95 and beyond* EL(94)20: This requires purchasers to make arrangements with each provider for clinical audit.
♦ *Comparative Cost Data: The use of HRGs (Health Resource Groups) to inform the contracting process* EL(94)51: This requires acute providers to 'cost at least one of three nationally selected specialties to HRG level'. It is part of the move to price contracts and measure performance using output rather than input measures.
♦ *Contracting for Specialist Palliative Care Services* EL(94)14: This provides guidance for contracting for palliative care services, which are largely or partly charitably funded in most cases.
♦ *Review of Contracting – Guidance for the 1994-95 Contracting Cycle* EL(93)103: This is to some extent superseded by the 1994 letter on contracting. However, it laid the foundations for breaking down 'whole unit' contracts into specialist-based

contracts. *Priorities and Planning Guidance* issued in 1993 also sought to ensure that 'no simple block contracts are negotiated for 1995–96. All contracts at a minimum will be required to have indicative volumes and thresholds in the form of floors and ceilings and agreed arrangements for managing over-performance or under-performance'.

The above guidance is probably the most significant in demonstrating the direction to be taken in NHS contracting: increasingly prices and performance standards will be set and measured in quantifiable units of outcome. Block contracts, e.g. 'ABC NHS Trust will continue to run ABC Hospital much as it has always done next year for the same money in real terms as it cost last year' are on the way out, not only for whole hospital units but also for individual departments and specialties.

The above are some of the more significant developments in contract terms. However, EL(94)88 is recommended reading for the 1995 contracting cycle.

SUMMARY   The following key points will help you through the contract minefield:

- ◆ Be clear about who are the parties to a contract.
- ◆ Be sure the terms are unambiguous and not left 'to be agreed'.
- ◆ Be clear about what a contract is and when one comes into existence.
- ◆ If you are presented with a contract to sign, read it and argue any terms you are unhappy with.
- ◆ If in doubt with smaller contracts, but only when you have employed common sense to its full, get legal advice.
- ◆ For guidance on NHS contracting, read EL(94)88.

CASE STUDY – THE
ARBITRATION
PROCESS

A health authority purchaser has traditionally purchased emergency activity at several provider Trusts. Most activity is bought at its two local main providers, Hospital A and Hospital B, who are both located within the purchaser's boundary.

A large amount of emergency activity is also purchased at Hospital C, that is located one mile across the health authority boundary within a neighbouring district.

Hospital B proposes to close its Accident and Emergency (A & E) Department as part of its rationalization programme and this has been supported by the purchaser in its Purchasing Intentions document. The purchaser proposes to increase the number of emergency finished consultant episodes (FCEs) in its contract with Hospital A to reflect this change.

During its contract negotiations with the purchaser, Hospital C pointed out that the closure of the A & E Department at Hospital B will also have an effect on its own A & E Department due to the proximity of the hospital to the purchaser's boundary. Hospital C, therefore, was seeking an increase in the emergency element of their contract for the coming year. They presented detailed forecasts to support their case.

The health authority refused to buy significantly more activity as its forecast predicted an increase in activity at Hospital A with only a limited effect at Hospital C. The authority wanted a simple block contract for emergency activity which would give Hospital C no additional income should emergency activity increase during the year.

Hospital C refused to contract on this basis and suggested to the purchaser that if they did not buy at the increased level suggested by them then there could be no contract. All activity would then be charged at the higher extra contractual referral (ECR) rate.

Despite several meetings between the authority and Hospital C, a contract could not be agreed within the timescale set down by the regional office and both parties were deemed to be in dispute and in need of conciliation and possible arbitration.

The regional office instructed both the purchaser and Hospital C to exchange written cases with each other by a predetermined date. Copies of these submissions were also required to be sent to the region. A 'conciliation' meeting was then arranged between the two parties and regional officers were present to offer guidance. The chief executives of both organizations were required to attend the conciliation meeting.

By the end of the meeting a final agreement could still not be reached and so the case proceeded to arbitration.

Both sides' written case, together with any supporting information available from the conciliation meeting, were then considered by a panel of regional officers. In these cases 'pendulum' arbitration is normally used, which means that a decision is made for one party or the other. There is no compromise between the two. One party will win completely, the other will lose completely. There are virtually no published standard criteria for the panel to use. The case judged most reasonable wins. This is in marked contrast to the criteria used by a court, which is the whole body of English law.

The decision of the panel is communicated to both parties together with a deadline by which the contract must be signed. There is no appeal against the regional office decision.

*FURTHER
QUESTIONS*

The following questions identify some issues from this chapter which you may wish to consider or discuss further with your colleagues.

♦ When is a NHS contract a contract?

♦ Would the NHS benefit from a stricter more 'legal' approach to contracts?

♦ Is the concept of an internal managed market flawed? If so what should replace it?

♦ Would it ever be beneficial for NHS bodies to enforce their contracts in the courts? Is the process beneficial in the commercial sector? If not, why does it happen?

♦ Could the NHS learn anything from the law which might improve the present NHS arbitration process?

♦ How is the shape of NHS contracting likely to change in the near future?

*STATUTES
QUOTED*

Statue of Frauds 1677
National Health Service Act 1946
Sale of Goods Act 1979
Unfair Contract Terms Act 1979
Limitation Act 1980
Supply of Goods and Services Act 1982
National Health Service and Community Care Act 1990
Sale and Supply of Goods Act 1994

*SCHEDULE OF NHS
GUIDANCE
LETTERS*

*Review of Contracting – Guidance for the 1994-95
Contracting Cycle*   EL(93)103
Risk Management in the NHS   EL(93)111
Contracting for Specialist Palliative Care Services   EL(94)14
Clinical Audit: 1994/95 and beyond   EL(94)20
*The management of the estate in the NHS: Fire Code policy and
principles - Directions from the Secretary of State*   EL(94)29
*Comparative Cost Data: The use of HRGs (Health Related
Groups) to inform the contracting process*   EL(94)51
Contracting timetable and signing off   EL(94)55
Improving the Effectiveness of the NHS   EL(94)74
Developing NHS Purchasing and GP Fundholding   EL(94)79
1995-96 Contracting Review: Handbook   EL(94)88
Energy efficiency in the low energy hospitals   EPL(94)26
*Energy efficiency in the NHS: Energy efficiency office good
practice programme*   EPL(94)29

Contracting out finance related functions   FDL(94)31
Guidance on capital projects   HSE(94)31
Procedure to be followed in the event of a dispute. Annex to Market Management 1995–96 ('Conciliation and Arbitration')
Priorities and planning guidance for the NHS 1995–96
CONCODE
ESTATECODE

FURTHER READING

♦ Finch, J. (1994), *Speller's Law Relating to Hospitals*, 7th edn. Chapman and Hall Medical, London.

A useful outline of most law affecting health services.

CONTRACTING OUT SERVICES

Elaine Hedgecock

OBJECTIVES

♦ To explain how and why NHS organizations are placing contracts for services which they used to employ their own staff to provide.

♦ To give practical guidance on the process of specifying and agreeing a contract with an external provider.

♦ To give guidance on how to manage a contracted out service.

INTRODUCTION This chapter addresses the issue of organizations such as NHS Trusts which are purchasing services from commercial suppliers under a contract. This process is known as *contracting out*. The reader may wish to refer to the examples of current experiments in contracting out within the NHS, listed at the end of the chapter. A fictitious case study, showing where contracting out might lead us in the future, is also included at the end of the chapter.

The first part of the chapter discusses the background to contracting out both within the NHS and in organizations generally. The discussion moves on to *make : buy decisions* – under what circumstances an organization might choose to buy in services rather than providing them internally.

The chapter reviews two important strands of government policy which impact on contracting out services – market testing and compulsory competitive tendering (CCT). These policies require organizations within the NHS to put certain services out to tender to determine whether or not better 'value for money' could be secured through contracting out.

The chapter steps through the contracting out process including preparing a tender specification, identifying potential suppliers, inviting and evaluating bids and awarding contracts. The chapter also discusses the management of external contractors.

An important point about contracts with private sector suppliers is that they are proper commercial contracts as opposed to the internal contracts of the NHS which are not enforceable at law. The chapter sets out some guidance for negotiating and managing commercial contracts.

Finally the chapter discusses the types of services which have been contracted out in the NHS and anticipates probable developments in the field.

INTEGRATED OR VIRTUAL ORGANIZATIONS

In the 1970s and early 1980s, conventional management wisdom was very much that organizations should be fully integrated. They should contain within them all of the important processes required to carry on their business. The philosophy was a simple one; the more we own and control, the more efficiently we will be able to run our business. Another ingredient in the philosophy was the notion that contracting out with another supplier entailed forgoing an element of profit which could have been retained in the business.

Organizations such as Shell and BP set out to become fully *vertically integrated* – that is to control all the steps in production and marketing from exploration and drilling, through refining to retailing. More typically, organizations wanted to own their own transport fleets, their own print shops, their own canteens, their own maintenance operations and so on. As a result organizations tended to become very large and capital intensive. They also ended up grappling with the management of very diverse operations.

There were some interesting exceptions, such as Marks & Spencer, which followed a philosophy of concentrating on their core business – retailing – and developing collaborative partnerships with suppliers to meet their other needs. For example, Marks & Spencer transportation was managed on their behalf by BOC (British Oxygen Company).

The National Health Service very much followed this self-sufficiency philosophy. With the exception of pharmaceutical products, supplies and utilities such as electricity NHS organizations sought to have all the services which they needed under their own roof. A typical NHS hospital would employ its own cleaners, cooks, drivers, maintenance staff and computer staff. At district and regional level, it also employed its own architects, surveyors, safety specialists and so on. Given that the core business of the organization was the delivery of health care, a surprisingly high proportion of the workforce had little or nothing to do directly with health care.

In some areas of the NHS, an element of pharmaceutical manufacturing was taking place and some hospitals had their own workshops for building and maintaining electrical equipment.

Towards the end of the 1980s this basic philosophy came more and more into question. There were some clear disadvantages:

♦ Organizations had to be good at managing very diverse types of activity.
♦ Organizations had to be quite large.
♦ A significant proportion of the workforce were only tentatively connected with the core business of the organization.
♦ Management attention could easily be diverted from the core business and into resolving difficulties with peripheral support services.
♦ Capital could be tied up in assets which were not very directly related to the core business of the enterprise.
♦ Each of the support services was likely to be quite small. As a result it was difficult to achieve economies of scale or to build up real expertise in a particular area.

A familiar example of these disadvantages within the NHS was the development and management of computer services. All over the country, small computer departments were building information systems from scratch. None of the individual departments really had the scale or expertise to do this efficiently or well. As a result, information technology in the NHS has become a major problem and a significant constraint on the ability of the organization to conduct its affairs in a sensible way.

The overriding problem with the fully integrated organization was its *inflexibility* – as its portfolio of internal services grew ever larger and more specialized, the organization's ability to manoeuvre and to respond quickly to changes in its environment became circumscribed.

Clearly, there are some advantages to the fully integrated organization.

♦ If the organization *can* manage its own services efficiently and economically it does not have to pay someone else to do so. The trade-off is between internal management and investment costs against external management costs and the profit taken by the external supplier.
♦ If the requirement of the organization is very specialized, it may well do better to meet that requirement internally rather than taking the risk of another supplier being able to meet such a specialised requirement. For example, theatre packs in a particular hospital might be so specialized that it is better to make them up internally rather than buying in general purpose packs.
♦ If a particular requirement is absolutely crucial – perhaps a critical component in an electrical assembly, maintaining the capability in house may be sensible both in terms of assuring your own supply and denying the component to competitors.

In the mid 1980s, an alternative view of organizations was starting to develop. Essentially, this suggested that an organization should concentrate on its core business and should buy in the services which it needed to support that core business. By implication, it would be buying services from an organization whose core business would be to supply precisely that service.

Thus, a hospital might buy its catering from an organization who were very good at catering, its information systems from a company which was very good at developing and implementing computer systems and its security systems from a professional security company. This approach was called *outsourcing*. The argument in favour of outsourcing was:

♦ Specialist providers would be likely to manage their specialist business best.
♦ There should be economies of scale. For example, a national catering company should be able to buy produce more cheaply than a local catering department.
♦ The capital required to support the specialist service would be provided by the supplier.
♦ The specialist supplier would be likely to invest properly in research and development.
♦ Internal management would be able to focus all their attention on the core business.

In the early 1990s, the outsourcing concept was developed into the idea of the *virtual organization*. This idea also rested heavily on the proposition that the real strength of an organization lay not in its plant and equipment or its buildings but in its *expertise* and *reputation*. Everything else could be bought – expertise and reputation had to be *built*.

A virtual organization would employ very few people and own very few physical assets. The people it did employ would be those who had the key expertise of the core business. Everything else would be purchased as needed. Buildings would be rented, components would be manufactured by a specialist manufacturer, transport would be undertaken by a transportation contractor, payroll would be administered by a payroll company and personnel management services would be provided by an external specialist supplier.

The advantages claimed for the virtual organization were two-fold:

♦ Managers could concentrate exclusively on the core business of the organization.
♦ The organization would be extremely flexible. It would have very few fixed costs and supplies and services could be turned on and off to meet the changing demands of the business.

COMPULSORY COMPETITIVE TENDERING AND MARKET TESTING

Partly for ideological reasons, the government in power in the mid 1980s were very attracted by the idea of outsourcing. The public sector workforce was growing inexorably, there were felt to be huge inefficiencies in areas such as the direct labour forces employed by local authorities and public sector capital was scarce and expensive.

The government, therefore, initiated a programme of *compulsory competitive tendering (CCT)* in all areas of the public sector. Under CCT rules, public sector organizations were obliged to invite private sector suppliers to tender to provide certain services which had been internally managed. Local authorities were obliged to put their works services and refuse collection out to tender. The NHS was obliged to put catering and domestic services out to tender. Internal departments were allowed to submit their own tenders but relatively few were successful.

This whole process was described as *market testing* – finding out whether the market (private sector suppliers) could provide equally good services at a lower price.

At first glance, few (other than existing public sector employees) would quarrel with the concept. If we can get equally good or better catering or cleaning at a lower price, we have more money available to spend on direct patient care. Unfortunately, the concept has not always worked out like that in practice.

In the case of the NHS, there was very little expertise available within the organization to enable effective tendering and contract management. Similarly, potential suppliers had little experience of providing services to hospitals and other NHS institutions.

As a consequence, many of the contracts which were placed in the first few years of CCT were very unsatisfactory. Very often the quality of the service provided was inferior either because the contract had not been specified very well or because the supplier was unable to deliver what had been contracted for. In some cases, the contractor had under-priced the contract and was unable to fulfil it. A number of small contractors went out of business as a result of contracts unwisely undertaken with the NHS.

As both the NHS and suppliers have been going up a learning curve, the situation has been improving and many contracts are now performing to the satisfaction of both parties.

An unexpected problem has arisen recently in the shape of a piece of legislation emerging from the European Union. The legislation is known as *TUPE (Transfer of Undertakings Previous Employment)*. TUPE stipulates that when an organization undertakes work previously done by members of another organization, the staff who previously did that work have a right to transfer to the new organization *on no less favourable conditions of employment.* One of the main reasons why private sector contractors had been able to undercut internal bids was that they reduced rates of pay and eliminated other expensive employment benefits. With the advent of TUPE, this convenient short cut to lower prices has effectively been blocked off and contractors must be able to compete by managing their services more effectively rather than simply by cutting pay rates.

Although early experiments with contracting out in the NHS involved services such as catering and cleaning, there is increasing interest in contracting out a wider range of both clinical and non-clinical services.

In the clinical area, services such as cold pathology have been contracted out either to private sector laboratories or to other NHS Trusts. In the non-clinical area, services such as organization development, personnel and payroll administration and computer services have been put out to contract.

The next section of this chapter outlines the factors which should be taken into account in developing a contracting out strategy.

USING CONTRACTING OUT EFFECTIVELY

Despite some unfortunate early experiences within the NHS, contracting out does have a role to play in creating NHS organizations which are better at delivering cost-effective care. Managers who are contemplating making use of contracting out need to address two fundamental questions:

◆ What is core to our business?
◆ What are our criteria for make : buy decisions?

The question of how core a particular set of people or group of skills is to your business is a matter of judgement. The judgement will be influenced by the structure of your organization and by how it functions.

For example, if your service is organized around multidisciplinary teams including physiotherapists, the physiotherapists will almost certainly be core to the work of those teams; they need to be members of your organization and members of those teams. If, however, physiotherapists work relatively independently delivering particular items of service for particular patients or clients, it may be quite appropriate to contract out your physiotherapy service.

An interesting example is that of the ward cleaner or domestic. As indicated earlier, domestic services were one of the earliest targets for competitive tendering within the NHS. The familiar ward domestic was replaced by a cleaning service. The staff providing this service often had no particular allegiance to Ward X. They went where they were told by their own supervisors and had a schedule to complete. Staff turnover and absenteeism were often both very high as a result of which there was very little continuity in the cleaning service provided.

A number of Trusts, often at the instigation of ward sisters and charge nurses, are reconsidering their initial strategy. Perhaps the ward domestic is an integral part of the patient care team. If he or she is trained to carry out a range of duties as a member of a relatively stable and flexible ward team, the gains in true efficiency and in the quality of patient care may well outweigh the apparent cost savings realized by contracting out the cleaning service.

The question of who is core is not a simple decision. It depends very much on the style and structure of the organization.

Contracting out services may be more flexible but that is not always the case.

Box 10.1 proposes some guidelines for deciding whether or not a particular service is core to your business:

Box 10.1
Core services

> ◆ Do the staff in this service have specialist skills which contribute to the overall expertise of your organization?
>
> ◆ Do they work within multidisciplinary teams within your organization?
>
> ◆ Is continuity of staffing important?
>
> ◆ Are most of the equipment and facilities which they need already an integral part of your organization?
>
> ◆ Does their performance and attitude contribute significantly to the reputation of your organization?
>
> ◆ Are you confident that there is enough work to keep them productively employed?
>
> ◆ Can you provide sufficient training and development opportunities within your organization to maintain and extend their expertise?

If the answers to most of the questions in Box 10.1 are affirmative, the probability is that the service in question is core to your business.

CORE STAFF AND WORKLOADS

Although a particular service may be core to your business, not all the staff within that service may be core. If workloads fluctuate, it is sensible to staff at a level which enables you to deal with the troughs with your own core staff and to top them up with contracted staff when necessary.

If managed well, this approach has a number of important benefits:

♦ You can provide a good measure of job security for your core staff.
♦ You have a smaller number of people in whom to invest in terms of training and development.
♦ You can flex your costs in line with your income.
♦ You can organize your services so that additional staff fit into an established structure.

MAKE : BUY DECISIONS Make : buy is a convenient bit of shorthand from manufacturing industry to encapsulate the decisions we take when considering contracting out all or part of a service. It means should we make this ourselves or should we buy it from elsewhere.

As a general rule of thumb, we should not consider contracting out core services for which we can provide a steady workload. The core people in core services constitute the real permanent organization.

For the rest, we ought to consider contracting out if the conditions shown in Box 10.2 are true.

Box 10.2
Contracting out: key points

♦ There is more than one supplier who can provide this service to the standard we require.
♦ There is no significant benefit in doing this ourselves.
♦ The total cost of buying is less than or equal to doing it ourselves taking account of elements such as redundancy costs.
♦ There is no major impact on employee relations or overall staff morale.
♦ We have the capacity to monitor and manage a contract.
♦ There is more than one potential supplier with an appropriate reputation, trading record and financial standing.

Dual sourcing It is dangerous to contract out in a situation in which there is only one supplier who can meet our needs. That supplier then has a very powerful negotiating position, particularly if we remove our own capacity to provide the service internally.

Quality It is critical to *specify* the standards of quality which you require and to *assure* yourself that a supplier has the ability to deliver to those standards consistently.

Intellectual property rights   In certain areas such as information technology, training and research and development, your supplier may be creating intellectual work of real value such as a computer program, a scientific discovery or a workbook. It is important that your contract be clear about the *ownership* of any such rights.

The area of intellectual property rights (IPRs) is something of a legal minefield and it would be prudent to get specialized advice if you believe this question may arise.

Cost comparison   Cost comparisons are rarely straightforward. You will need to consider the costs of negotiating, monitoring and managing the contract including any legal fees. You will also need to consider any redundancy costs or other costs of reorganization which you may incur. In some cases, there may be a cashflow penalty if the supplier requires a significant up-front payment.

In evaluating a bid, you will need to take account not only of the contractual price as such but also of charges for any *contractual variations* or *cost triggers* which may have been built into the contract. These topics are discussed more fully in the next section.

Impact on employee relations and staff morale   This is a very serious consideration particularly when you are moving from doing something yourself to contracting out. Trades unions or professional associations can be very disruptive if they decide to oppose your contracting out decision. In weighing up the make:buy decision, you need to think very carefully about the long-term impact upon the rest of your organization.

Capacity to manage a contract   As indicated earlier some of the contracts negotiated in the NHS were unsuccessful and very damaging to the organizations which negotiated them. Managing contract services is a skilled and specialist discipline not just something which can be bolted on to someone's full time job.

Financial standing and reputation   In considering a supplier you need to assure yourself that they have the capacity to deliver the service you need in the long run. It is not appropriate to regard that as the supplier's problem. If they go out of business, they will have their problems but so will you.

If you value the reputation of your own organization, you should make sure that the reputation of your supplier is at least as good. Their reputation will inevitably reflect on your own.

Reputation is not just a matter of ability to deliver. A supplier may be engaged in a line of business with which you might prefer not to associate your own organization – arms dealing or tobacco manufacture – or might be open to criticism on issues such as environmental pollution.

Conflict of interest   Many of the potential suppliers whom you might wish to use will already be supplying similar goods and services to your competitors. This is completely to be expected. You will need to assure yourself that they have in place adequate mechanisms for avoiding or resolving conflicts of interest.

New organizations   Although you would normally be well advised to deal only with suppliers with an established reputation, in some circumstances you may wish to work with a new company. Perhaps you want to support business start-ups in your local community or some of your own staff wish to leave and become a supplier. You should not let the absence of a trading record rule out such suppliers but you will need to use extra vigilance in the negotiation and management of the contract.

Advantages of   If we are able to buy rather than make, there are significant
contracting out   advantages in doing so.

◆ It enables us to concentrate on our core business.
◆ It allows us to use available capital to invest in our core business.
◆ It increases the flexibility of the organization by reducing its permanent workforce.
◆ It allows us to rethink and respecify the service we want.
◆ It *may* yield cost savings.

Cost saving, although the most obvious, is not the most important reason for contracting out. Being able to focus on your core business and to have a more flexible organization are of much greater significance in ensuring the long-term success of your organization. Even if the cash cost of contracting out is higher than doing it yourself, it may still be appropriate to contract out.

MANAGING THE   Let us suppose that you have decided to contract out a service, how
CONTRACTING   do you go about it?
OUT PROCESS

Specification   The first step is to prepare a *specification* of the service which you require. The question of service specifications is dealt with fully elsewhere in this book (see Chapter 5). However, the key points are:

◆ What quantity of service is required.
◆ What quality of service is required.
  - Type and qualifications of staff.
  - Response times.
  - Performance standards
◆ How long will the contract run for.
◆ What is included in the contract and what is excluded.
◆ How will the contract be monitored.

♦ How will disputes be resolved.
♦ What penalties will there be for non-compliance.

In preparing a specification remember that the service you currently get may not be the service which you would choose to have. Use the contracting out process as an opportunity to redefine the type and quality of service which you want.

Identifying potential suppliers

There are several ways in which you can identify potential suppliers:

♦ You or someone else in your organization may know of a potential supplier. Non-executive directors may well be a useful source of contacts.
♦ Other local organizations may be aware of potential suppliers.
♦ A trade association or professional body may be able to provide a list of appropriate suppliers.
♦ You can advertise for potential suppliers to express an interest.

For public sector contracts over a certain value, there is a legal obligation to advertise the contract in the official publications of the European Union. If your contract is substantial (over £100 000) you should seek specialist advice from your legal advisers.

For contracts for the procurement of information systems, there is a set procedure defined by the NHS Executive.

Remember that advertising for a supplier can be like advertising a job vacancy. You may get a lot of responses and it is sensible to set up a process for response handling in advance.

Shortlisting suppliers

You only want to spend time on suppliers who potentially meet your needs. It is helpful to establish a set of *qualifying criteria* which suppliers must meet if they are to be allowed to submit a bid. Qualifying criteria might include the size of the organization, experience in a relevant area, ability to start work on a particular date and so on.

Evaluating suppliers

Depending on the nature of the service, you will need to carry out a thorough and systematic evaluation of your short-listed suppliers. The questions which you are trying to answer are:

♦ Has this supplier got the capability to fulfil this contract now and in the longer term?
♦ Are the standards and values of this potential supplier consistent with our own?

For a contract of any value, you will certainly want to do all of the following:

♦ Visit the supplier premises, meet key people and inspect the facilities.

♦ Examine the financial records of the business to ensure that they have the financial strength to support your service in the long term.

♦ Talk to and visit current customers selected by you from a list of the supplier's current customers.

Some suppliers may be part of a national accreditation scheme such as BS5750 (British Standard for Quality Assurance Systems) or Investors in People (a scheme operated by the Department of Trade and Industry which ensures that acceptable standards of management are in place).

You may want to invite formal presentations from potential suppliers so that you have an opportunity to see them perform and they have an opportunity to meet with you.

Taken together, this investigation is sometimes known as a *vendor appraisal.*

Evaluating bids   In most contracting out processes, you are likely to invite bids from those suppliers whom you have appraised successfully. In most health authorities and Trusts, there are standing procedures governing the evaluation of bids. For example, it is usual for bids to be submitted in plain envelopes and for them to be opened in the presence of at least two directors or senior executives.

Bids should be evaluated item by item against the contract specification. Normally, you would expect to take the lowest bid which meets your requirements. You should not, however, allow cost alone to dominate the outcome. If you are convinced that a more expensive supplier will give you a better service, then go for that supplier. In the public sector in particular, it is helpful to make a very full record of your reasons for selecting anything other than the lowest bid. Chief executives of public services can be called to account for their decisions before the Public Account Committee of Parliament.

Negotiating a   For certain services, bidding is not an appropriate mechanism for
contract   awarding a contract. This is particularly the case where the service is very specialized and the supplier is more expert than you are. In these circumstances, it is more appropriate to discuss your requirements with a potential supplier, invite a proposal and then negotiate on the proposal. The process of negotiation is described more fully in Chapter 6.

In areas such as training and development or information technology it is almost impossible to arrive at an appropriate outcome simply through a process of bidding against a specification.

Placing the   As indicated earlier, contracts with non-NHS suppliers are legal
contract   agreements which can be enforced in the courts. Chapter 9

outlines some of the legal considerations but for a contract of any significant value, proper legal advice should be taken.

However, the key points of any contract include those shown in Box 10.3.

Box 10.3
Contracts: key points

- ◆ What goods or services are to be provided.
- ◆ What standards of quality are required.
- ◆ What price is to be charged for the goods or services.
- ◆ Under what circumstances can this price change.
- ◆ How are payments to be made and in what currency.
- ◆ How will invoices be validated.
- ◆ What information does the supplier have to provide.
- ◆ What facilities does the organization placing the contract have to provide.
- ◆ What warranties and indemnities does the supplier have to give (see Chapter 9).
- ◆ What insurances have to be in place.
- ◆ What qualifications do contractor staff have to hold.
- ◆ How will disputes be resolved.
- ◆ What penalties apply for non-performance.
- ◆ How long will the contract run.
- ◆ Under what circumstances may the contract be terminated.
- ◆ How will contractual variations be agreed and charged.

Contractual variations

It is worth discussing the idea of contractual variations (CVs) in a little more detail. For major capital projects they are a common cause of bitter disputes and huge cost over-runs. A recent example is the Channel Tunnel and some recent NHS building projects have attracted attention through the disparity between the estimated cost and the actual cost.

A contractual variation arises when the client changes his or her mind about something in the contract or the contract specification. Depending on the wording of the contract, the client may be liable not only to pay for the contractual variation itself but also for any associated costs and delays which the contractor may incur as a result.

The rules for managing contractual variations are simple:

♦ Avoid them in the first place by getting your specification right.
♦ Make sure that approval for a contractual variation can only be given by a senior management who understands the implications and who has overall budget responsibility for the contract of project.
♦ Ensure that your contract is drafted in a way which controls the effect of contractual variations on penalty clauses and completion dates.

MANAGING THE Once the contract is in place, it needs to be managed. A designated
CONTRACT senior manager in the client organization should have responsibility for managing the contract and should have the necessary authority to do so. It is essential that the contractor knows that he or she is dealing with the real decision-maker when talking to the contract manager. Similarly, the contract should specify that the contractor designate a senior member of staff who is responsible for managing the contract from their end and who has the necessary authority to take decisions about it.

The contract should specify the monitoring information which has to be provided, the format in which it is to be provided and the timing. The contract manager should review this information meticulously and discuss any matters of concern with the contractor at the earliest possible opportunity. Examples of monitoring information might include:

♦ Progress against milestones set out in a project plan.
♦ Quantity of service provided – meals served, tests carried out and so on.
♦ Complaints received and responded to.
♦ Invoices submitted to date.

In addition to the monitoring information provided by the contractor, the contract manager should personally evaluate the satisfaction or otherwise of end users in his or her organization.

If the contract is for ward cleaning, the contract manager must be in regular dialogue with ward managers and nurses and must carry out ad hoc inspections. Any problems should be raised immediately with the contractor and a satisfactory resolution sought.

If the contract is for pathology tests, the contract manager must be in regular conversation with clinicians about the quality of the work, the style of reports and the timeliness of the service.

The contract manager should monitor the financial performance of the contract. All invoices should be checked carefully and a rolling total of expenditure against budget should be kept.

Where part of an invoice is in dispute, it is usual to pay the undisputed part as usual and to withhold the disputed element until the problem is resolved. Do not pay invoices unless you are satisfied with the service and with the accuracy of the invoice. It is much harder to get the money back later.

The contractor may also, of course, have problems. The promised office is not available, the secretarial support is off on maternity leave, the last three invoices have been lost in the bowels of the finance department. It is very much in the interests of the contract manager to get these problems resolved quickly too. If the agreed facilities are not provided, the contractor may not be able to provide the required service and has a perfect excuse for not doing so. If invoices are not being paid, he may not be able to fund the cash flow to maintain the service contracted for.

SUCCESSFUL CONTRACTING OUT

Marks & Spencer was cited earlier as an organization which has contracted out its non-core services very successfully over a number of years. It is, perhaps, worth considering some of the features of their contracting relationships (Box 10.4).

Box 10.4
Features of Marks & Spencer's contracting relationships

- They are interested in building up good long-term relationships with their suppliers.
- They help their suppliers to do a good job by providing advice and support.
- They specify what they want very tightly indeed.
- They negotiate very hard but they never demand an unachievable price.
- They monitor performance very carefully.
- Their contracts are clear and simple.

LOOKING TO THE FUTURE

Contracting out is still at a very early stage in the NHS. Some of the early steps such as blanket contracting out of domestic services may well turn out to have been mistakes and are, in some cases, being reversed.

The nature of health care is evolving very rapidly in the UK which suggests that there will be a real premium on organizational flexibility. Our hospitals may never become virtual organizations in the true sense of the term but they will probably need to become considerably less monolithic and self-sufficient than they are at present.

The core staff of an NHS hospital are those directly engaged in the care of patients – doctors, nurses, therapists, technicians, porters, ward-based support staff and so on. Core staff probably also includes a small senior management team who lead and coordinate the organization.

At least, in principle, everything else *could* be contracted out. A hospital could contract out all of the following functions apart from a few key managers:

◆ Accountancy
◆ Payroll
◆ Supplies
◆ Estate management and maintenance
◆ Security
◆ Occupational health
◆ Personnel management
◆ Training and development
◆ Car parking
◆ Equipment maintenance
◆ Information technology
◆ Cold pathology
◆ Pharmacy dispensing and supplies
◆ Food preparation
◆ Laundry

Depending on its style of working, it might also be able to contract out services such as physiotherapy but only if the physiotherapists did not work as members of multidisciplinary teams.

As the contracting out is developing, new kinds of organizations are being created to meet the need for outsourced services. These are known as *facilities management organizations*. Their business is that of providing complete managed services for organizations which are outsourcing.

Organizations exist, for example, which will manage everything to do with the buildings which you occupy. They will build them, maintain them, heat them and light them and, if you wish, furnish and equip them. Organizations also exist which will manage all your transportation requirements, your computing and information requirements or run your complete purchasing and supplies function.

More recently, organizations are developing which will manage your entire human resources function on your behalf and certainly this model is being used within the NHS at the time of writing.

SUMMARY   Contracting out services can be of real value to an organization by allowing the key people within the organization to focus clearly on its core business.

Contracting out tends to make organizations more flexible and adaptive and this may be of great importance in a fast moving world such as that of health care.

Contracting out is a sophisticated management skill. Organizations which are contemplating contracting out services should ensure that they have people with skills in contract negotiation and contract management.

Contracting out should form part of an overall organizational strategy. There must be a clear view of how we wish to run our organization before we can make sensible decisions about contracting out. If you are in the business of healthcare delivery, there needs to be a clear and shared view of how care should be delivered before contracting out decisions are taken.

The scope of contracting out is widening over time. Services which would once have been regarded as integral to the business are now being shown to work perfectly well on a contracted out basis.

The government is likely to continue to exert pressure on public sector organizations to market test through compulsory competitive tendering.

Contracting out may yield useful cost savings. That is the least important reason for contracting out a service.

CONTRACTING OUT – SOME EXPERIMENTS

♦ A Mental Health Trust in London has contracted out all its residential care for adults with learning difficulties to a voluntary organization which is an offshoot of a housing association. Staff have been transferred from the NHS Trust to the voluntary organization.

♦ A number of Trusts in Kent have agreed to place contracts for speech and language therapy services for children and adults with learning difficulties with a voluntary organization – once again, an offshoot of a housing association. Staff have been transferred from the NHS Trust to the voluntary organization.

♦ An NHS Trust in London has contracted all its human resource management services to another NHS Trust.

♦ A number of NHS Trusts have placed total facilities management contracts for information technology services with private sector suppliers.

♦ Several NHS Trusts in London have contracted all or part of their training and development services to a Resource Group hosted by another NHS Trust.

CASE STUDY: CONTRACTING OUT – A VISION OF THE FUTURE

The following (at the time of writing fictitious) example illustrates where the contracting out process might take us.

The Care 2000 NHS Trust is a provider of secondary care in West London. The Central Clinic is an imposing building with facilities for 500 inpatients, a large day-surgery centre, a patient hotel and a set of outpatient facilities capable of handling 5000 patients a day. The Central Clinic provides an Accident and Emergency service which complements the minor injuries and primary care facilities provided through six Locality Clinics. Each Locality Clinic provides facilities for minor surgery, outpatient clinics and imaging.

All of the clinics are linked by advanced optical datalinks which allows clinicians working in Locality Clinics and in health centres to have access to expert help and advice immediately.

The buildings are provided on a fully maintained and serviced basis by Ptarmigan Construction. They pay for the capital costs of building and equipping the clinics and also pay for heating, lighting and maintenance. Cleaning of public and shared areas is also the responsibility of Ptarmigan as are transport services. The Trust pays an annual rent for the facilities which they occupy.

The Trust employs 800 people of whom 700 are directly engaged in patient care of one kind or another. The investment in information technology has led to a dramatic reduction in administrative and clerical staff. Clinical support staff carry out a range of support duties including patient care, internal transport of patients, clinic administration and day-to-day cleaning of their own clinical areas.

The Trust has placed a contract with Professional Services Plc (PSP), to provide additional clinical and support staff to cope with peak workloads. PSP employs a pool of about 200 people who regularly work at the Trust. When they are not needed there, they can be deployed in other organizations.

The Trust's management team is very small indeed. Most of their work is concerned with the development and support of clinical care. They do not have to worry about the buildings which they occupy, they are not managing hundreds of badly paid clerical staff or juggling establishments and vacancies to try to balance their budgets. Finances have improved very significantly now that there are few if any capital charges – the Trust has very few fixed assets.

An important feature of the building design was flexibility of use. Inpatient areas can be reconfigured for outpatient care and vice versa. Nearly all of the core staff are capable of working in at least two major specialties which means that resources can be moved around quite easily to deal with peaks and troughs in the mix of work coming into the Trust.

FURTHER
QUESTIONS

The following questions identify some issues from this chapter which you may wish to consider or discuss further with your colleagues.

♦ Which elements of your business are core?

♦ Which services might you consider contracting out?

♦ Have you contracted out anything which should really be core?

♦ Have you the right number and mix of staff for dealing with baseline volumes of work?

♦ Have you got the right skills to undertake contract negotiation and contract management on a significant scale?

INTERNAL SERVICE LEVEL AGREEMENTS

Glenn Douglas

OBJECTIVES

- ◆ To explain the importance of SLAs to the organization.

- ◆ To distinguish between SLAs and other forms of contract, both NHS and commercial.

- ◆ To provide a practical check list for those embarking on negotiating SLAs in their organization.

INTRODUCTION

This chapter distinguishes between internal service level agreements (SLAs) and other forms of contract and explains the role of SLAs in allocating resources, controlling expenditure and improving performance and quality within an NHS Trust.

The advantages and disadvantages of an internal trading environment are discussed and the reader is cautioned about getting too immersed in detail. The problems of dysfunctionality, which can be caused by the devolution of responsibility inherent in the operation of internal SLAs and occur where the benefits to a component part of the organization run contrary to the benefit of the organization as a whole, are discussed and recommendations on how to minimize the risk are offered.

The chapter highlights the characteristics which make a good SLA and recommends appropriate services where it can work and is beneficial to the organization and individual directorate.

The chapter concludes with a checklist for those wishing to establish this regime in their own organizations.

WHY HAVE INTERNAL TRADING?

A real dilemma for a Trust considering devolvement of responsibility to those who affect consumption arises in areas where the functional management structure does not reflect the control of consumption. The largest elements falling into this category will be imaging, pathology and paramedical services such as physiotherapy. Most Trusts operate a system of functional management for these services. The dilemma is who controls the activities and expenditure in these services. Is it the providers of the service or is it the users?

All these services have one thing in common which is that they are demand led. An example would be a consultant physician requesting a number of pathology tests for a patient. The pathology department has no choice but to provide those tests. If the demand for tests exceeds that budgeted for, the pathology budget overspends with no adverse effect on the budget of the referring directorate. Therefore there is no direct incentive on the referring directorate to control the number of tests requested.

A potential solution to this problem is to devolve the budget for these services to those directorates who consume the service and operate each provider department on a trading account basis. The income from selling these services would then be used to set against the expenditure of running the department. This would mean that the user would pay according to demand and could potentially buy more services by saving in other areas.

However, potential financial benefits are not the whole reason to have internal trading. SLAs are established to aid service management, providing a more effective support service based on user requirements.

WHAT IS AN SLA?   In order to facilitate the process between the internal providers of services and the internal users it will be necessary to come to some agreement. Essentially this is what an SLA is. A definition could be :

> *an agreement between the provider of a service and a user of that service quantifying the minimum acceptable level of quantity and quality to be provided.*

The key words in this definition are:

♦ *Agreement*: the negotiation of an SLA must be two-way, otherwise it has no validity.
♦ *Quantifying*: which means there has to be some way of measuring adherence to the standards set in the SLA. If there is not, then any agreement will largely be symbolic as it will have no firm base to judge successful performance. Avoidance of subjective words such as slow, poor or good should help ensure measurability. The establishment of an agreed currency is important to ensure performance is adequately measured.
♦ *Quality*: the SLA should stipulate the minimum acceptable level of quality. It is important to define this level carefully during negotiations. However, it must be remembered that there is a trade off between quality and cost and, as most internal purchasers will only have limited resources, through contract income, reaching an acceptable compromise is all important. An

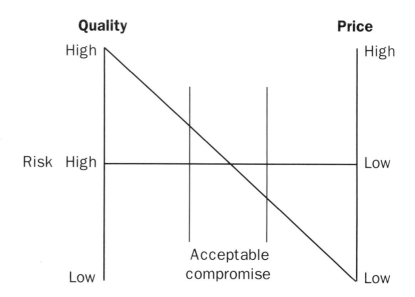

Figure 11.1
The trade-off between
price and quality

example of this could be in terms of response times for an examination or test. Because of the use of expensive on-call staff if it is stipulated that the service has to be provided within 4 hours it will incur greater costs than if it is within 12 hours. The purchaser then has to determine just how clinically necessary this is. It is also extremely important to take into account the effect this decision will have on the total delivery of care. It is pointless saving pennies in one area if it costs you pounds in others such as increased length of stay. This area of acceptable compromise is illustrated in Figure 11.1.

TECHNICAL CONSIDERATIONS In order to begin to achieve the benefits of internal trading, the technical solution needs to be in place in order to back up the SLA. A potential mechanism for dealing with this is illustrated in Figure 11.2.

This illustrates for the example of pathology that by using the general ledger system plus either a casemix system or a pathology system, the technical solution to internal trading can be found.

The mechanism illustrated assumes a clinical directorate model of management with a separate functional directorate of pathology. Each directorate incurs direct expenditure and the indirect charges for pathology (shown as a dotted line). The budget for the service would lie with the user clinical directorate and in order to function, the pathology directorate would need to charge the user directorates for their use of the service. Thus, the clinical directorate would have their usage shown against a budget for pathology, in exactly the same way as any direct expenditure. The pathology directorate would run as a trading account with no budget as such

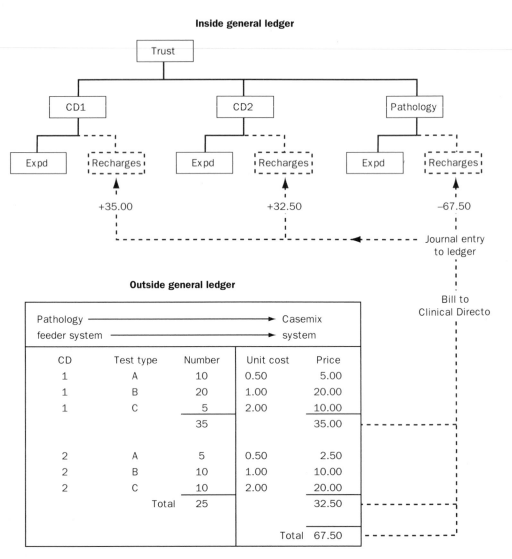

Figure 11.2
Trading in clinical support services. CD, Clinical Directors

but with the income derived from the services it provides offsetting the direct expenditure it incurs.

The information necessary to produce the recharge is also illustrated, this is fundamentally the activity units provided to each clinical directorate and the unit cost for each unit of activity.

The diagram further illustrates an important prerequisite: *it is necessary to have adequate information to feed such a system.* To be effective each test needs to be individually priced and accounted for. However, it may be that this optimum level of information is not available. In such cases an appropriate currency, based on what is available, needs to be agreed and monitored against, whilst working towards more appropriate information. Such a currency could include use of on-call; requests or allocation of staff numbers all as a proxy. Lack of information per se is not an excuse not to consider SLAs. In other key aspects such as quality, it is important to be explicit and an SLA is the mechanism for achieving this.

LINKING TO COMMISSIONER CONTRACTS

The majority of the income of a Trust comes from the sale of its frontline clinical directorates, healthcare activity to health commissioners and GP fundholders. In order to deliver these contracts, the front line directorate depends on a wide range of services provided by other parts of the organization. If a Trust moves towards the devolution of income to front line directorates, typically 50% of the costs and activities will lie outside the directorate. SLAs provide one mechanism for allowing the income to flow through the organization to the support functions. They also focus attention on the important role they play in successfully delivering healthcare contracts.

DIFFERENCES BETWEEN AN SLA AND OTHER FORMS OF CONTRACT

In the same way as a patient care contract between NHS providers and commissioners is not legally enforceable, so internal contracts do not have redress to law. Clearly, it would be nonsensical to settle internal disputes with a large expenditure on lawyers and courts. What is needed in the Trust is an internal mechanism for arbitrating between parties to settle any disputes. This process must be seen to be fair and acceptable to all players. The chief executive will normally be the final arbiter in any dispute. Where SLAs cross between Trusts, this creates a more complex relationship. Again there is no redress to law; instead the NHS Executive will arbitrate on contentious matters more cheaply and more efficiently. However, it is important that both parties agree, as part of the SLA, the mechanism for arbitration prior to using the Executive. Continual referrals to the Executive are likely to reflect badly on the Trusts in question. A possible hierarchy of arbitration is shown in Box 11.1.

Box 11.1
Hierarchy of arbitration

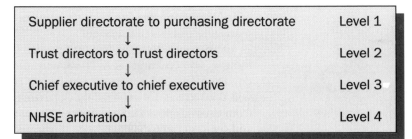

Supplier directorate to purchasing directorate	Level 1
↓	
Trust directors to Trust directors	Level 2
↓	
Chief executive to chief executive	Level 3
↓	
NHSE arbitration	Level 4

However, every effort should be made to solve issues at the lowest possible level.

Where the SLA is integral to the Trust the same process of arbitration needs to be established. However, it is extremely unlikely that the NHSE would be involved and the final level of arbitration would be by the Trust chief executive.

The basic principles of contract apply just as much for an SLA as any other form of contract in so far as for the creation of a contract all that is required is:

♦ *An offer* on certain (defined) terms (to provide goods or services or to pay for them if provided).
♦ *Acceptance* of the offer, which must be unconditional. The offer and acceptance together comprise agreement.
♦ *Consideration* (that is, payment which must not predate the agreement).
♦ *An intention to create relations* (which are not legal between NHS bodies). This means that both parties intend to have a contractual relationship with each other.

It follows that there are numerous traps for the unwary; it is an easy matter to create a contract when you do not intend to, or fail to create a contract when you wanted to. A contract need not be in writing. Although to some extent you may be protected by the Trust from particularly bad contracts, it is quite possible to enter into a contract that does not give you what you require by agreeing to a proposal without thinking through all the issues, particularly in terms of price or quality. This could then seriously affect how you deliver your own service or how much budget you have to do so.

In all other ways, SLAs are just like any other contract and even though they are 'internal' to the organization and not legally enforceable, they should be treated seriously and as if they were.

THE SLA AS A MEANS OF ACHIEVING EFFICIENCY

The major way in which an SLA can assist the Trust and/or directorate to achieve efficiency is by transferring the responsibility and control of support services to those who actually, by their actions, influence consumption. An example of this is in pathology, where traditionally the service is budgeted on a functional basis. The pathology manager argues that he cannot control demand because it is a responsive service. The users complain that they cannot obtain the service they want because the pathology manager controls the service.

An answer is to bring the two parties together on a more formal footing by creating SLAs between the parties, linked to the devolvement of budgets to the users. The providing department will then act as a quasi-trading department, dependent on income from users to provide the service. This is known as internal trading and the mechanisms have been illustrated in Figure 11.1.

Although this system appears to provide a better solution, there are a number of potential pitfalls. As mentioned in the introduction, the issue of dysfunctional behaviour can occur.

DYSFUNCTIONAL BEHAVIOUR What is dysfunctional behaviour? This is probably best answered by example. At the extreme, one clinical directorate may decide to buy a service from an outside source. If it does, it may get a better deal, but overall the Trust will probably suffer because the remaining directorates will have to pick up an increasing amount of fixed costs. This is illustrated in Box 11.2.

Box 11.2
Effect on pricing of a directorate going outside for pathology

Pathology costs of test	Based on 100 tests	Within year 80 tests	Next year based on 80 tests
Variable	20p	20p	20p
Semi-fixed	60p	75p	60p
Fixed	20p	25p	25p
Price to directorate	£1.00	£1.20	£1.05

Box 11.2 shows that the effect within year on a £1.00 test of losing 20% of work would be a 20% increase in costs to remaining customers. Given time to readjust semi-fixed (mainly staffing costs), the increase could fall to 5%, although this is probably optimistic. This, as far as the Trust is concerned, would easily outweigh any price gain received by the directorate going outside and may easily cut through a policy of encouraging a healthy pathology department. This position would become untenable and the service may fail completely to the detriment of those to whom having an in-house service is vital for their own success.

Thus dysfunctional behaviour occurs when the benefits of the component parts of the organization run contrary to the benefit of the organization as a whole. Potential exists for this to happen in any system of devolved responsibility.

How to address the problem A way of addressing this problem is by setting ground rules which limit the choice of directorates to using only the in-house service. There would be potential losses from this approach but it would ensure, from the lack of competitive pressures, organizational cohesiveness.

Targets for providers Other issues to be considered must include that of ensuring targets are available for the provider department to achieve efficiency if they are not to be at the mercy of commercial pressures. The potential solution here is to build in a cost improvement target into the annual price, which would have to be a Trust-wide agreement.

Stimulating demand   Another potential dysfunctional issue is that the provider department may seek to extend the volume of tests it provides to user departments, whereas the Trust is attempting to restrict them. Although giving the budget to user directorates should counter most of this, it may cause initial problems when system is first up and running.

Less demand   A user directorate may choose to buy significantly less of one service and more of another; potentially this would lead to an under recovery (loss) to one provider and an over recovery (profit) to another. If the gainer were to spend this surplus, the Trust as a whole may lose money and this loss could be the result of spending on items which the Trust may consider a low priority. This aspect of dysfunctional behaviour occurs when there is a combination of real and notional money put into the individual directorates' budgets. The solution is again to have clear rules of the game and clarity of understanding by all parties as to the effects of their actions both on the Trust as a whole and specifically on other parts of the organization.

BENEFITS   Despite the potential for dysfunctional behaviour, the benefits of devolved responsibility linked to SLAs are considerable and progress in this area is essential to meet the overall objectives of placing budgets in the hands of those who control consumption. Thus the SLA can contribute to achieving greater efficiency in the use of resources in the Trust.

CONFLICTS   In many clinical support areas such as imaging or pathology, the advent of external contracting, particularly with GP fundholders, has created a position where conflicts can exist between the priorities of internal and external users of the service. The rapid development of GP fundholding and the contracts for these services has placed pressure on support directorates to deliver increasing quality and access. The defence of this income has often become the major issue in the management of support directorates. The effect of this, particularly within a constrained budget, has been to put pressure on the service provided to internal users. This may be to the detriment of the Trust as a whole as the clinical contracts may be put at risk.

SLAs can help to address this issue and ensure that internal users of the service are assured of a proper level of service and are treated in the same way as external customers. It may not, however, be the complete solution as external customers can go elsewhere, whereas realistically internal users are likely to be constrained by the Trust as discussed above.

ACCURACY VERSUS COST

In common with many areas there is always a trade-off between generating good quality information and the cost of providing that information. What is needed to drive an SLA is an acceptable compromise. Firstly, it must be recognized that while information needs to be credible, it does not need to answer every question. When asking for information as part of an SLA the practicalities of obtaining that information and the danger of creating an over bureaucratic mechanism must be avoided. The answer is to be clear about what information is *essential* and what is merely *desirable*.

It may be that all the information required to inform an SLA is not immediately available but that should not in itself stop the process taking place. You may be surprised just how much is available but nobody has asked for it before.

Some examples of essential and desirable information are given in Box 11.3.

Box 11.3
Examples of essential and desirable information

Essential	Desirable
◆ Price for service ◆ Activity ◆ Operational policies ◆ Key contact points ◆ Quality standards ◆ Development plans ◆ Current budget available ◆ Expected demand from contracts/GPs/ECRs ◆ Specific requirements of individuals (dependent on service) ◆ Penalty clauses	◆ Breakdown per unit price ◆ Breakdown of activities ◆ Marginal costs for additional activity ◆ Organizational structure ◆ Contingency plans, i.e. major disaster. Recovery particularly in computing ◆ Historic data on performance against quality standards, activity and cost

Many elements of pricing may have already been done to inform outside contracts and the mechanism exists in most general ledger systems to effect the recharges to the devolved budgets and set up the support department as a quasi-trading department.

Whatever the level of information available it is probably beneficial to attempt some form of SLA even if it only monitors on one or two key indicators such as on call in pathology or imaging. In these circumstances, it will be important for the users to be involved in the development of information systems by the provider departments.

In summary, there is a trade-off between accuracy of information and cost. Do not seek to attain perfection, rather identify what is essential to inform the process. There will probably be more information available than you think.

IMPACT ON QUALITY OF SERVICE PROVIDED

SLAs are not all about financial efficiency and control. Quality management criteria form an important part of any SLA. Entering into negotiation with a service provider will lead to the definition of minimum acceptable criteria in areas such as:

♦ Responsiveness.
♦ Accessibility.
♦ Courtesy.
♦ Competence.
♦ Accuracy.
♦ Communication.

In most cases, this will be the first time explicit quality issues will have been discussed and agreed on. Clearly, this brings with it many advantages from just going through the process. Communication between parties will also lead to providers of services recognizing the importance of one issue versus another, which may be at variance from their own perceptions.

It may not be possible to cure all the ills of the relationship in one go because of lack of resources or physical constraints. However, it may well be that by understanding each other's issues and priorities, significant gains in quality may result. An agreed way forward may also form part of the SLA so that both sides share a commitment to a quality strategy over the next few years.

Measurement of quality will always cause problems mainly because of the subjective nature of it. However, as a starting point it should prove possible to agree key simple indicators in most services, for example turnround times in pathology and imaging. These should be agreed by both parties to the SLA and it should be possible to monitor them without expensive collection systems. It is important to decide which features of the service are of prime importance in delivering the service and, who under the SLA, has the responsibility for collecting the information. Normally this should be the provider of the service but the purchaser may wish to do this themselves to ensure proper standards are being met. It is important once these have been agreed to develop a simple system to monitor adherence to them and, also the mechanism for putting it right if performance is not up to agreed standards. This is prior to triggering any arbitration arrangements.

Again, the importance of this two-way dialogue in enhancing quality forms a major reason to attempt to establish internal SLAs.

CHARACTERISTICS OF A GOOD SLA The SLA should be the final part of a process of negotiation between the two parties. As such it should reflect the agreements reached in those negotiations and should not be imposed on one party by another. As it is not a legally binding document it should be written in simple unambiguous language with as few generalizations as possible. Box 11.4 shows the key components of a good SLA.

Box 11.4
Essential
characteristics of an
SLA

◆ Parties to the agreement

◆ Length of time of agreement and start date (including any possible review process)

◆ Notice period

◆ Mission statement for service

◆ What is to be provided (may include when and where service is provided if appropriate)

◆ What level of service (quantity)

◆ The price/cost of the service (including any triggers for inflation or increases/decreases in activity)

◆ The minimum quality levels acceptable and the mechanism for monitoring them

◆ Information requirements/monitoring information

◆ Signed agreement by both parties by authorized personnel

◆ A named contact point

◆ Mechanism for contract review

◆ Arbitration process

These characteristics can act as a guide to subheadings in your SLA. It is important that all issues are covered to ensure a robust agreement.

SERVICES SUITABLE FOR SLAS If a Trust is viewed as an organization with an end product of clinical activity which is contracted for by other agencies, then potentially all the services which support this end product have the potential for an internal SLA. Although this may be an ultimate goal, the first priority should be to address those services where the user can exert real influence on the service provision. These areas are likely to include:

♦ Pathology
♦ Imaging
♦ Pharmacy
♦ Theatres
♦ Use of outpatient departments
♦ Computing
♦ Catering
♦ Portering
♦ Provision of accommodation for clinical services
♦ Sterile supplies
♦ Laundry and linen
♦ Physiotherapy and other therapy services

This list is relevant for acute services but also likely to cover the majority of issues for community based or psychiatric services.

Each of these services directly impact on the quality of patient care in the widest service and can be altered by the actions of a user directorate. It is in these areas that the most benefits can be accrued from SLAs.

This does not mean that other areas should not be thought of as eligible for SLAs. The large central Trust functions such as finance, human resources, business development and hospital administration can also benefit by the discipline of an SLA. These should be seen as a second phase as there are major potential problems of conflicting priorities and objectives between the purchasing directorates and the Trust itself. For example, if a directorate could decide it did not need to buy human resources, yet the Trust wanted human resources to act consistently throughout the Trust. Again, these are solvable by the application of clear ground rules but, prior to embarking on this exercise, a clear cost-benefit analysis needs to be undertaken and the purchasing directorates need to be clear exactly what the implication of these actions are.

In summary, all support areas are suitable for an SLA. However, the benefits are likely to be greater in concentrating on those areas where the user can exert real influence over the support activity.

ALTERNATIVES TO SLAS

Are SLAs the only way forward? There are a number of other options, these including:

♦ The use of benchmarks to assess the performance.
♦ Performance indicators.
♦ Customer satisfaction surveys.
♦ The setting of targets on responsiveness and availability.

It is hard to see that any of these options will generate the potential benefits of an SLA. They do not involve a real agreement between the provider and user and do not align the service business needs in the same way. However, they do represent possible steps forward and a useful halfway house for some services such as the Trust central functions mentioned as a possible second phase above.

SUMMARY This chapter has explored the main issues surrounding both the appropriateness of SLAs and the essential ingredients of a successful agreement. It has demonstrated that they can improve the service provision within a Trust and also improve efficiency. All support services have the potential for SLAs but it is probably beneficial to target those areas where the user can exert real influence over the support activity.

Box 11.5 gives a checklist to those wishing to establish agreements in their Trust.

Box 11.5
Service level
agreement: checklist

> ♦ Treat all SLAs seriously, as if they were legally binding.
>
> ♦ An SLA is an agreement between two parties, therefore be prepared to negotiate.
>
> ♦ Make sure adherence to the terms of a SLA are measurable.
>
> ♦ Avoid loose terms such as good or on time.
>
> ♦ SLAs should be signed by people who have actual or ostensible authority to do so.
>
> ♦ It is vital to keep a copy of the SLA and if it refers to published terms not contained in the contract itself, ensure you have a copy of those terms (preferably before you sign the SLA).
>
> ♦ Ensure the process for arbitrating disputes is understood and clearly stated in the SLA.
>
> ♦ Make sure you understand the price and any variables such as inflation and triggers for additional activity.
>
> ♦ Make sure you can afford the price offered from within your income/budget. Make sure you can provide the service at the quality demanded for the price quoted.
>
> ♦ Keep in mind the wider Trust perspective and avoid the potential for dysfunctionality.

FURTHER READING

This work provides a much more detailed analysis of SLAs, in a wider context than the NHS.

◆ Hiles, A. (1993), *Service Level Agreements : Managing Cost and Quality in Service Relationships*, Chapman and Hall, London.

CONCLUSIONS: CONTRACTING IN THE FUTURE

Kim Hodgson

OBJECTIVES

- ♦ To pull together the ideas presented in the book and to tease out the implications for managers and clinicians who are, or may be, engaged in the contracting process.
- ♦ To sketch out some of the main features of the future landscape of the NHS in relation to contracting.

PROBLEMS AND SOLUTIONS

As several contributors have indicated, the creation of an internal market within the NHS was a response on the part of the Thatcher government to a fundamental political and economic problem. The problem which it sought to address was that of demand for healthcare resources out-stripping the ability of the economy to provide those resources.

This basic dilemma is by no means confined to the UK. It is a problem which confronts every society and every government in the world. Readers will be aware that healthcare reform was a central plank of the legislative agenda for the in-coming Clinton Administration in the USA. Interestingly, at the time of writing, the reform of health care in the USA seems to have been placed in the 'too difficult' tray for now. At the creation of the National Health Service, this dilemma was not foreseen. On the contrary, the founding fathers expected that the creation of a comprehensive national health service free at the point of delivery would actually *reduce* demand for health care once the health of the nation had been improved.

A number of factors conspire to create the incessant demand for more resources for health care.

- ♦ Disease processes which were once fatal are now susceptible to treatment. As a consequence, people live longer. There is clear evidence that per capita expenditure on health care for elderly people is significantly greater than for younger age groups.

♦ Advances in medical technology move illnesses from the untreatable to the treatable. Thus conditions which might once have required no resources simply because there were no appropriate treatments available may now require very significant resource commitments.

♦ The public expects and requires high quality care which is increasingly delivered in ways which are convenient for the consumer.

♦ The proportion of care which is delivered by informal carers has reduced steadily. This may be attributed to three factors:
   - A higher proportion of the population engaged in paid employment.
   - Changing social attitudes towards care.
   - The professionalization of care and the squeezing out of the voluntary effort from many areas of health care.

An important feature of healthcare systems is that, despite much rhetoric about the importance of maintaining good health, most of our resources are actually consumed by processes which seek to correct illness. Thus, even in an apparently obvious example such as smoking, most societies seem more willing to spend resources on coping with the illness which results rather than taking firm action to address the problem at a preventative level.

There is, therefore, a fundamental issue of balancing supply and demand in health care. As supply is limited by the size of the gross national product (GNP) and the proportion of GNP which we, as a society, are prepared to devote to health care is also limited, there needs to be some *rationing system*.

Chapter 1 discusses this concept in more detail and it is clear that the use of competition was the solution chosen by the Thatcher administration to address the underlying issue of balancing healthcare demand and healthcare resources in the UK.

In part, at least, this solution was adopted for ideological reasons. The government of the day and the 'think tanks' which informed government policy were strongly committed to using market forces to address public policy issues. The approach is reflected not only in the National Health Service but in the privatization of public sector monopolies such as BT, the creation of 'Next Step' agencies within the Civil Service such as the Driving and Vehicle Licensing Centre and the introduction of compulsory competitive tendering in local government and throughout the public sector.

Politics has been described as 'the art of the possible'. The somewhat chaotic way in which the creation and development of the internal market within the NHS has taken place and is taking place fully illustrates this proposition. The internal market is full of contradictions and paradoxes, of tensions between 'hands off' and 'hands on' management and control.

The reasonably clear vision at the creation of the internal market has become increasingly cloudy and distorted as political realities have been imposed on an apparently simple idea.

In a market, there are winners and losers. In theory, at least, the winners are the organizations which meet the needs of customers most effectively and efficiently. One of the complications of the internal market is that we do not much like the political consequences of losing. Allowing a local hospital, however inefficient or inappropriate, to close is a major and unpalatable political decision. Clinicians and local communities have proved themselves extremely good at orchestrating opposition to such closures.

Similarly, any attempt to apply notions of cost-effectiveness to health care have proven deeply unpopular. Healthcare decisions are simply too emotionally loaded to allow any form of 'objective' decision-making to take place. If it is your child who needs the £50 000 operation with a slim chance of success no amount of carefully assembled statistics will convince you that it is more appropriate to allow that child to die so that you can improve the quality of life for fifty other people.

The hand of the Treasury has also influenced the implementation of the internal market. First Wave Trusts were excited about the possibility of being able to secure capital from commercial sources. The Treasury were equally although very differently excited about the notion that an element of public expenditure should be 'out of control' and very firmly vetoed any attempt to give public sector bodies the freedom to borrow funds from private sources.

Overriding all of these considerations was the standing of the National Health Service in the view of the electorate. Whatever complaints anyone might make about the NHS, it is firmly entrenched in the national psyche and politicians tamper with it at their peril. Shortly after the formation of the internal market, directives were issued by ministers and by senior NHS executives to cut out the 'commercial' language of the internal market as it was sending out the wrong signals to the general public. Almost overnight, purchasers turned into commissioners and competition into contestability.

Health care will always be a high profile political issue and those of us who are engaged in the management or delivery of health care, particularly within a national system such as the NHS, will always have to deal with the complexity and volatility which the political spotlight brings. One of the more curious side-effects of the internal market has been to move some of the difficult decisions which were often taken by clinicians quietly on a case-by-case basis into the arena of public debate. This is an uncomfortable transition but one which probably had to happen.

A question which must occur to the reader is what will happen if there is a change of government. Unfortunately, it is not an easy question to answer. At the time of writing, the policy of the Labour Party towards the NHS is not readily discernible.

As we have suggested, underlying the particular ideological model which has driven the creation of the internal market are some fundamental problems which will confront a government of any political complexion. The reforms have, themselves, changed the political landscape in ways which are difficult to reverse. It seems likely, for example, that withdrawing from a statement of basic standards like the Patient's Charter would be politically very difficult. Similarly, we believe that many GPs would be reluctant to give up the increased influence which they have acquired through the reforms.

Some features of the internal market are probably here to stay even though the language and the detail may well change.

♦ Some form of split between the provision and the commissioning of health care is likely to be maintained. The freedom of hospitals to determine who they treat and how and when is likely to be constrained by some arrangement which will look suspiciously like contracting.

♦ A powerful role for GPs in shaping the nature of secondary and tertiary care seems likely to be maintained. Whatever mechanism is adopted, service providers such as hospitals will find themselves tailoring services to meet the requirements of GPs.

♦ Explicit statements about what patients are entitled to expect in terms of quality of service seems to us irreversible. The growth of consumerism has always tended to be a robust trend.

♦ Continuing pressure to *do more with less* is an inescapable consequence of the harsh economics of health care outlined above. It seems very unlikely that any foreseeable administration will simply say 'have all the money you need and tell us when you need some more'.

An issue which would very probably be addressed quite differently by the Conservative and Labour parties is what is known as the *democratic deficit*. Within the NHS at the moment, there is very little public accountability at a local level. Accountability rests solely, for all practical purposes, with the Minister to Parliament.

An incoming Labour administration would be likely to introduce some form of representative democracy at local level. This could be achieved by having members of health authorities and NHS Trust Boards elected directly or indirectly. More radically, as some have suggested, the role of local authorities could be extended to include the commissioning of health care. The latter solution would have certain advantages in facilitating the interface between health and social care.

The Conservative Party has indicated that its approach to the problem of accountability would be to bypass representation by elected members and go straight to consumer choice as the lever of accountability. They argue that strengthening the role of the GP as commissioner/purchaser of health care would enable individual consumers to exercise very direct influence over decisions by GPs. If patients do not like the way in which their GPs are exercising influence, they are 'free' to register with another GP.

At the time of writing, a 'think-tank' on health policy has been established under the chairmanship of the former NHS Chief Executive (Sir Duncan Nichol) with funding from the pharmaceutical industry. The 'think-tank' is considering some very radical alternatives to the current model of the NHS.

Perhaps most interesting is the concept of the Health Maintenance Organization (HMO) – a model which has developed in the USA. In essence, an HMO is an organization which undertakes to meet the health care needs of its subscribers for a given fee. One of the advantages claimed for the system is that there is an in-built incentive to *prevent* ill-health rather than undertaking costly 'repairs' at a later stage. It is not inconceivable that, within the current framework of contracting between health authorities and providers, contracts could be placed on a total health maintenance basis.

PRIMARY CARE LED PURCHASING

The declared strategy of the present government is to move towards a system of primary care led purchasing through an extension and elaboration of the current GP fundholding scheme and by changing the role of health authorities.

Under this model, commissioning of secondary and tertiary care would largely be in the hands of GPs who would hold the funds to purchase services on behalf of their practice populations. The role of health authorities would be to support, facilitate and regulate the work of GPs. The arguments advanced in favour of this model are threefold:

♦ It addresses the democratic deficit issue by creating a channel through which patients should be able to directly affect the shape of local services.
♦ It supports the governments wish to see a transfer of resources from hospital-based care towards community-based care.
♦ It should place a greater emphasis on promotion and prevention.

In common with past reforms, much of the detail is vague and important issues such as provision of care for small populations and strategic planning do not seem to have been addressed. The government proposes to introduce legislation to establish new health authorities in 1996 and, no doubt, they will be left to work out the details.

Primary care led purchasing presents a number of interesting challenges and problems:

◆ How will a sensible balance be struck between GPs focusing in a fairly parochial way on the immediate needs of their patients and the need to take some wider and more strategic approach to healthcare planning?

◆ How will GPs develop the skills needed to specify, negotiate and monitor contracts for a complete range of healthcare services?

◆ How will the commissioning activity of a large number of GPs be managed and controlled?

◆ How will the tension between GP as provider and GP as commissioner be managed?

It seems that just as the NHS has the end of one learning curve more or less in sight, it is about to embark on another and yet more difficult one.

THE SHAPE OF
THE NHS
This book is about contracting. Having considered both the fundamental issues associated with publicly funded health care and the political agendas, it seems very likely that some form of contracting process, perhaps with a different name and between different bodies, will still be central to the process of healthcare planning and delivery.

As an absolute minimum, we believe that there will be formal agreements which require doctors and hospitals and community units to deliver specified services in exchange for the funding which they receive.

We also believe that there will continue to be a move towards contracting for outcomes rather than processes. The implications of such a move are formidable and present three major challenges:

◆ Developing robust and appropriate methodologies for measuring the outcomes of clinical processes.

◆ Allowing for the huge number of variables which influence outcomes. Health care is not a straightforward business and conventional scientific methods may not prove adequate for handling the range of variables involved. It seems probable that we may have to look to some of the research techniques developed in the social sciences to inform our approach to outcome measurement.

◆ Developing information systems which will support the quantity and complexity of data needed to relate data about individuals, data about clinical interventions and data about outcomes. As yet, our systems are hopelessly inadequate for the task.

We believe that there will have to be a process of reinventing healthcare organizations. Developments in clinical practice such as day surgery, hospital at home and home dialysis are already challenging our concept of what a hospital is. It is becoming increasingly inappropriate to think of a hospital primarily as a building or collection of buildings. It is even more inappropriate to think in terms of numbers of beds when we describe the size of a hospital.

We envisage a trend towards some very different kinds of healthcare organizations. A possible pattern might be:

◆ High technology centres with very specialist expertise and facilities serving relatively large catchment areas.
◆ Integrated secondary care providers which offer a range of secondary care services delivered across a whole spectrum of settings from hospital wards to specialist GP clinics to care delivery in the patients home.
◆ Primary care providers with a health maintenance role but which also deliver some of the care which we currently tend to think of as secondary. One of the roles of secondary care providers and of high technology centres may be to provide support services such as pathology and imaging to primary care providers. Developments in information technology will make this a much more feasible option and 'teleconsulting' will become a normal way of delivering specialist health care.

In some ways, the managed market inhibits the development of new kinds of institutions. One of the effects of the Tomlinson report was to create splits between hospital and community services. As a previous chapter indicated, competition between hospital and community providers can be very dysfunctional in terms of care delivery.

There are many other obstacles. Both the general public and healthcare professionals have a real attachment to bricks and mortar. There is something reassuringly solid about a hospital both as a place in which to work and as a place to which to go for treatment. Local MPs have proved themselves very vocal in resisting any proposals to reconfigure services in ways which require closure of hospital facilities.

There is a view amongst many healthcare professionals that demand for hospital beds has, in fact, stabilized. They take the view that the number of beds available influences demand rather than vice versa. Bed availability changes our rationing decisions and our admission criteria.

It also seems probable that private sector finance will come to play an increasingly important part in the provision of health care. The present government requires that any major capital proposal shows that private financing options have been thoroughly explored before public funding will be allowed.

There has been some cautious experimentation with private sector provision for entire clinical services. Tenders have been sought from the private sector to build and manage complete facilities and, in some cases, to provide the clinical services which are run in those facilities.

THE SHAPE OF CONTRACTING

The changes which have occurred in the NHS over the last five or six years have seemed dramatic. They have challenged traditional ways of working and traditional values. Managers have often felt overwhelmed and clinicians threatened.

Yet, in many ways, the changes which have taken place have been relatively simple ones. Most contracts are still very broad in their scope. Quality specifications are relatively superficial concentrating as they do on the processes of service delivery rather than issues of clinical efficacy.

The great majority of NHS Trusts only have to negotiate contracts with one or two health authorities or commissioning agencies and with a few fundholding GP practices for a limited range of services.

Despite the claims of both the media and politicians, there have been few fundamental shifts in resources from the acute sector to primary care and community-based services. Where health authorities have published even relatively modest plans, public and political opposition has often been such that these have been rapidly shelved.

Despite the great wave of change with which people in the NHS have been coping, we are, at best, at the end of the beginning of the reinvention of the NHS. The challenges ahead are more formidable than those with which we have already coped. The future will create enormous opportunities for clinicians to shape the future provision of health care in the UK but to do so in a partnership with the consumers of that care.

In view of the changing shape of the NHS, how will the contracting process develop in the future?

There will be a move from the current short-term one year contracts towards longer term 'fixed' or 'rolling' contracts. This development will help provider Trusts to develop their strategic planning as they will have greater certainty over their contract income. The introduction of longer term contracts will also help purchasers as they probably could negotiate 'loyalty' discounts from providers.

The present contract currency of finished consultant episodes (FCEs) will change as contracts become more sophisticated. Purchasers will buy Care Packages for their patients with more emphasis being placed on the outcomes of treatments offered by providers. In the future there will be progress towards using Healthcare Resource Groups (HRGs) as a currency for certain specialties such as orthopaedics, gynaecology and ophthalmology and this is seen as the first stage towards purchasing care packages.

As contracts are made with commissioning authorities and an increasing number of GP fundholders, care will need to be taken to ensure that a wide range of contract documentation and service specifications reflects the intentions of all parties. More precise monitoring will be required to ensure that contract terms are being complied with.

For all purchasers there will be a greater involvement of the public as patients are encouraged to influence the decisions of GP fundholders and commissioning authorities. This debate will lead to more explicit rationing of health care as more open decisions are taken on priorities for the use of scarce resources. Contracts will, then, be set to specifically exclude certain types of treatments or care packages.

As contracting becomes more sophisticated there will be a need to support the function with more timely and accurate information on cost, prices, contract performance and quality.

The skills of GPs in assessing health needs and commissioning for those needs, both at practice and locality level will require strengthening. They will also need to develop their contracting skills and refine practice based information systems to support this.

Clinicians within provider units will also need to increase their knowledge of the contracting process if they are to take a stronger role in negotiating and delivering contracts for their services.

THE CHALLENGES FOR NHS TRUSTS

1. NHS Trusts will have to be in a position to negotiate separate contracts with each of the GP practices which they seek to serve. GPs will tend to have a sharp focus on the needs of their own patients and will expect and demand services which keep their patients well and happy. Many will also expect to be equal partners in the management of care. Some GPs will wish to push back the current boundary between what hospital consultants do and what they do.

2. NHS Trusts will be competing to win tenders for the supply of clinical services not just against other NHS bodies but against private and voluntary sector suppliers. Although the NHS is relatively efficient, it still carries a significant bureaucratic overhead and can be very resistant to change. Opportunities exist for new organizations which are lighter on their feet to enter the market and to offer real advantages in terms of cost and quality of service.

3. NHS Trusts will have to be able to assemble and offer complete packages of care which can be shown to demonstrate measurable benefits for groups of patients.

4. NHS Trusts will be dealing with patients who have much more information about the performance of particular hospitals and, possibly, particular clinicians. Some might quarrel with the relevance of the kinds of statistics which are being piloted in Scotland at the time of writing. At the very least, they signpost the way to a future in which we are dealing with much better informed patients.

5. NHS Trusts will be dealing with patients who have a clear idea of their rights as users of the NHS. The Patient's Charter has had a real and lasting impact on the attitude of patients towards the

NHS. Many will demand that services be provided in ways which are convenient for them rather than efficient for us.

6. NHS Trusts will face downward pressure on costs for the foreseeable future. In many cases, the obvious 'fat' has already been trimmed off. Future productivity gains will probably have to come from fundamental changes in the ways in which services are delivered. They will require Trusts to become much more flexible organizations with a much smaller fixed cost base.

7. NHS Trusts will be taking risk management decisions in conditions of much greater uncertainty than currently prevail.

8. NHS Trusts may have to carve out specialist niches for themselves in the healthcare market. Very few will find a successful future as generalist providers of undifferentiated secondary care.

THE CHALLENGES FOR NEW HEALTH AUTHORITIES

With the advent of primary care led purchasing, the role of health authorities will be transformed from that of purchaser into that of facilitator, enabler and regulator.

1. New health authorities will have to develop strategic visions of health care in collaboration with GPs *and* secure the support of GPs for that vision. Theirs is the unenviable task of persuading GPs to balance the sharp focus upon their own patients against the needs of the wider community. If they are unsuccessful, health care will become balkanized with each GP pursuing his or her own agenda. The effect will be great instability for NHS Trusts, gross diseconomies in healthcare provision and gaps in the pattern of provision. In essence, the market would no longer be managed.

2. New health authorities will have few powers of coercion. Successful ones will be extremely competent at persuasion, influence and facilitation.

3. New health authorities will have to support NHS Trusts in understanding the new, very volatile market and in working out viable survival strategies.

4. New health authorities will have to support GPs in managing the commissioning process. They may do this by providing:
   - Information about health needs.
   - Information about the performance of different providers.
   - Competitive pricing information.
   - Collective or consortium commissioning services.
   - Consultancy services.

THE CHALLENGES FOR GPS

1. GPs will be faced with the challenge of taking their own make : buy decisions. Which services should they provide from within

their own practices and which should they buy in from other healthcare providers.

2. GPs will have to learn how to evaluate providers across a range of performance indicators, price being only one.
3. GPs will have to learn how to specify, negotiate and manage contracts with a number of different providers. Some may be in the NHS, others outside.
4. GPs will have to make quite big investment decisions, some of which may be shared investments with other organizations. For example, a practice might decide to invest in the information technology necessary to enable 'teleconsulting'. They will do this in partnership with another healthcare organization. In so doing, they tie themselves to some extent to that provider.
5. GPs will have to face some of the rationing decisions which are currently taken by hospital consultants. They will not be able to say that the Trust has long waiting lists or that the health authority has failed to commission enough services. They will hold the purse strings and the difficult decisions which accompany that power.

THE IMPLICATIONS FOR CLINICIANS

There are three major implications for clinicians:

1. If commissioning is to be clinician led, the probability is that those doing the commissioning will want to talk directly to the clinicians providing the services. The role of managers in the contracting process will shift into that of providing specialist *support* to clinicians and away from leadership of the process.
2. If future productivity gains are to come not from 'fat trimming' but from real changes in the way in which we do things, the success of healthcare providers will be determined by their ability to innovate quickly and effectively. This innovation process will have to be clinician led.
3. If hospitals need to reinvent themselves and to exploit specialist niches, clinicians need to play a central role in shaping the strategies of their organizations. In many cases, being a district general hospital (DGH) is likely to be a rather poor survival strategy. Helping an organization which was conceived as a DGH, and which has spent many years learning to be good at being a DGH, to become something different is not a trivial problem.

Against this background, clinicians still have to find ways of discharging their primary duty of care to their patients. In some ways, the challenge is to shift the focus up from the particular individual patient being treated to a world view that includes the whole system of health and illness.

THE CHALLENGE
FOR NHS
MANAGERS

The first five years of the reforms have, on the whole, been good times for NHS managers. Certainly they have been very busy, they work long hours and many of them are highly stressed. Quite a number have been sacked or otherwise fallen by the wayside. On the other hand, they are better paid, have more interesting jobs and are able to exercise much greater power within their organizations. They also have exotic job titles and some of the trappings of directors in real companies.

In the next phase, there will be a subtle but important shift in the role which managers play and the skills which they need to perform well. The platitude that they are only here to *support* clinicians will have to become a reality.

In some ways, their challenge is the same as that facing the new health authorities. How do they make sensible things happen when they have little or no power to command?

Many of the best managers already see their jobs in this way. They spend their time working alongside clinicians and they measure their successes by how well they are able to support clinicians in doing what they want to do. Managers who persist in thinking that they really run the organization will almost certainly fail.

A particular competence which managers will require is the ability to build different organizational cultures and to manage different and more creative kinds of employment relationships. If organizations are to become more flexible and lighter on their feet, managers need to develop policies and ways of working which enable staff to feel sufficiently secure and committed that they can embrace very flexible working practices.

This is not a book about organization development but the ability to develop very different kinds of organization should be high on the priority list of both managers and clinicians.

THE TIMING   Four major factors will influence the pace of change:

1. Politics

The political dimension occurs again and again throughout this book. Health care and the NHS in particular is a highly political issue. Changes in the pattern of service provision have been held back to a very great degree by unwillingness to take politically unpopular decisions. The Labour Party has indicated that it would impose a moratorium on bed closures in London were it to form the next government. It would also phase out GP fundholding and end Trusts' independent status. It is also uncertain what the attitude of the Labour Party towards private sector finance would be.

2. Medical opinion

Medical opinion is important in determining the pace if not the nature of change. The growth of GP fundholding is an informative example. The British Medical Association was initially deeply opposed to the scheme. They were not able to stop it but they were able to influence the pace of change. The stance which GPs take as primary care led purchasing evolves will strongly influence the pacing of many of the changes discussed.

3. Medical technology and health sciences

Fundamental changes in medical technology and in health sciences are on the near horizon particularly in areas such as genetics, molecular biology, gerontology, imaging and minimally invasive techniques. It is difficult to make an accurate prediction as to the pace at which developments will move from the laboratory into daily practice. There is some evidence, however, that the rate of change in the application of new technologies is speeding up. The spread of minimally invasive techniques is an example which will be familiar to most readers.

4. Information technology

The speed of development of more sophisticated contracting processes will be influenced by the development of and, more particularly, the rate of investment in information technology. There is now, for the first time, a national information technology strategy for the NHS. The strategy includes the development of a national information network for the NHS and the development of nationwide patient identifiers.

Information technology will also enable the development of different models of clinical practice such as teleconsulting and will facilitate the development of organizations which are less to do with buildings and institutions and more to do with people and skills and cultures.

Most of the information technology which is needed to transform the NHS actually exists. The real question is about the rate of investment and the vigour with which a comprehensive national strategy will be pursued.

CONCLUSIONS – A PERSONAL VIEW

If I had to stick my neck out, I would be fairly confident that most of the predictions in this chapter will have been realized by the end of the first decade of the next millennium. Many will have been realized by the end of the century.

The times ahead of us all will be very turbulent but, nevertheless, I am quite optimistic about the outcome.

Whatever else we may say about the NHS, it contains within it a disproportionate number of our brightest and most committed citizens.

GLOSSARY

Accreditation   A method used to address the issue of evaluating quality: in this case, of health service provision.

Agency   The relationship which arises when one person is authorized to act as the representative of another person.

Assignment   One process by which rights under a contract may be transferred.

Block Contract   The payment of an annual fee for access to a defined range of services at a given indicative level of activity.

Breach of Contract   An act by one party which is contrary to the terms of the contract and entitles another party to a remedy.

Case Mix   The mix of types of clinical case specified in a contract or actually receiving care.

Clinical Directorate   A common form of organization in provider units. Normally led by a practising clinician.

Commissioning Agency   An Agency created, usually jointly, between one or more District Health Authorities (DHAs) and one or more Family Health Services Authorities (FHSAs) to carry out purchasing (commissioning) functions on their behalf.

Community Information Systems for Providers (CISP)   An information and operational support system for community providers.

Compulsory Competitive Tendering   A policy of the current government which requires public sector organizations including Local Authorities to seek tenders for the provision of certain services which have traditionally been provided by directly employed staff. The clinical aim of the policy is to ensure that the best possible value is secured for the tax payer.

Consortium   A group of two or more GP practices which combine to enable them to achieve the minimum list size to qualify for GP fundholder status.

Contact   A unit of currency commonly used in community services and for services from the professions allied to medicine, e.g. physiotherapy.

Contract Currency   The unit of measurement of activity in the contract.

Contract Minimum Data Set   A minimum data set that can be provided to purchasers in order to 'bill' a spell of care.

Contract Specification   The overall contract which includes overarching measures of service performance, quality measures, penalty clauses etc.

Core Business   The term used to describe the main task or mission of an organization. For a hospital, for example, clinical care would be the core business. Having a clear idea of its core business should help an organization to determine what services might be considered for contracting out and which should be managed internally.

Cost and Volume Contract   The payment of an annual fee for access to a service or a number of services at a defined level and mixture of activity.

Cost per Case Contract   The payment of a fee for a particular service, the frequency and number of which may not previously have been agreed.

Delivery   The process by which a contract signed by one party is received by another. This is usually done by exchanging two identical drafts, one executed by each party.

Diagnosis Related Group (DRG)   An early attempt to group patients according to the resources which they are likely to consume based on the primary diagnosis. Now no longer used.

Directly Managed Unit   Provider sites which are still supported by regional funds and as yet have not become 'Trusts'.

Enforcement   Methods of sanction by which the Court ensures that the remedy it has ordered takes place.

Execution   Signing or sealing the contract. However, a formally written contract is not in force until it has been delivered.

Extra Contractual Referral (ECR)   A referral by a GP or consultant to a provider unit for which there is no existing contract with the patient's 'home' health authority.

Finished Consultant Episode (FCE)   The period of care a patient receives as an inpatient from admission to discharge whilst under the care of one consultant. For outpatients, an attendance or series of attendances related to a particular episode of illness.

Fund Manager   The person identified by the practice to take the lead on the management of the fund.

GP Fundholder (GPFH)   A general practitioner who holds funds to purchase hospital and other forms of care for his or her patients.

Health Maintenance Organization   An organization that contracts to meet all the healthcare needs of a member, over a given period of time, which may be a lifetime.

Health Resource Group (HRG)   An experimental method for grouping together patients who are likely to consume similar amounts of resource. Used as a basis for price comparisons between providers.

Hospital Information Support System (HISS)   A Provider Information Support System which covers PAS, OCS and nursing (care planning).

Indemnity   A promise or obligation entered into by one person to cover another person's liability or potential liability. For instance NHS Trust 'A' may indemnify NHS Trust 'B' against damage that A may cause in B's building. This is separate from the question of insurance.

Integrated Care Pathway   This shows the type of care which it is anticipated will be required by a patient of a particular kind at each point in the episode of care. By analysing variances between actual and anticipated pathways, it is possible to identify ways in which care delivery can be improved.

Internal Market   The general name given to the system whereby the provision of NHS services is orchestrated through the negotiation of contracts by purchasers with provider organizations.

Managed Market   In contrast with a normal 'free market' in which various suppliers compete freely for business, the NHS internal market is managed through policy directives from government and the NHS Executive. The purpose of market management is to protect patients (and politicians!) from the adverse effects of free market forces.

Market Testing   Similar in purpose to compulsory competitive tendering. Market testing requires public sector organizations to compare the value for money offered by their own services with the best available in the general market place.

NHSE Regional Office   The NHSE is managed through the NHS Executive based at Leeds and eight Regional Offices. The Regional Office has no power in its own right but merely carries out functions delegated from NHS HQ. The Regional Directors sit on the NHS Executive Board. Regional Office staff are, in effect, civil servants.

Order Communication System (OCS)   An electronic ordering and reporting system which can also contain alerts and reminders.

Outreach Services   Specialist services provided by hospital staff in community locations.

Outsourcing   The practice of using an external supplier to carry out certain organizational functions. Typical examples include catering, printing, car fleet management.

Patient Administration System (PAS)   Patient Administration System which supports contracting and basic management of patient care.

Pendulum Arbitration   A process used to resolve contractual and other forms of dispute. Each side presents its position to an independent and mutually agreed arbitrator. The arbitrator must then decide completely for one party or the other. A compromise settlement is not permitted. The advantage claimed for pendulum arbitration is that it encourages both sides to adopt moderate rather than extreme positions.

Preparatory Year An opportunity for a potential GP fundholder practice to familiarize itself with the requirements of the scheme. It is a period during which the fund operates in shadow form.

Remedy Compensation in some form, usually ordered by a Court. Note this is different from enforcement.

Service Level Agreement An agreement between a service provider and its customers quantifying the minimum acceptable level of service to be provided.

Service Specification That part of the contract which defines the objectives, delivery and quality measures for the particular service to which it applies.

Transfer of Undertakings – Protection of Employment (TUPE) Legislation originating in the European Union which requires that when ownership of an enterprise is transferred from one organization to another, the new owner is required to employ existing staff on their current terms and conditions of employment. The significance of TUPE in the context of contracting out services is that it prevents a potential supplier reducing costs simply by re-employing staff on much lower wages and poorer conditions. This has been very much the practice of private contractors taking over NHS services.

Trigger Mechanism A device built into contracts which stipulates that when volumes of activity pass a certain level, the provider is entitled to expect additional resources to be made available or for a compensating reduction to be made in some other element of the contract.

Vendor Appraisal The process of ensuring that a potential supplier is competent to provide the goods or services which you require. Typically vendor appraisal will cover financial stability, quality assurance, staff skills and facilities.

INDEX

Note: terms explained in the Glossary are indicated by **bold page numbers**; text in Boxes, Figures and Tables by *italic page numbers*. Index entries are arranged in letter-by-letter order (ignoring spaces).